THE
STOCKBROKERS'
BATTALION
IN THE GREAT WAR

Dedication

To James, Alex and Simon Valder and Oliver Janikoun
in the hope that they will keep alive the memory
of those who served in the First World War.

THE STOCKBROKERS' BATTALION IN THE GREAT WAR

A History of the 10th (Service) Battalion Royal Fusiliers

David Carter

Pen & Sword
MILITARY

First published in Great Britain in 2014 by
PEN & SWORD MILITARY
an imprint of
Pen and Sword Books Ltd
47 Church Street
Barnsley
South Yorkshire S70 2AS

ISBN 978 1 78303 637 0

Printed and bound in England by
CPI Group (UK) Ltd, Croydon, CR0 4YY

Typeset in Palatino Light by CHIC GRAPHICS

Pen & Sword Books Ltd incorporates the imprints of
Pen & Sword Books Ltd incorporates the imprints of Pen & Sword
Archaeology, Atlas, Aviation, Battleground, Discovery, Family History,
History, Maritime, Military, Naval, Politics, Railways, Select, Social History,
Transport, True Crime, and Claymore Press, Frontline Books, Leo Cooper,
Praetorian Press, Remember When, Seaforth Publishing and Wharncliffe.

For a complete list of Pen and Sword titles please contact
Pen and Sword Books Limited
47 Church Street, Barnsley, South Yorkshire, S70 2AS, England
E-mail: enquiries@pen-and-sword.co.uk
Website: www.pen-and-sword.co.uk

Contents

Acknowledgements

Thanks to Stephen Booth, Laureen Ellington, Stanley Jenkins, Jane Jones, Alan Metcalfe, Kate Mills, Graham Morley, David O'Carroll, Sir Julian Horn-Smith, Paul Reed and David Underdown for allowing access to their information and photographs to enliven the story of 10RF. To Anthony Richards and his colleagues at the Imperial War Museum for their advice and support in trying to contact the holders of copyright material. To Robin Sharp for agreeing to my using his father's diary and photographs, and for his memories of his father and to Christopher Sharp, who provided additional information about his grandfather's service. To members of Chris Baker's Great War Forum who unselfishly share their knowledge and answer questions. To Henry Wilson and Roni Wilkinson at Pen and Sword who had faith in my ability to deliver, and to Irene Moore who has made the editing process enjoyable. Last but by no means least, thanks to my wife, Jan, who has encouraged when necessary, tolerated my absences and surprised herself by how much she enjoyed the trip to France when we followed the route taken by the battalion.

The maps are sketch outlines to assist those who want to follow the routes and actions using maps and atlases. The list of members of the battalion who fell in action, with details of their service and family information, where this has been found, is available on www.10throyalfusiliers.co.uk. The site is always being updated as more information becomes available.

I have made every effort to contact holders of copyright and my apologies to anyone I have failed to thank. Finally, all errors in the text and maps are mine.

Introduction

This book grew out of research into my family tree and the discovery of a great uncle, Ernest Lionel Carter. One of eight children living in north London, Ernest took up employment as a clerk in a shipping company. When war broke out he was an early volunteer to join the 10th Battalion (Stockbrokers), Royal Fusiliers (10RF). The Commonwealth War Graves Commission records show that he was, at the time of his death in October 1918, a second lieutenant in the 13th Battalion, Royal Fusiliers (13RF). Further research showed that he had joined 13RF in September of 1918 having obtained his commission after service with 10RF where he was number Stk (Stockbroker) 925[1]. He had reached the rank of sergeant and was awarded the Military Medal (MM) for his part in a raid in 1917. This book is the result my search to find out more about him and the men he served with in a battalion about which little has been written.

In his *History of the Royal Fusiliers* O'Neill described 10RF as the first completely new battalion in the regiment; the Imperial War Museum describes 10RF as the first 'Pals' battalion. Whether the battalion is qualified to hold this distinction is a topic for full discussion outside the scope of this book. However 10RF displayed many of the features of the Pals 'locally raised' battalions in that it was raised from within a locality by an individual. It differed in that it received accommodation and supplies from the Army. What is indisputable is that it was raised outside of the normal army recruiting processes of the time.

The battalion was formed at the suggestion of the Director of Recruiting who asked Major the Honourable Robert White to begin recruiting in the City of London. Getting sight of White's diary in the collection of the Imperial War Museum was followed by finding the diary of Second Lieutenant Maurice Sharp. The outline provided by these diaries was supplemented by the very detailed letters and cards sent home by George Wilkinson from the time of his departure from The Tower of London to Colchester. Further collections of letters by Roland Mountfort and George Knight Young added additional points of view. A published account of events, including the work undertaken during the formation of the battalion, as well as his thoughts during training and action, is provided by the autobiography of William Babington Maxwell, *Time Gathered*. These all form the basis of the account, combining the experiences and differing viewpoints of these men.

Other members of the battalion: Ray Zealley, originally a member of the 18th (Public Schools) Battalion, Royal Fusiliers, Rupert Whiteman, Sydney Sylvester and Charlie Miles wrote of some of their experiences in papers and letters after the war. Zealley described in some detail the attack on Pozières in July 1916. Whiteman, an Australian, who had arrived for a holiday in Europe which was extended by his volunteering, wrote with Sylvester and Miles a retrospective account of the 1917 attack on Monchy-le-Preux. The different perspectives on the formation and actions of the battalion give a range of views and descriptions, sometimes of the same training event, or varied responses to experiences of training and life in barracks, under canvas and in action. The view from the position of Major, later Colonel, White gives the overall picture of the development of the battalion, including difficulties with the War Office. The other officers, Sharp and Maxwell, record events from their positions within a company and the Transport Section respectively. The views of the recruits, although sharing common elements, give different stories, partly because they were in different companies, Young in A, Wilkinson and Mills in B, and Mountfort in C.

All the writers demonstrate a common belief that volunteering to serve their country was an essential responsibility of all able-bodied young men. The differences of class are evident, though subtle, as all come from what are broadly the upper and middle classes: a retired professional soldier working in the financial sector of the City of London; an author; bank clerks; insurance clerks; shipping clerks; draughtsman; lace shop assistant and sales clerk. Many were educated at grammar schools and had professional qualifications and degrees. Most had decided that joining the ranks would ensure that they would see action before the war ended by Christmas 1914; waiting for commissions would mean that they could not get to France until 1915, when the war would be over.

The diaries and letters give insight to the excitement, the tedium, the new experiences and the maturing of these young men. The pace of events is sometimes slow, but the experiences build up to describe how a fighting unit was formed. The training was made as thorough as it could be in the time available, but they were by no means skilled professional soldiers when they arrived in France, though in contrast with later volunteers and drafted men they were a cohesive unit, following commands from officers they trusted. The heroism of the war was not the bravery in action of a few as part of a thrilling story. It was the underlying courage of men pulled from their routine lives and volunteering to participate in defending their country, resulting in daily tedium, constant danger from random shells and bullets and occasional adrenaline filled hours of action in an attack. The battalion was lucky in that it was not thrust into the maelstrom of the attack at Loos, the First Day of the Somme or the early Ypres campaigns. It spent time gaining experience in trench warfare, raiding, small scale attacks and defence before being involved in the attack on Pozières.

The letters and diary notes written before the departure from England differ in style from those written from France; once near the front they become terse and lack detail. The desire for normality, a life away from the mud of the trenches and to give some impression of life, without causing concern among relatives, particularly mothers and sisters, comes through, often by what is not there. Occasionally the reserves are removed and real feelings are expressed.

This book uses the main sources with others, from books or accounts of specific events by individuals in the battalion, to create a chronological account. For the period from when White was asked to form the battalion until it leaves for France his diary provides the frame for the other sources; from the time the battalion arrived in France the Battalion War Diary provides the linking role. For various reasons the sources cease to provide information at different points in the story. Diaries were not permitted in France, although fortunately some flouted the rule; some men were promoted and transferred; soldiers who were wounded left the battalion and did not return to it; some were killed. Once these events have removed a source others take a more central position to complete the account. Reading the letters and diaries without knowing the individual outcomes was part of my exploration and allowed the story to evolve. The extended quotations are offered without apology as they provide the voices of the participants. As Siegfried Sassoon wrote: 'Anyone can find out photographic details of the war. What they can't find out is the secret drama inside a soldier's head.'[2]

The Writers of Diaries
and Letters

The Hon Robert White

Robert White was born on 26 October 1861, the sixth child of eight born to Luke White and his wife Emily, nee Stuart. In 1873 Luke White succeeded to the title of 2nd Baron Annaly of Annaly and Rathcline, County Longford.

The Honourable Robert White was educated at Eton and Trinity College, Cambridge before he joined the Royal Welsh Fusiliers. All of his four brothers served in the army seeing service in the Sudan, Matabele Wars and the Boer War and two of them served in the First World War.

Robert White was a professional soldier reaching the rank of major and later brevet lieutenant colonel in the Royal Welsh Fusiliers. He fought in the Nile Expedition between 1884 and 1885 and then the First Boer War of 1886. He next served in the Rhodesian

Letter to Robert White asking him to raise a battalion, dated 19 August 1914. White gave it to the battalion. Sharp Collection IWM

WAR OFFICE,

WHITEHALL,

August 19th, 1914.

My dear White,

LORD KITCHENER is anxious to get a further supply of recruits for the London Regiment, the Royal Fusiliers.

I understand that there are many City employés who would be willing to enlist if they were assured that they would serve with their friends, and I suggest that you collect names and addresses of those who would be willing to serve in the Service Battalion of the Royal Fusiliers in Lord Kitchener's new Army.

The battalion—which would be composed entirely of City Employés—would then require a few months' training before they would be fit to serve on the Continent of Europe, but it is the intention of the Military Authorities to send this new army abroad as soon as it has attained a sufficient standard of efficiency.

Yours sincerely,

(Signed) H. RAWLINSON,

Director of Recruiting.

Mounted Horse and as a magistrate in Bechuanaland, where he became involved in the ill-fated and historically controversial 1895 Jameson Raid. This resulted in his being tried in London with his brother Frederick and eleven others all charged with 'having fitted out an expedition in December, 1895, within Her Majesty's dominions, without her permission and marching against a friendly state, the South African Republic'.

The trial began in March 1896 and ended with Jameson being sentenced to fifteen months imprisonment and both White brothers were given five months imprisonment. Frederick White was released after five days and stripped of his army commission, but this was later reinstated. Robert White returned to the army and served in the Boer War of 1900-02 on the Staff of 6th Division.

Following this colourful career the 48-year-old Robert White settled into business in London at Govett and Sons, an investment company in Throgmorton Street. After the declaration of war by Britain on 4 August 1914 Sir Henry Rawlinson, the Director of Recruiting for Lord Kitchener, Secretary of State for War, arranged to meet White at the Travellers Club in London on 19 August. Rawlinson asked White whether he thought men working in the City of London would volunteer to join the New Armies. White thought that they would, if serving with men of a similar background and given the right leadership; Rawlinson then asked him to raise a battalion of 1000 men to form a 5th Battalion of Royal Fusiliers as part of the 2nd Army.

He records in his diary the actions taken by him and others to raise and establish what became the 10th Battalion Royal Fusiliers.

William Babington Maxwell

William was the illegitimate son of the writer Mary Elizabeth Braddon, one of the most successful novelists of her day, who had a long relationship with her publisher. Born in 1866 William is listed in the 1871 census with his mother, named as Mary Elizabeth Maxwell, wife of the head of household, novelist. John Maxwell, a journalist, is shown as head of household, and there are eight children, including William. John Maxwell's first wife was in an asylum in Ireland until her death in 1874. It was not possible for John Maxwell to obtain a divorce and so it was necessary to accept that any children born to him and Mary would be legally illegitimate although the relationship was publicly acknowledged.

William attended the local day school in Richmond, but his autobiography makes little mention of his experiences there other than to comment on the good quality of the education he received, describing it as 'very modern'. Rather his book is filled with accounts and descriptions of the many visitors to Lichfield House, the family home in Richmond, and visits to Broadstairs, Brighton and Switzerland. One event he links to his school was an injury to his foot, a bad strain with some broken bones which was neglected and resulted in extreme pain, limiting the amount of walking, and later golf, which he was able to indulge in, until he undertook route marches with the Fusiliers at the age of 48.

Aged 14 he convinced his father that he should attend art school. Three notable artists of the day, Frith, W.C.T. Dobson and Edward Duncan had all made flattering comments about Maxwell's drawings and sketches. His indulgent parents duly enrolled him in Calderon's art school in St John's Wood which, he records in his autobiography, had a very traditional 'severely old fashioned' curriculum. For the first term he worked hard, but became aware of what he describes as his incompetence. After a few more terms he stopped working altogether and spent his time going for walks, playing billiards and watching the trains on the Great Western line from Paddington as it passed through Royal Oak. He managed many boys' dream of convincing a Metropolitan Railway driver to let him take the controls on the journey back to Richmond, not always totally successfully. Eventually he left Calderon's and enrolled at Ridley's art school in the Uxbridge Road. But again after an enthusiastic start he drifted away to pretend to work on his own at the British Museum. He says 'there, at that noble institution I finally left my easel and drawing board and never returned to fetch them away. It was the end of a career slightly before it had started. I renounced my dream of being an artist'.

The family pattern of life was also undergoing a change because John Maxwell had built Annesley House at Lyndhurst in the New Forest, and they were spending their time there in summer, the south of France in the winter and Richmond in spring. William spent his life moving in the literary and artistic and theatrical circles of a young man of means in London. He met many notable actors and his autobiography is a Who's Who of the famous of the day as they visited Richmond and made the acquaintance of 'my people'.

At the age of 21 his father gave him the 'Mistletoe Bough', a Christmas annual edited by his mother and to which she contributed a story each year. It had been very popular but as time passed the revenue, which was at first sufficient to keep William Maxwell for a whole year on the income from the single edition, began to wane. He looked for ways to make improvements but admits that instead of radically changing the style and content he just improved the illustrations and tried to get better content. For a few years he tried to make improvements but after a particularly bad year he records 'a queer sort of listlessness had possession of me. I let time pass without preparing for the publication. It was as if I thought that the Annual would come out of its own accord. Naturally it failed to do so. That autumn there was no Mistletoe Bough. I had allowed it to fade and die.'

After his father's death in 1895 William took on the role of secretary and manager to his mother. He looked after the houses in Lyndhurst and Richmond and dealt with her correspondence. After a period of depression during which he felt guilty at what his parents, particularly his mother, had done for him with little in return, he began to write short pieces and articles for magazines. His writing improved and he researched and wrote some books. In the summer of 1906 he married Sydney Brabazon Moore and they quickly produced two children while living in Richmond with Mary Maxwell.

In the early years of the twentieth century Maxwell was attending a house party at Stoke Poges where he met Major Robert White, Bobby White as he was called almost universally. 'Bobby and I were soon very great friends as close and affectionate friends as is possible with men who do not meet until middle life. So to speak we were as brothers who had been brought up at a distance from each other. Anyhow the bond was strong enough to hold us together tightly until death snapped it.'

His autobiography describes the opening days of the war, his attempts to get into uniform at the age of 48, paints a picture of some of the officers who arrived to lead the raw recruits and records the movement of the battalion in England and France.

Percival Maurice Sharp

Employed at Coutts Bank in the City at the outbreak of war, Sharp's military career began as a private in the Civil Service Rifles (1/15th Battalion London Regiment), part of the Territorial Force. He took ten days holiday leave in July 1914 to attend the annual training camp. They were moved into London to guard Somerset House and on mobilisation in August 1914 they moved again, to St Alban's. He was called to see his commanding officer and told that he had been given a commission and was to report to the CO of 10RF at Colchester. The announcement of his appointment to the rank of second lieutenant was in *The London Gazette* on 8 September 1914.

Maurice Sharp, facing the camera, second from the left of those in uniform. Sharp Collection IWM

OUR "TERRIERS" ARE KEEN FOR THEIR DAILY DIP

As at home, so abroad. Our young men in khaki are ever keen for their daily dip, and scenes like that depicted above are of daily occurrence wherever there are public baths. Just before the fierce fighting began near Mons, on August 22nd, British soldiers were seen bathing in the canal, as coolly as though they were just about to go on parade. They live clean, they are clean fighters; and, so far as possible, if die they must, they prefer to die clean

Born in Thame, Oxfordshire in 1894 Maurice, as he was always known, lived with his family on the site of the school of which his father, originating from Warrington in Lancashire, was headmaster. He was the fourth of five children with an older sister, Evelyn, and two elder brothers Hugh and Francis as well as his younger sister Helen. His mother died in 1907 and by 1911 his father had given up the school and was tutoring individual pupils from the family home in Christ Church Gardens, Reading.

His diary commences on 1 January 1915 as he is serving with B Company in charge of 6 Platoon and records events until the battalion leaves for France in July 1915. He wrote of later events in France after the war.

George Wilkinson

Born in London in 1892, George Wilkinson lived at 30 Avenue Road, Hammersmith with his parents and siblings. His father, also called George, was a railway booking clerk. He had a sister, Emily Irene, an office clerk, whom he called Rene in his letters, and a brother Leonard. George was one of about 100 employees of a motor manufacturer called Million Guiet. He was a cost clerk at their works in Longton Road, Cricklewood.

Million Guiet, as the name suggests, was a French company. They were described in Whittaker's Red Book of 1914 as having 'a range of specialties: high-class motor carriages of all descriptions, landaulettes, limousines, torpedoes and cabriolets'. After a period of financial difficulty at the beginning of the war they became increasingly involved in the production of lorries and cars for the military.

A keen Boy Scout, Wilkinson, Stk575, enlisted in the first day or two of recruiting with Arthur Parnell, Stk488, whose brother was scoutmaster and George's letters include messages to his troop at the church in Hammersmith.

His letters and cards commence with the departure of the battalion from The Tower of London on 3 September 1914. He was a member of Number 8 Platoon, B Company.

George Knight Young

George Young was born on 21 June 1894 at Heyford Avenue, London. He was the second son and third child of Charles and Kezia Young, his father a salesman for an india rubber firm. At the time of the 1901 census the family was living in Winsham Grove, West Side, Clapham Common, having moved there in 1900. The introduction to the collection of his letters, which were edited by his elder sister Florence Cole, records that the young George had a good voice and at the age of six a neighbour who was a professional singer suggested that he have it trained. He attended the Balham School of Music where his teacher was the Italian singer Madame Caviella. Victory in a boys' solo singing competition at Battersea Town Hall led to him being in demand to sing at local concerts.

A pupil at Battersea Grammar, and later at the

George Knight Young Stk 293, a fine baritone singer. Kate Mills

Guildhall School of Music, George developed what his sister described as a 'fine baritone of outstanding quality which in the years leading up to 1914 became well known at the Broomwood Road Wesleyan Church which the family attended and in a much wider field of entertainment'. In 1911 he was employed as an assistant in a shop selling lace and in 1914 was a very early volunteer with the number Stk293.

His letters are often undated but begin with his experiences while undergoing basic training in Colchester.

Roland Mountfort

A volunteer in the first days of recruiting with the number Stk771, Roland Mountfort, an employee of the London Prudential Insurance Company, signed up alongside a number of his friends and colleagues, including Ernest Pickering, Stk791, with whom he shared lodgings, and Stk875 Valentine Woolley, an insurance broker, who was born in Bundaberg, Queensland, Australia but who in 1911 was living with his parents and siblings in Leytonstone. At this very early stage of the war 140 men from the Prudential head office had volunteered to serve, and the company was giving support by making up wages and keeping their jobs open. Others had formed a men's detachment of the Red Cross and 150 lady clerks had formed six Voluntary Aid Detachments.

Mountfort was born in Coventry in 1890 and enjoyed a successful period as a pupil at the city's grammar school. By 1911 he was living with his brother, Bernard Dormor Mountfort, a clerk in the Royal Insurance Company and Ernest Pickering, a clerk in a mineral water company, in Sistova Road, Balham, London. Although clearly able academically Roland, along with many others in 10th Battalion, Royal Fusiliers, chose to enlist in the ranks rather than take a commission.

His letters commence in May 1915 when the battalion was at Windmill Hill, Ludgershall near Andover.

Alfred Mills

Stk759 Alfred Mills was born on 10 October 1894 in West London. His parents, Alfred John Mills and Mary Ann (nee Pooley) were both born and bred in west London and his mother's family were well known brick makers in the Fulham area. His father owned a tobacconist's in Ealing Broadway, west London, initially living in Shepherds Bush and later moving to Southall.[3]

Alfred was employed as a draughtsman by Anglo Saxon Petroleum, the shipping arm of the Shell Company, working in their offices in the City of London. He joined the Stockbrokers in August 1914 at the age of 19 years and 9 months, and after completing his training went to France in July 1915 as a member of 5 Platoon, B Company. His diary begins with the arrival of the battalion in Armentières in August 1915.

Rupert Stanley Whiteman

Stk868 Stanley Whiteman was an Australian businessman living in Sydney. In April 1915 the *Sydney Morning Herald* included an item which announced: 'Mr Rupert Stanley Whiteman, of Sydney, who went to Europe on a business and pleasure trip last June, has joined the 10th Battalion of the Royal Fusiliers'.

Alfred Mills Stk 759, aged 19 when he volunteered. Graham Morley

A member of C Company, Whiteman wrote his memoir, which focused on the attack on Monchy-le-Preux, after the war. He corresponded with Charles White and Sydney Sylvester who added their memories and comments to his original version. They give their opinions on the effectiveness of certain of their officers and colleagues who served with them.

Chapter 1

Formation and Settling in at Colchester

The 10RF attracted volunteers from firms in the City and the War Office appointed some regular officers and NCOs, with other junior officers coming from Territorial units. There were a number of characters in the battalion who were well known at the time, or destined to become famous after the war. The man charged with recruiting, Major the Honourable Robert White, had been in the Welsh Fusiliers in Egypt, then he served in the Rhodesian Mounted Horse and as a magistrate in Bechuanaland, where he and two of his brothers became involved in preparing for and leading the Jameson raid on Johannesburg; this resulted in a short spell in prison.

Brigadier General the Hon Rober White. Stanley Jenkins. Ox & Bucks LI Museum

A man of evident energy and patriotism, White had already been to Belgium in uniform having escorted a contingent of Red Cross nurses to Brussels, where the populace believed that he was the advance guard of the British Army come to save them. Sadly this was not the case, Germans entered Brussels on 20 August and the nurses were all taken prisoner but White had left forty-eight hours before. Rawlinson met White on 19 August and, having been asked to recruit men, White set to with a will to set up 'his' battalion using City contacts, including the Lord Mayor, to encourage men to enlist in what was effectively the first Pals Battalion, locally raised with men from a similar background.

White was assisted in recruiting by William Babington Maxwell, a dilettante author keen to offer his services to his country but with no military experience. On the outbreak of war he applied to, and was turned down by, three Yeomanry Corps, but although lacking a commission he went ahead to buy a field dress uniform. Unable to tell the tailor what badge of rank to sew on he discovered the man had given him a collection of stars and crowns in one of the pockets ready for any eventuality. Proceeding to Oxford Street he ordered riding boots from Peel, his boot maker, and then moved further down the street to Champion & Wilton to obtain a military saddle. On their advice he ordered a staff saddle, which was much more comfortable than a regimental officer's saddle.

White recognised in Maxwell the enthusiasm of a patriot keen to be involved. He asked for his assistance in recruiting, so Maxwell obliged by acting as chauffeur, collecting

Crowd outside Royal Exchange July 1914. Pen & Sword

News vendor announces closure of the Stock Exchange. Pen & Sword

Crowd in Throgmorton Street July 1914. Pen & Sword

Crowd in Throgmorton Street July 1914. Pen & Sword

White from Pembroke Lodge in Richmond Park, where he was a long-term guest of the widowed Lady Dudley. Maxwell later wrote that 'with gaiety and high spirits off we went to London'. They observed the changes already taking place, red uniforms were disappearing, the Household Cavalry reserve regiment had put away their fine uniforms and horses and could be seen standing in lines on Rotten Row in Hyde Park.

White and his contacts got busy on 20 August contacting City firms. He was assisted in contacting Lloyds by Sir David Kinloch, director of Leslie and Godwin, insurance brokers, veteran of the Boer War and later brigadier general commanding the 70th Infantry Brigade. Also assisting was Leigh Wood who had links with the Baltic Exchange. White wrote to many City firms and consulted the chairman of the Stock Exchange, which had closed immediately after the declaration of war and remained closed until its partial reopening on 4 January 1915.

Recruiting began at the office of White's firm, Messrs Govett, 6, Throgmorton Street, on 21 August. Two hundred and ten men enlisted on the first day. White arranged for *The Daily Telegraph* and other papers to put in notices regarding recruiting for the battalion. City employees like Ernest Lionel Carter prepared to leave their families and join their friends.

Ernest Lionel Carter, back left, with his family c1906. Author

Maxwell described the process in a little more detail:

'We had our recruiting station at the offices of Messrs Govett and Sons, Bobby's firm, in Throgmorton Street. Sir David Kinloch had a place for recruits somewhere else. Smith-Bingham, a partner of the firm, was in another room getting the names down more expeditiously while Bobby walked from room to room talking patriotism.

'They loved his talk these recruits. From the entries that I myself made out I would cite two or three chartered accountants, a leader writer from The Times, a doctor of science; Delbos, the son of a French professor; Beevir (sic), President of the Oxford Union; Oswald Birley, the painter.'

Second Lieutenant Raymond Bevir, he joined as a Private, was promoted to Lance Corporal and received his commission in January 1915. World War One Photos

All three of the recruits named by Maxwell were commissioned while the battalion was in training. Delbos, commissioned on 30 November 1914, was transferred late in 1915 to the Intelligence Battalion (10 IB) of the Royal Fusiliers, because of his ability to speak French. He finished the war as a captain in the Machine Gun Corps. Bevir, born in London in 1889, had been educated at Shrewsbury School and Hertford College, Oxford where he was President of the Union. He took up the law as a profession becoming a barrister of the Inner Temple. He reached the rank of lance corporal before being commissioned on 28 January 1915 in 10RF. Oswald Birley was 34 when he enlisted. The son of a Lancashire family, he had been educated at Harrow School and Trinity College, Cambridge. He was an established artist and sculptor who enlisted in the ranks but was commissioned on 28 November 1914. He remained with the battalion until it left for France, when, like Delbos, he transferred to the Intelligence Battalion where he made maps and models based on aerial photographs. The numbering of the Intelligence Battalion as 10IB is something of a mystery as the two were never linked. It has been suggested that as it was set up about the same time as 10RF it was a security device, although as will be seen, the numbering of 10RF was not a seamless process.

For the next week White recorded the rush of recruits, beginning on Saturday 22 August.

'22nd Enlisting all day. W. B. Maxwell and David Kinloch assisting. Recruited up to 425.
'23rd With W.B. Maxwell recruiting.
'24th An immense rush of recruits. Enlisted up to 900.
'25th Enlisted up to 1300. First batch of 320 medically examined.
'26th Enlisted up to 1510. Second batch of 340 medically examined.
'27th Enlisted up to 1600, refused any more. 3rd batch of 360 medically examined. Secured the services of 25 ex-guards NCOs, invaluable.
'28th 4th batch medically examined. War Office suddenly announced they would take only 920 of 1600 recruited. This occasioned immediate confusion and disappointment.'

This limit on numbers was just the first of what White saw as frustrating interventions by the War Office into the approach he took in establishing the battalion. He would describe his task as patriotic and commissioned by Kitchener himself. Just ten days after receiving his commission to raise the battalion 1,147 (in White's diary) or 1,156 (in *The City Press* of Saturday 5 September) men paraded in Temple Gardens. White recorded:

> *'Lord Roberts inspected in Temple Gardens. Headed by the band of the Grenadier Guards we marched to Tower Ditch. The Battalion was sworn in as a whole by Sir W. Vansittart Bowater, Lord Mayor of London. Marched back with bands of Grenadier Guards and Scots Guards by Tower Hill, Cornhill, Mansion House, Queen Victoria Street, St Paul's, Fleet Street, the Strand through immense cheering crowds to Trafalgar Square where we gave three cheers for The King and were dismissed.'*

The report in *The City Press* of 5 September 1914 reflected the confusion of the start of the war in referring to the 'newly formed 7th Battalion of the Royal Fusiliers recruited as it has been entirely from the City.' There was already a 7th (Special Reserve) Battalion of the Royal Fusiliers which had been sent to guard the docks at Falmouth. The place where they took their oath, the Tower Ditch, gave the founding members of the battalion their nickname of 'Ditchers' which they each carried with them for life.

The City Press reported:

> *'Thousands of Citizens lingered in town last Saturday to witness the formal inauguration. Formed into eight columns the recruits mustered in Temple Gardens and were inspected by Earl Roberts. Addressing the Officers and men the veteran hero welcomed them as brother soldiers and congratulated them on the splendid example they were setting to their fellow countrymen, coming forward as they had, as private soldiers and not seeking commissions. He contrasted their patriotic action with that of men who went on playing cricket and football and concluded:*
>
> *'This is not the time to play games wholesome as they are in times of piping peace. We are engaged in a life and death struggle and you are showing your determination to do your duty as soldiers and, by all means in your power to bring this war, a war forced upon us by an ambitious and unscrupulous nation, to a successful result.'*

Maxwell later wrote:

> *'I should have mentioned that we had been given Claude Hawker of the Coldstream for our Colonel, and Bobby White was to be our Second-in-Command. Hawker asked me to occupy this pause by going forward to Colchester on a reconnaissance - to gather information and pave the way for improvements in our accommodation, if this appeared to be necessary.'*

The appointment of Lieutenant Colonel Hawker as commanding officer must have been a blow to White who does not mention it until 4 September. It is possible that White's age at 53, combined with a lack of recent military experience and his links to the Jameson Raid may have raised questions as to whether he was fit and able to take command of a battalion in the field.

Volunteers for 10RF in Temple Gardens cheering after listening to an address by Lord Roberts on 29 August 1914.
Pen & Sword

Others who brought more than their military enthusiasm and aptitude included Herbert Rubens, Stk219, a member of a stockbroking family. His brothers, Paul and Walter, were both musicians and composers of popular musicals before the First World War. In addition to providing piano accompaniment to the singers of the battalion, Herbert attracted the involvement of his sister-in-law, Mrs Walter Rubens, a singer, and Miss (later Dame) Maggie Teyte, a young singer discovered by Walter and supported by his family. Maggie Teyte performed in at least two of the battalion's concerts while they were in training.

Men joined with their friends and brothers. William and Alfred Warman, Stk269 and 270, one a jobber in the Stock Exchange and the other a carpenter; Roland Mountfort, Stk771, who worked for Prudential Insurance, joined with his friend and colleague Ernest Pickering, Stk731. Of the 331 men identified through the 1911 census 168 had jobs in the stockbroking, banking, insurance and trading sectors. Others came from a wider range, gardeners, surveyors, engineers, clerks working for local councils and civil servants.

Officers and men arrived from overseas to join. Frederick Russell-Roberts, Ralph Cobbald and Geoffrey Harley were all known as big-game hunters, as well as soldiers and landowners. Valentine Woolley, Stk876, born in Australia, had arrived in England with his family in 1908 and worked as a clerk, he joined in August 1914. Rupert

Whiteman, Stk868, had, according to an article in the *Sydney Morning Herald* of April 1915, left on a business and pleasure trip to Europe in June 1914 and joined the battalion; Oriel St Arnaud Duke whose family lived on the island of Montserrat in the Caribbean, signed on, having served in the British West Indian Regiment; later arrivals came from other parts of the Caribbean, Malaya and India.

On 3 September in the early afternoon the men paraded at The Tower:
White's Diary:

'*Parade in the Tower Ditch. Marched to Liverpool Street, proceeded to Colchester in two trains. Lieutenant John Egerton Warburton, Scots Guards, had preceded us and prepared an excellent camp at Reedhall. Weather lovely. We all settled down in tents very quickly.*'

George Wilkinson sent his first two postcards home, in the days before text and tweet he was using the available technology to reassure his family:

'*3rd September 1914. Just leaving the Tower. OK, George.*
'*3rd September 1914. Arrived Colchester, lovely and comfortable. My address will be B Company, 8 Platoon, 10th Battalion Royal Fusiliers, Reed Hall Camp, Sobraon Barracks, Colchester.*'

Egerton-Warburton was clearly of great importance in providing current army experience and White depended on him. Maxwell exhibited his usual enthusiasm with something new and, although he still had no commission or actual authority, he took important decisions and his report to Hawker on the conditions at Colchester helped to establish his position within the battalion:

'*I said I had the honour to inform Colonel Hawker that the site of our camp at Colchester was airy and salubrious; that the water supply was all that could be desired, with a pressure sufficient to allow for providing the men with shower baths at the washing places when we made them; that ample space for the camp was allowed; that it was planned on the regulation pattern, with two main streets crossing at right angles; that the tents standing together with their floor boards, were almost new; that they would hold our numbers with eight or nine to a tent; that certain large square tents had been provided for quartermaster's stores, guard room, sergeants' mess and so forth; that at Blanks in the High Street we could hire a large marquee as officers' mess, and, since time did not admit of delay, I had assumed authority to hire this and it was already being erected; that blankets would be issued and taken to the camp by the ASC before our arrival; that on each of the three days after our arrival clothing would be fitted and issued; that rifles of the new pattern would be issued to us within a week. This nonsense I wrote out on foolscap paper and delivered to Hawker. (He) was frankly enraptured with it and he said I simply must have been a soldier either in this life or a previous one. Praise, from such a quarter. A Colonel! A Guardsman! It brought too the more solid satisfaction that Hawker asked me to go to Colchester with the Battalion on Friday.*
'*On Friday therefore I put on my uniform and joined them at Liverpool Street Station.*'

His efforts were rewarded and he later recounted the events which led to his being granted his commission:

> 'One morning Hawker told me of a new regulation by which General Officers commanding Brigades were temporarily empowered to appoint officers to commissions without further formalities. I received a Lieutenant's commission my Gazette being dated September 3rd. When for some time I continued to receive notices from the War Office and Territorial Associations to say that my applications could not be considered I felt proudly amused.'

The battalion was clearly in some excitement when settling in at Colchester. White spent time getting things in order and establishing routines with help from Egerton-Warburton. Maxwell continued to make himself indispensable to those in authority. For many of the men, as we shall see from a letter of George Young, this was the first time they had been away from home and they needed to reassure their parents. The novelty of camp life, the discipline, the drill and the routines all brought bright-eyed excitement to many of their faces. George Wilkinson was particularly keen to share every step of his new experiences with his parents and brother and sister. George Young wrote less frequently and was more restrained about army life; he was keener to talk about more personal and musical matters.

White's Diary:

> '4 September: First parades. Major Boileau (late Northamptonshire Regiment), B Company; Major Cobbold (late Kings Royal Rifle Corps), A Company; Major Maclean, C Company; Major Gouldborn (late Grenadier Guards), D Company. Lieutenant Colonel Hawker (Coldstream Guards) in command of Battalion.
> '5 September: A lovely day. Drill under Egerton-Warburton and the Guards NCOs. Men most keen and enthusiastic. Warburton a tower of strength.
> '7 September: Major the Honourable George Keppel[4] arrived and posted Second in Command B Company.'

Maxwell remembered:

> 'Our officers were as good as our men. Major Keppel grand to look at, arrived in characteristic style with a large motor car and two footmen; Major Raymond Boileau[5], another fine handsome man, was with George in the Norfolk Artillery Militia; Major Ralph Cobbold, a fine distinguished soldier of the 60th Rifles, explorer and big-game hunter, followed quickly. Major Gouldborn, a Grenadier and Major Maclean were two more of Field rank.'

George Wilkinson wrote home on more prosaic matters, he had a habit of writing a running letter over a few days before he eventually signed and posted it.

> '5 September. Dear Dad, Have had a very jolly day. I am in a tent with L. Bannister, Gratwick, and Scoutmaster Parnell's brother. Bannister (nicknamed Banny) is tent

commander and Gratwick keeps the tent dry. Mr House of the church house is a serjeant (sic) in the 9th Battalion in the barracks nearby. Yours George

'7 September. Dear Mother and Dad, Yesterday, Sunday, after about 3 hours drill in the morning we were free from 2pm to 9pm so I went out with Parnell and had tea at Wivenhoe a sweet little village on the estuary of the Colne. Tuesday, The Lord Mayor has telegraphed that the City Corporation are prepared to stand the expense of a machine gun and band instruments.

'Reveille goes at 5:30, Coffee and biscuits 6:00, Physical Exercise 6:30 – 7:30, Breakfast 8:00 Drill 9 – 12 noon, Dinner 12:30, Parade 2:00 Drill 2:00 – 4:00, Tea 4:30 free from 5pm. Some of our battalion have had their uniforms issued but I will not get mine until tomorrow. The equipment is very fine.

I am free every evening from 5 – 9pm and on Sundays from 2pm – 9pm in case anyone thinks of coming down.'

Stk677 James Farrar in his new uniform. Another picture of Farrar looking less formal appears on p106. Sir Julian Horn-Smith

One who got his uniform about this time was Stk677 James Farrar a 21-year-old auctioneer's clerk who lived in Putney.

Domestic and personal needs featured in the letters home from Wilkinson and Young; Wilkinson wrote on 9 September:

'Dear Mother and Dad, I hope Dad can come over on Sunday. You remember Captain Howard of the Church Army who gave the lectures with lantern illustrations during the Scout Exhibitions at Wandell Park, Parnell and I walked right into him last night and found that he is in charge of the tin church.

'Cakes!!!! If you please by all means send some. Small currant buns are best and we are <u>always</u> hungry.

'Ta Ta once more, the time is flying past in a succession of delights – fatigue is unknown to me – I never say "I feel a bit tired now" that is a thing of the past.

'Yours George'

White's diary of 11 September included an entry which pointed to the different experience of men being allocated to other battalions:

'All men clothed today, some queer figures. I am ordered to take over command of 960 men who are to form 11th Battalion, Royal Fusiliers.'

O'Neill wrote about the formation of the 11th Battalion in his *History of the Royal Fusiliers in the First World War*:

'Recruited at Mill Hill as a battalion of the Middlesex Regiment, they were received at Colchester by Colonel (sic) the Hon R. White (of the 10th), who asked them if they would care to be a sister battalion to his own. This was agreed to unanimously. At this time the battalion was simply a body of enthusiastic recruits from Manchester and Notting Hill; and they slept their first night in Colchester under hedges. During the next week officers began to arrive.

The contrast between this level of disorganisation and the relatively smooth transition of 10RF from civilians to soldiers is stark. In addition to receiving the men for 11RF White was faced with a major crisis on the following day, but tackled the problems with his usual vigour.

White's Diary:

'12 September. A fearful blow. Egerton-Warburton ordered back to rejoin the Scots Guards. Very bad blowy night. Tents knocked about.
'13 September. Most of the day paying men of 11th Fusiliers who have no Officers, no boots and are in a terrible state.'

Also written probably on 13 September, the first in the collection of Young's letters home dealt with some pressing business.

'Dear Dad, I have signed and am enclosing the notice of withdrawal which Charlie sent yesterday. You were quite right about my not mentioning to you before and I am very sorry I have not done so. However, you can believe me I shall not borrow money like that again except for some very important reason without telling you of it. I do hope you are not worrying about me in any way. Now that I am away from home I have got to take care of myself and I hope you can trust me to do it honestly and not to get mixed up with the wrong kind of people.

'I am singing at two concerts next Thursday one at the Town Hall which is to be given by the Band, the other at a Wesleyan Church where Professor John Duxbury is giving a recital. I expect it will be a bit of a rush to do both.

'Give my love to mother and tell her to write to me soon. I enclose a 1d stamp for the knife and quite agree about the custom of it[6]. With fond love, Yours ever, George.'

The following week saw White dealing with matters of concern to him and the battalion; he wrote in his diary:

'14 September. After a big day at the War Office succeeded in getting Warburton back and brought him back to Colchester where we had a great ovation from the men. Warburton and I lectured on advance guards etc. W. B. Maxwell appointed Lieutenant and put in charge of transport.'

White had boundless energy to tackle the problems which presented themselves. Maxwell continued to make himself indispensable:

'I had care of the battalion funds. I did all the correspondence relating to officers and much else of an official and semi-official character. My assumption of all this clerical work gave Egerton Warburton of the Scots Guards, our splendid young Adjutant, freedom to be out in the open drilling and instructing, and he was particularly grateful for this benefit.'

Being a man of independent means Maxwell was also able to purchase necessary extras for the senior men around him.

'I had brought down a couple of horses and Hawker and I rode about together very happily....Not liking to ride past Bobby and Warburton while they remained on foot I bought two more horses, mounting the Second-in-Command and the Adjutant, but I intended to be recouped eventually by Government for this outlay.'

One man who benefited by the purchase of the horse for White was 26-year-old Stk415 Stanley Greenhill. He served as White's groom and valet and in October 1914 attended a course at the Army School of Cookery at Aldershot. He became a member of the Battalion Transport Section.

Maxwell listed the newly arrived officers:

'Among the junior officers we had Fleming who had been a militiaman and "something in the City"; Geoffrey Harley, six foot six in height and noble of aspect, a Shropshire[7] landowner and another big game hunter and explorer now just returned from the Kalahari desert; and Fred Russell Roberts, one more big game hunter really famous for his exploits; brave as the lions he used to kill, gentle and kind as a child, brimming over with amiability and good fellowship and possessed of only one failing a queer sort of sleepiness that attacked him in unexciting hours. He used to get me to sit next to him and wake him up from time to time during military lectures by Bobby or anyone else. Another of our juniors was Maurice Sharp affectionately called 'Sharpey', a clerk in Coutts Bank; very young and nice to see, modest but never clumsy.'

Percival Maurice Sharp, a private in the Civil Service Rifles of the Territorial Force, was gazetted second lieutenant on 8 September. Writing later he recalled being summoned to the adjutant's office and told of his commission.

'I was told to report to 10th Royal Fusiliers, I trekked 2 miles back to my billet and was invited to lunch with my Company CO. After a hurried lunch I quickly got out of and

Second Lieutenant Sharp in his new uniform. Sharp Collection IWM

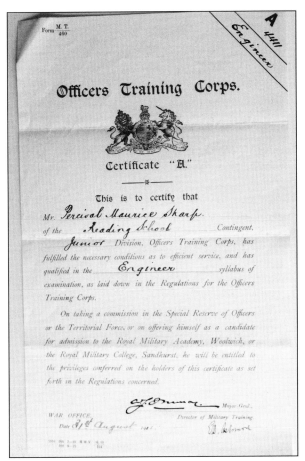

Maurice Sharp's OTC Certificate A from Reading Grammar.
Sharp Collection IWM

handed in my uniform and, armed with a railway warrant and clothed in a crumpled pair of grey flannel trousers etc, set off for Colchester.

'There I reported to a very military officer, Major the Hon Robert White of Jameson Raid fame. He took one look at me and said 'Go away and don't come back until you are properly dressed'.

'I returned weary and rather depressed to London getting there about 5:30pm. The Regimental tailors could not fit me out before Christmas so I went to Moss Brothers near Covent Garden. I was told I could have a fitting in 3 days and delivery in a week or so. I then went home to my father in Reading for a few days.

'I had made no application for a commission but my old school had been approached by the War Office and asked to recommend suitable candidates. As I held Certificate A and had been a Colour Sergeant in the Cadet Corps my name had been sent in. So I became a Second Lieutenant in the Royal Fusiliers and when I reported to Colchester again I got a good mark for being the first of the 'young officers' to turn up in uniform and ready for duty.'

On 20 September Wilkinson wrote home to his sister and referred to the concert which included the contribution from George Young.

'Dear Rene, On Thursday last 650 of us were invited to a concert in a big hall in Colchester where we had a very enjoyable evening. Today we have been visited by the Daily Mirror who gave us a huge cake which has been divided between the whole 1100 of us. We had stewed steak and potatoes as usual today but as it is Sunday this was followed by boiled rice and treacle and this for some unaccountable reason was again followed by boiled suet pudding and treacle. I expect the cook made a mistake.

'We had our first route march on Thursday morning before dinner for about eight miles on Friday we had an hour's night march in the dark. We marched along the dark country roads in absolute silence except for the tramp of our feet on the hard road.

'We have had our webbing equipment issued. When it is all fixed together by slipping two braces over our shoulders we can in the space of two seconds load ourselves with belt, bayonet, trenching tool, haversack, water bottle, 150 cartridges and overcoat etc etc and the whole lot can be as quickly taken off.

'I have just been to tea which consisted of bread and butter and cake. We didn't like the idea of stale bread and butter as the canteen is not yet open, we clubbed together and bought a tin of Lyle's Golden Syrup from another tent for 3d.'

The last couple of weeks in September saw White moving from recording the drama of getting the battalion established to logging the routine of training. Evidently bureaucracy had caught up with the cavalier approach taken by White and Maxwell in getting

10RF at Colchester, presents, especially cake, were always welcome. Laureen Ellington

Thomas Driver Stk661, seated left, and friends with cake. Laureen Ellington

equipment. On 21 September White noted that they'had to hand in the short rifles which we had practically stolen'. Companies were sent out into the training areas around Colchester to begin their basic training and familiarisation with army procedures, drills and musket practices.

Medical matters took priority towards the end of the month with the men paying visits to the dentist and being inoculated. The men were in good heart, keen to start their army life and to make the best of the conditions; the good weather experienced that month was clearly helpful. White had made an extremely good job of recruiting over 1000 men. He, supported by Egerton-Warburton and Maxwell, had put the camp together using the facilities provided by the army, and adding to these from their own or City funds.

Wilkinson was typical in recording that his general level of fitness was improving. The men had come from the smogs and fogs of London into the relatively clean and clear air of Essex. They were having regular, if boring, meals and exercise; they were stimulated by the new situations but not all were physically fit as over the next few weeks and months individuals were returned to the Fusiliers depot as being not yet fit for active service. The officers were mostly experienced and men of some style, big game hunters, explorers, professional soldiers. Maxwell commented on the fact that thirteen of the officers were over six feet tall. This quality was in contrast with that experienced in other parts of the army. Guy Chapman who joined 13RF, later a sister to 10RF in 111 Brigade, 37th Division, wrote that

> *'Many [officers] displayed only too patently their intention of getting through the war as quietly, comfortably and profitably as possible.'*

Similar to the 'Pals' battalions of workers from one factory, or inhabitants of a town joining the same battalion, 10RF although coming from all over London and the neighbouring counties, had experiences in common. Their near neighbours in Colchester, 11RF, had recruits from Manchester and Notting Hill and their embryonic sister 13RF, was:

> 'broken off from a swarm of men at the depot some three months earlier and from then left almost completely to its own devices. It never had more than three Regular officers and those very senior and very retired.'

Most of 10RF were employees in offices in the City of London. Early references to the battalion in *The City Press* refer to the 'City Battalion', which is accurate though wide in scope; it is not clear at what point they adopted the more specific name 'Stockbrokers' Battalion'. The support from the City gave advantages not shared by others in Kitchener's Second New Army (K2) battalions.

The City Press of Saturday, 3 October carried a report of the presentation of the band instruments:

> 'In a very appropriate and patriotic way the Musician's Company, of which Mr Clifford B. Edgar DL, JP, Mus Doc, BSc, is the Master, has associated itself with the new 10th Battalion of the Royal Fusiliers by presenting it with a complete equipment for a band...The instruments have already been forwarded to Colchester where the battalion is being trained.'

In addition to obtaining the band instruments and the promise of a machine gun, Maxwell recorded the advantage of the City connection and of having rich men in the ranks:

> 'One fund we called the Lord Mayor's Fund and I think that Sir Vansittart Bowater must have obtained donations for it. Another and lesser fund had a name but I have forgotten it. The third we called the Lyon Fund from the name of its founder. One of the wonderful people in our ranks was Rothschild[8], a member of the illustrious family, and a friend of his coming to see him said he would like to give us some money to increase our comfort. He seemed to imply that he would give us as much as we would like to take. Finally we accepted three thousand pounds from this generous Mr Lyon. We had not the face to take any more.'

The present day (2013) value is estimated as being over £250,000.

Chapter 2

Training at Colchester: September to December 1914

September was spent in settling into the new accommodation, becoming used to being away from home and adopting the routines of army life. Drill, marching and some route marches were combined with miniature range firing to get the men working together and to assess their level of skill in the basic arts of the soldier. Having completed firing on the miniature range more physical training started in earnest. On 1 October White noted:

> *'First big march out to Wivenhoe whence we did a rearguard action.'*

George Young reported the events of his week:

> *'Sunday 4 October*
> *'Very many thanks for your welcome letter which I received safely yesterday. By your specially arranged balance sheet I can clearly see that before very long I shall have a nice little bit in the Post Office. Re The Guildhall School of Music, the deposit fee is 5 shillings which they should send home. Will you let me know if they haven't sent it in a few days time and I will write to them about it? By the way that concert I was going to give has been postponed until October 29. I will let you know more about it later on.*
> *'Well Dad, things are going on much as before. I was inoculated for the second and last time yesterday and am feeling just as fit as ever. I have entirely lost my pale complexion by living in the open air. We are not going into barracks until the middle of this month and we are not sorry either. I think it is very improbable that I shall get another weekend leave for a while but should stand a chance of getting leave from 9am Sunday morning till midnight. If I do I shall come home if only for an hour or two. What about the cake mother was going to send? I hope she is quite well. I hope Charlie will have a jolly good holiday. Best love to Florrie and Doris.'*

George Wilkinson wrote to his sister on 5 October telling her that he's finished with seeing the dentist and has also finished his inoculation and vaccinations. He continued the letter on the 7th because while writing earlier in the week:

> *'The battalion was paraded and are now living in married quarters, twelve men to a house and we have two rooms and a scullery, coal cellar with a supply of coal, electric light, meat safe etc, etc.'*

Living in married quarters, Colchester. Much better than the accommodation available for other K2 battalions. Paul Reed

In his next letter, which is undated, George Young also told his mother of moving into the new accommodation:

> 'You may wonder why I haven't written thanking you for the beautiful cake and sausage rolls but there has been such tremendous excitement here for the last few days that I have had no time for anything. The fact is that we have been moving into married quarters

Preparing for bayonet practice, Colchester. Although much promoted as a weapon few attacks were 'at the point of the bayonet'. Paul Reed

which is a kind of barracks only much better. It is a positive luxury compared with tents. It is just like an ordinary flat and we sleep 4 in a room about the size of Florrie's bedroom, so you can imagine we are quite comfortable. Instead of candles there is incandescent gas and besides that there are various luxuries like cupboards and scullery etc all of which make it so much easier to keep everything in order.

'We were delighted with the cake you sent and had it Sunday tea time and of course we should like another whenever you feel inclined to make one. I sang at a concert in Colchester last night but have got rather a bad cold. However I went down all right and got a tremendous encore.'

In his diary on the 7th White recorded that the four companies moved into Connaught, Cambridge and Victoria blocks of married quarters. He also attended the funeral of Sergeant Hurden, who died aged 38. Alfred Hurden, born in Truro, a draper's apprentice in Truro in 1891 and a warehouseman in a company lodging in St Saviour's London in 1901, was married in West Ham in 1905 and in the 1911 census was listed as a dressing gown manufacturer living in Walthamstow with his wife and two young children. He had suddenly collapsed and died in the sergeants' mess tent at the camp on 4 October. Following an inquest on the following day the Coroner recorded that the cause of death was apoplexy. After the war his widow remarried and lived in Maida Vale, London.

The training syllabus followed by the volunteers was aimed at raising fitness, with drill to instil the instinctive following of commands and field craft. For much of the time at Colchester the training was up to the level of the company and the letters record how this differed slightly.

Personal matters were still contained in the letters home and once leave began both Wilkinson and Young gave details of trains to be caught, routes to be followed to meet friends and family and how late they could be to ensure they get back to Colchester in time. Complaints about the life were virtually non-existent. Stoicism was very much the vogue with Young commenting in one letter that 'it was rather horrid having to sleep again in rough blankets but we soon got used to that'.

The enthusiasm of young men having an adventure continued to shine through with Wilkinson giving particularly clear accounts of events. Parcels with cakes and other delights were greeted with great warmth and thanks. On Sunday 18 October he wrote home:

'Yesterday was full of interesting events commencing at 8am when the battalion paraded. We had had an earlier parade for Swedish Drill, presumably on account of the bad light. We marched into the country for about five miles and practised skirmishing during the morning in stubble fields returning for dinner at 12:30. It was a delightful morning the country is simply glorious now and the weather still continually dry. We drilled again from 2 to 3 and rested till 4 o'clock.

'At 4 o'clock we set out to clean the house. I washed the linoleum in the bedroom. Gratwick scrubbed the landing and stairs and Parnell washed the scullery. We had lighted the copper at 3 o'clock and had heaps of hot water. We resumed our labours after

tea and cleaned the windows and the knives and forks. At 7 o'clock Parnell took me to some friends he has discovered in Colchester and we stayed chatting all the evening. They are florists and fruiterers who have their own fruit farms. Mr Rice is a churchwarden and has invited us both to dinner next Sunday.

'I was on orderly duty and heard that the band instruments had arrived; supplied by the Worshipful Company of Musical Instrument Makers and the twenty-six bandsmen are all good musicians.'

White began to assess his officers and how the men responded to training.

'19 October: To B area. Keppel's Company (B) did the attack. I criticised and analysed.
'20th: To E area. D Company (Gouldborn) did attack. Badly carried out.
'22nd: A Company (Cobbold) attacked in F area from Lower Houses to Layer House. Very well carried out.
'23rd: 1st battalion attack from Peldon to a line Abberton Church to Badcocks Farm. I commanded Reserves. Fairly well done.
'24th: A area. D Company Taylor and Walters brought convoy from Heckford Bridge to Bottle End. Convoy attacked by B (Boileau) from Kingford (Fane, Sharp). Fleming reinforced the convoy at Brickwall Farm.
'27th: C Area McLean commanding C and A Companies attacked from Smithy and Barechurch towards Abberton Church and Farthinghoe across the river. A good, useful scheme.
'28th: Night march left 5pm via Maypole Farm through Barechurch to Kingsford thence Olivers to Bottle End. Home at 8:30pm.'

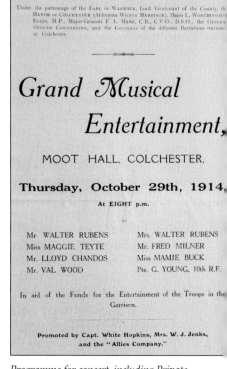

Programme for concert, including Private Young. Private Rubens played the piano.
Sharp Collection IWM

Culture and education were not forgotten among the training. Wilkinson began to attend classes in French at Colchester Grammar School. Lord Baden-Powell, Chief Scout, paid a visit to Colchester towards the end of October to meet all the scouts there who had joined the army. He shook hands with each of the 400, a source of great pride for Wilkinson. White noted in his diary that there was a concert on 29 October where Mrs Walter Rubens, Miss Maggie Teyte and White Hopkins all sang; he didn't mention the fact that Private George Knight Young also appeared and featured in the printed programme.

October was a busy month for Maxwell. He visited a doctor to try to find a cure for his foot which he had injured as a child and which for years had limited his mobility. He followed the advice and this, coupled with regular exercise, meant that he could walk quite well before the end of 1914. Hawker asked him to become Regimental Transport Officer, with fifty men to train, with the help of a sergeant. He discovered some fundamental problems:

> 'The fact that we had no horses available made riding lessons difficult to organise. I therefore bought some more horses, again trusting to the Government or the Lyon fund to defray the cost in the end.'

Colonel Hawker was concerned for the safety of his house on the Bosphorus, purchased when he was in command of the Turkish Constabulary. Maxwell undertook the task of visiting the American Embassy to obtain from the American Ambassador, Page, a guarantee that the house would be safe. He persuaded Page to break off from a meeting with the French Ambassador to see him and promise that all that could be done would be done to protect the house.

Letters from Young and Wilkinson recorded life in the ranks. Wilkinson on 30 October gave the information that:

> 'We have just been taught how to make bread and stew etc in our mess tins and we expect shortly to go out for the day and cook our own food. We are still having our outings in the country and the trespass boards have no terrors for us.'

Like many of his fellows Young was keen to get comfortable as the weather became colder:

> 'Tell Charlie I got the Phospherine⁹ and I am sure it is doing me a lot of good. Now that the cold days are coming on we have to take care of ourselves and I was thinking that a pair of woollen cuffs would be very acceptable. Quite a lot of the fellows have them and find them jolly comfortable.'

Medical matters and duties also featured:

> 'Yesterday I was on cookhouse fatigue which means that you have to chop wood, peel potatoes, carrots, turnips etc and various other delightful jobs. It was really good fun. Did I tell you we were vaccinated this week? The arm is going on splendidly.'

As did social and musical news:

> 'We knew that the King was coming to Colchester but he didn't come to see us, I suppose he was too busy. I have received some very nice songs from Messrs Boosey and Co so I shan't have to spend much money on songs now.'

The battalion was keen to get to France. Many men had enlisted believing that this would be a quicker way of getting to grips with the Germans than going through selection and training as an officer. White was equally keen to get fully involved in the war. In his diary for 31 October 1914 he wrote:

> *'Motored to see Lord Roberts re the Battalion. Up to the War Office to see Kitchener's secretary (Sir G. Arthur) re getting into the First Army.'*

The First Army had been raised by Regiments as adjuncts to their existing Regular and Territorial battalions. The Second Army was raised from volunteers and not all the battalions were adopted by the War Office until they had completed much of their training. They were, therefore, going to be later in crossing to France than the First Army.

Training became more varied and White logged the process of training and other events:

> *'November 2: B and C Companies out at Layer de La Haye and Layer Hall areas.*
> *'November 12: I area. Judged distance and made range card from Collars Farm with 2 platoons of C. Passed 3 sections of D and one of B.*
> *'November 13: To D Area. Companies had dinner out at Birch Hall. Wet. Colonel Hawker received instructions to sail to Egypt.*
> *'November 16: Took over temporary command of the Battalion. Hon John Fortescue lectured in the evening on 'Albuera'.*
> *'November 21: Warburton had a very bad fall with his horse, dislocated hip.*
> *'November 27: Digging and advanced guard at Kingsford. First concert in the double canteen.*
> *'November 28: Colonel Hawker sailed for Egypt.*

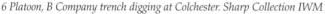

6 Platoon, B Company trench digging at Colchester. Sharp Collection IWM

Trench digging. Once in France many days were spent digging and reparing trenches. Paul Reed

On 2 November Wilkinson wrote:

> *'We have had an interesting time today. We went firing this morning and got rather wet and this afternoon we dug a trench. This is the first trench digging we have done and we all prefer it to drill; it thoroughly warmed us up after a rather cold morning.'*

On 11 November he wrote:

> *'We have had an interesting week so far and were sent to the hospital this morning to be vaccinated. There were three doctors in attendance and they were exceedingly careful. I went to the dentist on Monday and he stopped my tooth. I have now finished with the dentist for some time now I hope.*
>
> *'The army is very generous lately we have had sardines, celery and watercress for tea, not to mention bread pudding at dinner time.*
>
> *'I have heard nothing more about us going to the continent so we must wait and see.'*

Wilkinson sent his sister a postcard on 18 November showing B Company digging trenches.

> *'To fill up the time lectures have been arranged. On Monday evening the greatest authority on military history, a Mr Fortesque [sic] came up from London and lectured us on the deeds of the Fusiliers. On Tuesday we had one of a series of lectures on 'The German Empire', on Wednesday the Army Act was read to us, it lasted about an hour*

and a quarter and details the various offences for which 'the penalty is death or any punishment' etc etc. In the afternoon we had a lesson in knot tying and in the evening a lecture in elementary first aid. This morning three men with instruments assisted the Bandmaster in teaching us some fine marching songs. All these lectures take place in the 'Double Canteen' which has a large hall and stage like our church house.'

To carry on the traditions and maintain the reputation of a proud and ancient regiment was usually done through lectures by officers and the passing on of tradition through memorial events and tales told by the NCOs. With the speed of formation of the New Armies this was not possible and so White found other ways to at least give the outlines of the key points of the Fusiliers' history by engaging Sir John Fortescue, military historian and librarian of Windsor Castle to lecture the battalion. Again the contrast with the 13RF is of interest as Chapman complains:

'It never had more than three regular officers and those very senior and very retired. In consequence it learned nothing of the traditions of its name – few could have told you anything of Alma or Albuera – and knew nothing of its four regular battalions.'

In his letter of 19th Wilkinson told his family of the changes in command:

'You will be surprised that our Commanding Officer Colonel Hawker, was suddenly sent off to Egypt as he has had a lot of experience with the Turks. Major White as second in command is now temporarily in command of the Battalion.'

Hawker, formerly head of the Turkish Constabulary was fluent in the language. As Turkey was an important element in the alliances of the war, the command in Egypt wanted to create a strong intelligence service and during the last months of 1914 moved a number of serving officers, and other experts with relevant experience, to Cairo. Those lacking the military standing were quickly given commissions and formed the core of the Intelligence Service which was of great importance during the Gallipoli Campaign and afterwards in other actions in the Middle East.

Hawker's departure apparently had little impact on the battalion as neither Maxwell nor Young make mention of his going or the appointment and later promotion of Major White who on 6 December was gazetted Lieutenant Colonel and appointed to command the 10RF. He wrote in his diary on that day that 'O. Birley made a drawing of me', presumably to celebrate his appointment.

Training in November and December continued in increasingly wet and wintery conditions with marches, cross country exercises, skirmishes and some drill. All companies did entrenching work during the day and at night and incorporated attack and defence using the trenches they had just dug. On 11 December White commanded the right of the attack in the first brigade tactical exercise and as he says in his diary 'took out Cobbold, Maclean and Keppel and twelve despatch riders and kept them busy'. A new activity, which doubtless made the battalion think of leaving Colchester, was when White took two companies to St Botolph's Station to practise training and detraining.

One effect of a change in weather was that on 4 December White recorded that the officers' mess tent blew down. Each company in the battalion had five days Christmas leave in rotation: Wilkinson and B Company from 11 – 16 December; C Company from 16th, D Company from 21st, and A Company, including Young, from 29th.

In an undated letter, but probably written in the middle of December, Young wrote:

'Darling Mother and Dad, I expect you were rather surprised to hear that I was at Felixstowe, although the card I sent you didn't contain much information.

'As a matter of fact we have had a most interesting and enjoyable three day route march. We started from barracks on Wednesday morning about 10 o'clock and marched to Ipswich, a distance of about nineteen miles, arriving there at 6 o'clock in the evening.

'We slept there in a skating rink. It was a most picturesque sight to see 300 men all huddled together in the middle of a big skating rink.

'Thursday we marched from there to Felixstowe and stayed the night in wooden huts with straw to lie on. Felixstowe is now a most deserted place, barbed wire entrenchments being strewn out all over the place. Then yesterday we crossed the water to Harwich, the trip being most enjoyable but much too short, and marched from Harwich back to Colchester. Yesterday's march was about twenty-five miles so that in all we covered roughly fifty-six miles in the three days which we thought a very creditable performance considering we had to carry about fifty pounds on our backs. Today we made out our passes for Christmas leave on 29th so I don't suppose we shall have it stopped on account of this Scarborough business.'

Preparing for lunch break, the men with white bands on their hats were officer cadets, identified for commissions.
Paul Reed

All the major ports were guarded by members of Special Reserve Battalions and fortified by the Engineers. There was a real fear of attack from the German Fleet. Scarborough, on the Yorkshire coast, was, along with Whitby and Hartlepool, subjected to a naval bombardment on 16 December 1914 adding to the fears of invasion. It is thought that the Germans were targeting the coast guard station and the Naval Wireless Station but they succeeded in hitting the Grand Hotel, lighthouse and shops and houses with some of the 500 plus shells that were fired. Some passed over the town and landed on farms and villages inland. Seventeen people, all but one civilians, were killed and about twenty injured. In all three raids a total of 137 people were killed and nearly 600 injured.

Wilkinson returned from leave on 16 December and the following week wrote home about the activities he had been involved in:

> 'We have had quite an interesting time since we returned although the ground is damp. Last Saturday we went across country, jumping ditches and lying down in muddy fields, and returned home absolutely plastered in clay. Poor Parnell fell over a bank headfirst into a soft clayey field and his rifle stuck in about a foot. He had to buy a hat pin on Sunday to pick the mud out of the barrel! We thoroughly enjoyed ourselves however and on Sunday Parnell and I walked eleven miles without a stop, we like a change.
>
> 'Monday morning as it was wet we were taken into the canteen and watched fellows boxing and in the afternoon I was included in a party who motored into the country and cut a wagon load of holly to decorate our happy homes.'

Christmas, the first away from home for many, was prepared for by both the men and their families. Young wrote to thank his parents:

> 'Darling Mum and Dad, I have just received the splendid parcel which you have so kindly sent and of course must thank you immediately.
>
> 'Tremendous excitement pervades the whole company just now. Everybody is either expecting a Christmas parcel, or has just received one and even in camp the spirit of Christmas is making itself felt.
>
> 'We have erected three huge marquees where we are going to have our dinner on Friday and I believe they are going to give us a real good time.'

His finances were still giving him problems as he wrote:

> 'I wrote to Hind Bede and Ellis asking them to send my money straight on here as I want some badly and thought it would save time.'

Christmas Day arrived and those not on leave were entertained in camp. Wilkinson wrote an account of the day, not entirely matching the description given by his commanding officer.

White's diary:

> 'December 25: Christmas Day. To church with the Battalion. Dinner at 1pm. Concert and play 3pm. Dance 6pm. Lights out 11:15pm. Good little boys.

Getting ready for Christmas. Laureen Ellington

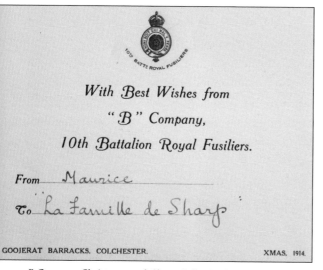

With Best Wishes from
"B" Company,
10th Battalion Royal Fusiliers.

From Maurice
To La Famille de Sharp

GOOJERAT BARRACKS, COLCHESTER.   XMAS. 1914.

B Company Christmas card. Sharp Collection IWM

CHRISTMAS
1914

NEW YEAR
1915

*10RF Christmas card, possibly designed by Private
Oswald Birley R.A. Sharp Collection IWM*

'December 26: Very Wet. Battalion route march through Colchester to Mile End and back. Band gave a dance in the evening.'

On 29th Wilkinson wrote a joint letter to his whole family:

'Christmas Day was a festive event. Dinner was provided by the officers and in the afternoon there was a concert in which the officers gave a touching sketch and a dance was arranged for the evening. Parnell and I went out after tea and called in at the canteen on our return to see how the dance was getting on. With the exception of a few sergeants' wives and two or three bar maids from the town and a programme seller from the Hippodrome there were no ladies but the hall was full of chaps in heavy boots, some even with overcoats careering in couples round the room to the robust strains of our military band. Parnell and I passed on.

'Boxing morning the whole Battalion paraded with the band and had a route march through the town. Then it began to rain – it continued! it rained still more!! and we arrived back soaked to the skin. We spent the rest of the morning changing our clothes and drying our rifles. In the evening we went to the Hippodrome where B Company, from the Circle, bombarded A Company, who were sitting in the stalls, with peashooters.

'On Sunday morning, as it was raining, the welcome 'no parade' sounded but it was followed shortly by the order to thoroughly oil all rifles. We started to do so when the order was countermanded and we were told to 'dry clean' all rifles for inspection. This

took about three-quarters of an hour. Our officers then minutely inspected the rifles to see that there was no rust and after that we had to smother them with oil again to prevent them rusting. At 12 o'clock we were paraded again and the rifles were collected. At 2 o'clock we had issued to us a brand new rifle of the latest pattern so that we are now quite proud of our arms which we pat and fondle to an extraordinary degree. It took me about an hour and a half on Sunday afternoon to clean mine and get it free from the Vaseline in which it had been packed but the operation was a pure pleasure.

'Yesterday (28th) at 8:15am we marched out with full packs and our rifles to a place called Fingeringhoe where we dug trenches on the side of a hill overlooking lovely country. It rained while we marched back but soon ceased. Parnell and I went to tea with Mrs Peak.'

That night, the last of the year recorded by any of the authors, was one of wild weather as Wilkinson wrote in his letter:

'When we came out after supper the wind was blowing a perfect hurricane and we had quite a struggle to make headway. We had just got comfortably into bed when the bugle sounded and men were rushing up and down shouting 'fall in B Company'. Then followed a scramble into trousers and coats. We couldn't keep our hats on so I tied Rene's scarf round my head and went out into the sleet. Here everybody was shouting to make themselves heard above the gale. 'What's up?' 'German's have landed at Clacton?' But we were dismissed within 5 minutes without any information and found this morning that our marquees had blown down.'

Chapter 3

Colchester and Andover:
January to March 1915

Equipped with their new short rifles the battalion spent most of January on the ranges at Donylands. Lieutenant Sharp got a new diary for Christmas and his voice joins the narrative. White's diary recorded simply that 'nearly all January the battalion was occupied at musketry'.

Sharp listed the daily turn of events; in addition to the routine of the ranges he recorded more personal social activities with his brother officers:

'January 1st Dug all day at Donyland
'January 2nd 3 rounds of ball ammunition on the miniature range. Tea at Miss Lockwood's
'January 4th Recruits musketry course, Middlewich 200 yards
'January 5th As yesterday Middlewich all day 500 yards application
'January 6th As before

B Company photograph, George Wilkinson mentions his company photographs on a number of occasions. Paul Reed

10RF marching at Colchester, not enough rifles to go round. Paul Reed

'January 7th   Very wet, more shooting
'January 8th   My 21st birthday. Musketry at Middlewich, tea with Roberts, dinner in mess, health drunk in champagne. Played bridge, lost heavily.'

Wilkinson writing home on Sunday 10 January wrote about the ranges, was grateful to his sister Rene for sending him a warm belt and expressed the hope that she and her friend Ada would come to Colchester where 'I can provide you with tea in my sitting room if you would like to sample soldiers' grub'. He continued: 'We have been on the ranges firing every day since last Monday and including today. We shall finish our course tomorrow. I am very fond of shooting and have done very well.'

Second Lieutenant Sharp continued to log events but a visit from his older sister Evelyn (Evie), gave a diversion:

'January 9   More musketry. Evelyn arrives, met her, lunch at Miss Lockwood's. Dinner party at the Officers' Club, Evelyn and I, Roberts and his sister.
'January 10   No church for me. Musketry until 2pm. Birley and I motored to Wivenhoe with Evelyn.
'January 11   Last day of musketry. Evie came out to ranges with Miss Lockwood. Finished about 3pm. Dinner at Miss L's in evening from 7pm. I sang, Evie played and Miss L played, said good-bye to Evie.
'January 12   Half Holiday Inspected houses in the morning and handed our rifles over to A Company. Motored with Roberts and Birley to Braintree for lunch, had dinner at Langley's.
'January 13   Wet all morning did nothing until the afternoon. Took B Company for route march. Seven miles via station to Leseden and Shrub End.

'January 14 Glorious day. Route march by half companies, 5 and 6 [platoons] go via Birch to Layer de la Haye, Fingerinhoe to Ipswich. Motor back to lecture in organisation of a platoon.

'January 15 Company to Langenhoe Lodge. Attack Plane Hall for General Drummond's benefit. Go to London by 2:15pm. Coutts, photo taken at Lafayetts. Catch 6:50pm home [Reading] go to Adams with Helen [his younger sister] after supper.'

B Company had passed their rifles to A Company on January 12 to allow George Young and his colleagues to begin their musketry course on that day. He wrote home on 17 January:

Darling Mother, Ever so many thanks for the splendid cakes you and Doris so kindly sent. They really are excellently made and we could not resist trying them at tea time yesterday.

'It is now Sunday and, contrary to the usual custom of Church Parade we have to go to the ranges to continue our rifle practice. This afternoon Rubens and I are going to Captain White-Hopkins' place to tea. I sang at the last concert of the season which he arranged and his wife asked us there today. The bright weather of spring will not be long now.

'Your affectionate son, George'

Second Lieutenant Maurice Sharp, a formal portrait, probably taken on his visit to London 15 January 1915. Sharp Collection IWM

After his weekend at home Sharp returned to Colchester for the start of the new week. He took up the new role of butts officer for the week, supervising and marking the shooting of C Company. The weather was cold, and he wrote on Wednesday 20 January 'life not worth living at all'. He did manage a couple of games of bridge, losing four shillings one evening but winning six shillings towards the end of the week. A visit on Thursday evening to Miss Lockwood included two hours of playing works by Berlioz and Chopin on the piano.

Sharp noted that B Company did a route march on the 25th, covering twenty miles taking five and three-quarter hours. They also took part in an attack at Fingeringhoe and 10RF beat 8 Battalion, Norfolk Regiment two goals to one in a football match. Wilkinson was similarly matter of fact about the week writing to his mother on 27th that:

'On Monday we marched twenty miles with full packs and rifle and on Tuesday we did ten miles and an attack. Today we have had an inspection of houses and kits and are to parade at 5:15pm for a night march.'

Sharp wrote that 27th was a slack morning with kit inspection as usual.

> 'In the afternoon at tea with Roberts at Wright's. Night marching by platoons. I took Nos 5 and 6 as far as Lexden then No 6 alone; arrived Gryme's Dyke exactly on time.'

Young wrote home about life in A Company:

> 'Dear Dad, Many thanks for your letter which I received yesterday. I am very glad that you are all quite well at home.
>
> 'Apparently the fall of snow was heavier in London than here although it was a most beautiful sight to see all the country covered with white. Naturally we had some sport out of it and on Friday we had a fine pitched battle of snow balls.
>
> 'We have now practically completed our course of shooting and I am pleased to say that A Company beat all the others and is now the finest shooting company in Kitchener's Army. Unfortunately one day a man was shot a mile and a half away from the rifle range and has since died. Today is Sunday and all is slosh and mud so that we are not sorry to go to church and have the rest of the day around a barrack room fire. There is a rather well-founded rumour that we are going to Aldershot before long but of course we don't know for certain.
>
> 'Give my love to all at home, tell mother not to work too hard.'

The mention of a man being killed on the range referred to the shooting of Private W.G. Hayden, number 7604, a member of 11RF who is buried in Colchester Cemetery. The incident is recorded in 'The 54th Infantry Brigade 1914-1918 History' which says:

> 'The first casualty in the Brigade was a man in the 11th Royal Fusiliers, who was badly wounded on January 18th 1915, whilst walking over the entrenching area behind the butts of the rifle range at Donyland.'

Sharp and Boileau inspectiong 6 Platoon B Company at Donylands, the training area near Colchester. Sharp Collection IWM

Sharp and B Company spent the last few days of January digging trenches at Copford where 'B Company entrenched themselves in two hours'. Sharp, accompanied by Roberts then went to see the Royal Engineers completing other trenches; he failed to see the point of the exercise. The Sunday morning began with breakfast in bed and after getting up at 10:15am he went by car with Roberts and Hall to Harwich; 'Lunch and tea there, a lovely day'.

Young wrote to his mother on 2 February about what he was seeing as tedium and an illness which affected a number of the men:

> *'Darling Mother, I am sure you will be wondering why I have not written to you before this but I have been expecting a letter from you and thought I would wait till I got that.*
> *'Well, dear, there is not much news to tell you as we are simply doing the same old things which are now becoming frightfully tedious.*
> *'This week we have got to practise drills in view of the forthcoming inspection by the General. It is a most monotonous performance and makes me wish for London and the end of the war. On Saturday night I sang at an Officers' Club concert but owing to a sore throat could only sing 2 songs. Everybody here seems either to have a cough or a cold. I suppose it is because of the changeable weather. There is not much to do in Colchester of an evening. An order has just been issued forbidding lights of any description to be shown in shop windows which makes the place look duller than before. Generally Dudley[10] and I go down to Dace's the music shop in Colchester and he plays to me and I sing to him. He is really a most lovely pianist and an extremely nice man.*
> *'Expecting to hear from you before long.*
> *'Your ever loving son, George'*

All was not tedium and dullness for the other three companies as on 2 February Sharp noted that having spent the morning filling in trenches there was an afternoon conference of officers regarding the forthcoming battalion scheme and a night exercise. On the pouring wet night 'I took Boileau out to attack C & D'. Writing to his sister on 3 February Wilkinson told the story of the evening's event for the entertainment of his family; but not before he confirmed that the 10RF were a proud bunch of men, determined to set a high standard of dress and deportment:

> *'Dear Rene, Thank you very much for your letter and the Brilliantine and Denta Cream. I was surprised to find when I used the Denta Cream that it lathers up like soap and gave me the appearance of a gee-gee after a gallop. Yesterday evening we had quite an exciting affair. C and D Companies, numbering some 500 men, paraded at 5pm with wagons containing picks and shovels and marched away for some night trench digging quite ignorant that B Company were to parade later and give them a surprise attack.'*

He described the approach through the dark and rain, whistling 'Somewhere the sun is shining'. They followed the man in front by holding his coat tail; the officers (he named Lieutenant Roberts, and Second Lieutenants Fane and Knox) got lost and had to turn back.

'Lieutenant Roberts, having marshalled the main company, started off at a breakneck pace to make up for lost time. About six of us stuck to his heels but the remainder gradually dropped behind. We came upon the Major who was waiting for us. "Hulloa", shouted the Major, "Boi——leau" came back the answer from the Colonel "Go———Home", "Ri——ght" bellowed the Major.

'We turned back. The rain stopped, the stars came out and lighted up the country just to show its nasty temper. We got back to barracks at 9:15pm and were served with hot cocoa and biscuits.'

Sharp on right with, from l-r Fane, Boileau, Roberts. Sharp Collection IWM

On the 3rd the battalion carried out its first full scale attack from Abberton to Peldon. The weekly kit inspection was carried out in the morning of Wednesday the 4th. In the afternoon Sharp stayed in prior to carrying out a night attack with Roberts and B Company. On the 5th Sharp and B Company marched 9.5 miles in three hours. After this he took to his bed with a sore throat and was out of action ill and on home sick leave until Tuesday the 16th.

Rumours about future movements were constant. After leave at home the previous weekend George Young wrote home on 9th:

'Darling Mother, I got back safely on Sunday evening after a very enjoyable weekend but need not have left so early as there was no train between the 6:39pm and 8:40pm.
'The cakes and apples were excellent although I liked the big cakes you make better of course. Today the weather is beastly and we have got the morning off.'

George Wilkinson avoided the colds and sore throats as on the 10th he wrote home:

'I am still feeling very fit and well and have taken to reading a good bit in my spare time. Yesterday we marched twenty miles with only four or five breaks of ten minutes. It poured with rain all the time and the water drained off our overcoats into our boots which was quite cool and refreshing. We changed immediately on our return and hardly felt any fatigue at all, neither have we felt stiff or tired today. We have today been issued with canvas shoes for indoor wear, we shall get collars and cuffs next I suppose.'

More battalion training filled the coming days of February, when weather permitted. Sharp recorded that rain prevented the Battalion Day on the 17th but when it was held on the following day he was complimented by the general on taking Parange Farm. The following day saw B Company doing more forced marches and practising going through woodland in extended order. Sharp with No 6 Platoon was in reserve for the Battalion Day at Fingeringhoe. That afternoon the footballers beat those of the Suffolk Regiment nine goals to two in a semi final.

Company parade. Laureen Ellington

The war came to Colchester on the night of 21 February. A Zeppelin dropped a bomb which caused damage to a house in Butts Road; Sharp went to see it, White wrote in his diary…

> 'German bomb fell in back garden of some houses in Butt Road near Artillery Barracks. Advanced billeting party went on to Andover.'

…and Wilkinson sent a postcard home two days later showing the damage.

> 'Colchester Tuesday: Parnell was within fifty yards of where the bomb dropped in Butts Road. He was taking his mother to the station.
> 'We are off to Andover tomorrow and HM The King invited us to march past Buckingham Palace but train arrangements won't allow us to.'

The two days before the move took place were spent in cleaning the houses. Wilkinson and Young were probably too busy cleaning to write before the move so the only records written on the day were those in the diaries of White and Sharp. Sharp was very brief:

> 'Miss Russell-Roberts arrived. We don't go until 1pm.'

White gave a more detailed account of the move on 25th February:

> '9:30am Battalion parade. 10:38am First train left with all the Transport and 180 men of D Company. 12:25pm second train with the balance of D Company, all baggage and 240 men of C Company. 1:25pm 3rd train with A, B Companies. The Adjutant and Regimental Sergeant Major travelled by the first train which arrived at 4:25pm. Travelling by Stratford, Hackney, Gunnersbury and Richmond. Lieutenant Hunter, Quartermaster and twenty men sent on made good arrangements for billeting, Orderly Room and Battalion HQ in cricket pavilion. Sergeant Major at 78 High Street, a guard post opposite the White Hart. All in by 7:30pm.'

On the following day the battalion paraded at 8:45am and the officers spent the rest of the day inspecting the men's billets. Wilkinson wrote a long letter home to get the family up to date with events:

'C/o Mrs Noyse, 6 Alton Terrace, Vigo Road, Andover, Hampshire

'I've arrived. We got here last night at 7pm and marched through the town headed by our band to the Town Hall. There are six of us here, Parnell, Cordingley, Hulford and one or two other fellows in a tiny cottage. It is a tight fit but we are thoroughly comfortable and the food is A1. Mrs Noyes, who is the mother of ten grown up children, treats us as if we were a further addition to the family and we are feeling quite at home.

'Four of us have mattresses on the floor in one room the other two have a double bed in a small room upstairs, we all feed in the kitchen and have use of a front room for reading etc. (Our Company Officer Major Boileau has just inspected our quarters and banged his head on the ceiling while climbing upstairs to the bedroom)…

'When I reached barracks in the evening all lights were out on account of the bomb dropping. On Monday we had to turn everything out of the houses into the street. Pettycoat [sic] Lane was eclipsed. Jam jars, beer bottles, books, old clothes, rifles, tables, chairs, homemade sugar box sideboards etc etc, covered the street and a chap next door wacked [sic] out old English melodies on a clarinet, like some street musician outside a pub on a wet day. We scrubbed the houses from top to bottom and strewed newspaper about so that in the words of Colonel White we could give a clean "(H) 'Andover". We carried out six bathfuls of rubbish to the refuse heap, where 'old-clo' men were picking and stealing, and put the little that remained back in the houses.

'Parnell and I intended to call on Mr Rice and Mrs Peck on Monday evening but it rained so that we stayed in. I went to a lecture by Lieutenant Harley on his personal

Platoon at Colchester. Laureen Ellington

experiences shooting elephants, lions, rhinoceroses, hippos etc. It was intensely interesting.

'The Major General complimented the regiment in Orders. The King's Equerry wrote to our Colonel saying that HM the King would be pleased for us to march past Buckingham Palace on our way through London. Yesterday we were played out of our barracks by our band and that of 11th Fusiliers. I went by the third and last train which left at 1:30pm and arrived at Andover at 7pm. We went via Stratford, Caledonian Road, Acton, Kew, Richmond, Woking and Basingstoke.

'We are all writing home now. I am now empty of ideas, devoid of interest and my pen won't write. I will try a pen sketch of myself marching to the station behind the band with my overcoat, equipment, rifle and kit bag.'

George Young wrote on 26 February to give his new address and assure his family that all was well in his new lodgings.

'2, York Villas, Victoria Park, Andover

'After a very tedious journey on Wednesday lasting nearly seven hours we arrived here about 7:15pm and have now got billeted in a very comfortable house.

'Andover is a much prettier place than Colchester although not such a large town, but the class of people and the whole aspect of the place is far superior to Colchester, which as you can imagine, we were not sorry to leave after having been there for nearly seven months.

'The weather the last few days has been priceless and we are beginning to like Andover immensely.

'I am enclosing the withdrawal form properly signed and witnessed by the Post Office official so shall hope to hear from you soon.

'Give my love to all at home and thank mother for her letter which I was so glad to get.

Training resumed on 26 Feb. White recorded:

'A fine day. Battalion marched along Salisbury Road to Abbot's Ann, Barrow Dean Farm, Upper Clatford and back to Andover. Three hours and fifteen minutes, 1015 men on parade. Marched just under three miles per hour. Column extended along 350 yards (say one foot per man).'

The speed of march and length of column were important facts for the colonel and senior officers to know, and be able to recognise instinctively. Movement in France was predominately on foot and when large numbers of men were changing positions their routes and timings were carefully planned and published in orders to ensure there were no bottle necks and hold ups, particularly at road junctions and in towns and villages. The orders were very precise about the times for battalions to begin their moves from different rest camps or points of congregation to ensure that accumulations of troops could be avoided as they would make a target for enemy artillery. Unfortunately perfection was not always achieved, particularly when troops were moving into trenches at the same time as others were leaving and diaries and letters tell of being stuck waiting

Fane, Roberts, Boileau, Sharp ready for a Sunday outing. Sharp Collection IWM

for battalions or transport to pass. Route marches also developed fitness and being able to maintain a regular speed for a long period was important. Officers and NCOs were held to account if too many of their men dropped out of the march and had to be picked up and returned later. As will be seen later White was proud to relate, and the Battalion Diary to record, the very low dropout rate among 10RF when in France.

Sharp had been on the march with B Company and in the evening he sang and talked in the drawing room with the Herberts, presumably the people he was billeted with. On the following Saturday, 28 January, Birley drove him in his car to Reading.

> *'Evie at home. Then sing and talk. Father and Evie and Helen play duets. Leave 6:20pm and arrive 8:15pm.'*

The new week saw the training continue and intensify. Sharp wrote on 1 March:

> *'Company in wood training. Went through Harewood Forest by platoon in fours and came out at Fox's Farm. Nothing in afternoon. Conference at 5pm. Night march across country by platoons 6pm till 8:30pm.'*

On Tuesday 2nd:

> *'Battalion Field Day at Cow Down, B in reserve with Cobbold. Roberts is o/c Company. Returned 1:30pm. Rifle inspection 3pm. Went to HQ tea at 5pm. HQ for papers and conference. Returned 7:30pm.'*

10RF Officers at Andover.
Back l-r Taylor, St John, Delbos, Dexter, Bonnett, Knox
Middle l-r Hall, Fane, Shurey, Pike, Bevir, Huntington, Brown, Campbell
Front l-r ?, Popham, Keppel, McLean, White, Warburton, Henning, Roberts, Sharp. Sharp Collection IWM

Also on the 2nd Wilkinson wrote to his mother giving more impressions of the town, some evidently gleaned from his landlady:

> 'I am already very much in love with Andover despite its quietness, the civilians tell us we are quite the smartest battalion they have had here. They are very impressed with our band and flocked out to hear it on Sunday at church parade. The band played outside the Town Hall for an hour on Sunday morning in front of an admiring crowd and is to give a concert in the Assembly Rooms on Thursday.
>
> 'And the town gossip; how a barmaid married a gentleman who on his death left her £65,000 which she ran through in a few years. Mrs Noyes has her opinions about such people. And the two brothers, one killed at the front and the other was run over by a traction engine "poor thing". And the vicar, over 60, kind enough but no speaker, but you should hear his wife. The vicar invites people to supper, forgets about it and the guests arrive to find he has gone to bed. On one occasion he went to the station to see his wife off on the train. When the train came in he gave his wife sixpence and kissed the porter. Oh it's so interesting.
>
> 'Cordingley went into a shop the other evening to buy a small battery but his patience was exhausted after waiting 10 minutes. He left a polite note saying he would call back in the Spring. We have recommended our training over beautiful country, it is very hilly and chalky and quite a change from Essex.'

And on the 3rd Sharp wrote in his diary:

'Company field day at Knights Enham. Roberts and I watch others attack Birley. No afternoon parade. Night operations in Doles Wood. B Company march five and a quarter miles then do mile and a half in the wood and march back four and a half miles.'

On 3 March Wilkinson found and sent a postcard showing the house where he was staying. On the same day White recorded the evening marches in his diary:

'B Company from Hurstbourne Hall to Wildhern. D Company marched from Dales House to Boxers Bottom; C from Middle Wykes Farm to Little London and A from Hurstbourne Hill to Little London. Very wet and dark.'

He ignored the 5-mile marches to the start points and almost as far returning from the Doles Wood, Ridges and Rags Copses where the companies practised their night woodcraft.

The following day Sharp led his company to Charlton to Redhouse Park.

'Did manoeuvres in large field. Came back across country. Bath in afternoon. Tea at HQ. Conference about field day at 5pm. Went with Mrs Herbert to Band concert, very good.'

The battalion field day on Friday 5 February consisted of B Company attacking the others at Abbotts Ann just south of Andover. The company did well in the field day on the 9th, also held at Abbotts Ann, when White recorded:

Officers' lunchbreak. Sharp Collection IWM

'10th Fusiliers held passages of the Anna. C Company on the Right, B in the Centre. The latter prepared a position about three quarters of a mile back. C and D retired by the flanks and fell back another half mile. A Company attacked and were completely surprised by B who were well dug in and concealed. John Warburton commanded.'

Young was feeling in a positive mood when he wrote home. The letter is undated but it was probably written on 9 March:

'York Villas Tuesday, Darling Mother, Just a line to let you know I got back safely on Sunday night after an enjoyable weekend.
We have had a field day today which has really been quite enjoyable and the weather is delightful. Will write again soon.'

The following day, 10th, Sharp recorded an incident which is not mentioned in White's diary:

'Digging in the morning, back by 1pm. Help find error in billeting at Orderly Room. Early tea. Night manoeuvres at 5:30pm under Keppel. A complete fiasco, Roberts and the Colonel lose tempers. Home 10:30pm.'

Sharp at Andover. Sharp Collection IWM

Keppel and D Company had a bad day on the Battalion Field Day two days later on Friday, 12 March as White noted:

'D Company vanguard, C and D mainguard advancing through Andover and Charlton to Tangley. Keppel's company (D) reported Charlton all clear. When mainguard got into the village a machine gun opened fire from the church tower on the road defile and cut us to pieces.'

Wilkinson wrote to his mother on Sunday the 14th:

'You ask me to send you a long letter. Now if there is one thing I cannot do to order it is to write a long letter. It's taken me about an hour to start this one much less make it long. The 'J' pen is out of action and this one is like a needle and the ink was so low in the bottle that I had to add some water. (I'm afraid this pen will pierce the paper before long and ruffle my patience in which case you'll probably never receive this letter at all). The doings of last week although not very striking would fill pages if written in detail and I am afraid to start my narration at the beginning of the week for fear of losing heart and not reaching the end. I will start from this very moment and work backwards wedging in any titbits haphazard as they occur to me. (Which reminds me of the strange effect produced by playing a gramophone record backwards.) Church bells 'fade' forward into a roar and break off with a snap).

'Today has been a glorious one, a real Spring day. A warm sun has made everything seem cheerful, made the birds sing and brought to life numbers of tiny flies in the lanes. I have already seen a butterfly.

After church I had a walk through the town where I had a chat with Bannister who appears to be getting along happily in his married state. I got back to a steak pudding as big as a football. Parnell and two others being on leave the attack on the pudding had to be very determined but we won the day. There followed an hour of luxurious repose and then I strolled out for a solitary wander along "The Ladies Walk". It runs along a hill overlooking the town and about 13 miles of country and today with the bright sun shining and the larks singing it was quite a treat to be there. Twice this week I have been perched similarly on a hill overlooking miles and miles of country digging trenches in the chalk. It reminds me very much of my happy trench digging days at Nobesdown as we pick away in the sunshine without a care in the world and with the prospect of a healthy dinner when we return. Air, sunshine and exercise make the heart light.

'Yesterday the Gordon Highlanders came in from Tidworth to play us at football. The match was a grand one and ended in a draw. Their pipe band was in attendance and played them out of the town. Many of them were "jolly" some even before the match began, but they did waken the town up with "wee" this and "aye man" that.

'Yesterday morning I was sent out with 4 others to make our way right across country by means of map and compass. It's really quite fascinating not to mention the excitement of going through a field in which a cow, which I thought was a bull, would persist in staring at me. Curiosity in these creatures is developed to an alarming degree.

'Mrs Noyes has now come in to get a "bit of supper" so love to all and kisses to some.'

George Young writing on Tuesday, 16 February, was less enamoured with, or accepting of, the training:

> 'Darling Mother, Ever so many thanks for your lovely letter which I was so glad to get. You know I look for letters from you dear far more than from anyone and it is always a delight to see your writing on the envelope.
>
> 'I expected to get one from you on Monday as I know Sunday is your best day for writing letters and I can just imagine you sitting in the kitchen then asking Doris how to spell some difficult words.
>
> 'It was certainly rather wonderful for both Dad and you to go for a walk together on Sunday morning. I only hope you would do it again always, but of course it is difficult to both get out together.
>
> 'Well dear there is nothing of very great importance to tell you about Andover and our life is necessarily monotonous and uninteresting but we have been having a much easier time so far while we have been here than at Colchester.
>
> 'This week we have had a week of trench digging so I cannot say very much about that except that we get very white as it is all chalk here. Your suggestion about another pair of pyjamas is an excellent one and I should love to have another pair so that Mrs Puddock can wash the pair I have here.
>
> 'I cannot possibly tell when I am likely to be home again but I hope to be able to arrange something before long.
>
> 'Darling I think I have written enough now so will close. God bless you dear and keep you safe and well. Give my love to Dear Dad and the others.'

The whole battalion was digging trenches in various places around Andover. Sharp in his diary in early March wrote about having to go out to 'prospect for digging places'. On the 17th he wrote

> 'Dug as usual. Adjutant's Parade of the Battalion in the afternoon for rehearsal of inspection. Saw my billets again.'

The next two days, were busy with inspections by General Campbell and the Battalion's Honorary Colonel, the Lord Mayor. Sharp commented in his diary:

> 'Thursday 18 March: A terrible wet and cold day. Sleet and rain all morning. Inspected by Lieutenant General Sir I. Campbell at Hundred Acre Field. Very cold but General, was very pleased. Night ops at Ben Hill Farm. Roberts, Bevir and I attacked Bevin from different quarters, a great success.
>
> 'Friday 19: Usual Field Day. Only six miles out at Hurstbourne. Lord Mayor Bowater came down, lunch party in his honour. Dinner party to which Keppel invited me at Star and Garter. We all went to Battalion concert at the Assembly Rooms.'

White made no mention of the general's visit in his diary but did write up the inspection by the Honorary Colonel:

'Battalion Field Day at Hurstbourne Tarrant. The Honorary Colonel Sir T. Vansittart Bowater (Lord Mayor of London) inspected. Passed through the village and attacked the high ground on the right. Lunch in the open; Mrs G Keppel, Mrs Jenkins, Lady Gussie Fane[11] etc.'

The City Press of 27 March reported the visit by the Lord Mayor:

'As Honorary Colonel of the 10th Battalion Royal Fusiliers Alderman Sir Vansittart Bowater Bt, visited Andover on Friday of last week. The Alderman who was accompanied by Miss Bowater wore the full uniform (khaki) of the Regiment. He was escorted by a Subaltern to the field of operations where he was met by Colonel the Hon Robert White and Major the Hon George Keppel. Among others present were Mrs George Keppel and Lady Augusta Fane. The 10th Royal Fusiliers took part in field operations with several other units. Luncheon was served in the woods. There was a march past and Sir Vansittart took the salute.'

The weekend saw Sharp at leisure with few duties:

'Saturday 20th Kit inspection in morning. Finished by 10:30. Caught 11:31 to Salisbury. Visited Cathedral. Walked out with Joanna to Old Sarum and back. Gave her chocolates and marzipan. George Herbert comes on leave.
   'Sunday 21st Took Church Parade under Boileau. Motored with Shurey[12] to Farnborough to Frensham Pond for tea. His mother, aunt and brother down from London and join us. Motor back by 6:30. Supper with him and [?]Gazelli at White Hart Hotel.'

On Monday 22 March Wilkinson wrote home to his mother setting out plans for his leave on the following weekend, hoping to be home about dinner time on Saturday.

'I had a letter from Mr Short[13] yesterday saying they are still busy with lorries etc and wishing me luck. I sent him a five page reply telling what a fine time I'm having. So I am.
   'We've still no idea when we are leaving England and have, in fact, almost forgotten that there is a war. Nevertheless when the time does come for us to go we shall be ready and confident.
   'And now mother I do hope you are fit and well and that dad is quite himself again. I feel quite a monster to be so hearty and cheerful and leave to you all the worries of war and war prices.'

Sharp and B Company were again digging trenches at Wherwell.

'Tuesday 23: Battalion Field Day through Harswood Forest. Very wet and very hot. B Company lead was a great success.[14]
   'Wednesday 24: Dug all morning as usual but back fairly early. In afternoon sat on Audit Board for battalion accounts with Cobbold and Hall.

'Thursday 25: Dug all day until 2pm. Very boring indeed. Had hot bath in the afternoon. Wrote to Ruby and Evie.

'Friday 26: Battalion Field Day as usual Rearguard action at Penton Mewsey.'

Young wrote to his parents on Wednesday 24:

'Darling Mother and Dad, I expect you are both thinking it is about time I wrote to let you know what there is to be known about Andover and our life here.

'But life in the army goes on in the same monotonous and uninteresting way that the news is very limited.

'Tonight writing this letter I have come back all muddy and unclean from trench digging, a very dull performance I can tell you in the dark especially after a stiff day's work doing other things. But there is consolation in having a decent bed to sleep in.

'They are continuing to have concerts here almost every week but the Bandmaster has promised that instead of paying me for each separate concert he is going, on the last concert we give, to divide the takings between Rubens, Dudley, myself and 2 others, so that I shall get about £5[15] then if he keeps his promise.

'There is a rumour that on April 6 we are going to a place called Chistleton near Swindon for another course of musketry but one doesn't know whether to believe it or not.

'Well dear mother and dad, I do hope you are keeping absolutely fit and happy at home. I am always thinking of you and hoping you are well. I got the book from the Minister of Romney Street and am writing to thank him.

'Please give my love to Charles, Florrie and Doris.'

The next week began with an inspection by General Sir Archibald Murray who was Deputy Chief of the General Staff, Sharp wrote:

'Monday 29: Preparation for the great inspection Battalion under Adjutant. Knock off at 10:15 get hair cut. Inspection a great success, a great tribute by Sir Archibald Murray "Finest Battalion in K's Army". Tea at billets.'

The next day in a letter to his mother Wilkinson also reflected the pride felt by the battalion. He enclosed a Fusilier brooch for his mother to wear:

'The inspection by Sir Archibald Murray went off very well on Monday and he said we were the smartest Battalion in K's army that he had inspected. (We spent all Monday morning cleaning every tiny piece of brasswork on our equipment, some dozen buckles and endless other fiddly bits. It cost me 5d for Globe polish, cherry blossom and emery cloth).

'Poor old X is sitting opposite me looking very worried about the proposal to close all the pubs.[16]

'Our Colonel addressed us this morning telling us how pleased he was [that] we had done so well yesterday. He has been to the War Office who tell him that with the exception

of a few drafts of old soldiers none of K's army have yet gone but they hope to send the First Army within a month. The whole army is held up by delay in the supply of munitions of war. The light is fading so I must write another time. Hoping the brooch is to your taste.

'PS Probably be home 2 days the week after Easter.'

On the last day in March White received a great blow. He simply recorded:

'Wednesday 31: Egerton-Warburton left us, a terrible loss.'

One attempt had already been made to get him returned to the Scots Guards but had been successfully opposed by White and Warburton had become battalion adjutant. White had depended on Warburton and the battalion maintained its link with him.

Chapter 4

Windmill Hill, Ludgershall:
April to July 1915

Work in April 1915 began as it ended in March, digging trenches. Some of the battalion, including Sharp, got home on leave for Easter, others, including Wilkinson and Young were stuck in camp for four days where they picked up the news of an impending move.

On Sunday 4 April, Easter Day, Young wrote a short letter to his sister Florrie's fiancé:

'My Dear Frank, Should be very much obliged if you would send the second volume of "Sinister Street" as soon as possible. I think the first volume is distinctly original and true to life and feel sure I shall not be disappointed with the second.

'Easter down here is frightfully dull. The weather is glorious but it is impossible to appreciate it.

'Kind regards, yours affectionately, George
PS Moving to Salisbury Plain shortly.'

On the same day Wilkinson wrote to his mother:

'Dear Mother, Never have I spent such a rummy Easter. We had the prospect of 4 days off duty with nothing to do but walk and read. Parnell and I decided to hire bikes and ride in to Salisbury and Winchester but we were forestalled, all the bikes were already out. Thursday evening I went to the pictures alone, Parnell was on duty. At supper time we were warned for Church Parade at 8am on Good Friday. Parnell and I strolled languidly round the lanes in search of something interesting and an appetite for dinner. We found three beetles beside the road and talked to them in baby talk which attracted the attention of a passing carter who pulled up his horses and volunteered the information that they would 'spit blood' if we waited a bit. One beetle kindly obliged so we went on in search of further adventures. A football match filled the afternoon and H.G. Wells' "First Man in The Moon" took up the evening.

'Saturday morning we were dismissed, after waiting for about an hour, to dress our leather equipment with tallow. Two hours gently rubbing and then dinner. I kicked a football about with a few others for an hour in the afternoon and then retired indoors to read and cool down. Parnell wanted to go to the pictures in the evening so I went with him and saw it a second time.

'Church Parade this morning at 9am followed by an hour at the Sunday papers. Dinner finished at 1:30, Parnell and I set out on what turned out to be one of the most enjoyable rambles I have had. Golden sunlight, blue sky, green hills, pine woods with their lovely green tops against the bright sky all had their place in enhancing the quiet joy of our walk though they seemed to fade from existence as we exchanged our innermost thoughts on life and its perplexities. And Abbots Ann, about 3 miles away was a lovely old village heaped round its church. On our return we came to a chalk pit and sat on the grass in the now warm sun. I climbed to the top and finding the view worth the effort signalled by semaphore for Parnell to come up and share it. It took a lot of arm waving to make him stir. Behind us on the crest we explored an old 'camp' made probably by the Romans or Early Britons.

'But supper awaits me. Tomorrow Parnell is on fatigue all day and I go on guard at 6pm until 8 on Tuesday morning.'

Sharp returned from leave on 6th, arriving at Andover at midday, and learned of the move to Windmill Hill scheduled to take place on the following morning. His diary for the following day, Wednesday 7 April:

'Roll call as usual. Visit all billets of 5 and 6 Platoons. Dinner at 11:45am. Route march 1:15pm arrive Windmill Hill 4:15pm. Tea with Lady A. No luggage arrives so sleep on floor.'

White's diary gave a brief explanation of why there was no kit:

'7 April: Marched at 1pm from Andover with the battalion. A lovely day. Reached Windmill Hill 4pm, eight miles. Mess contractor from Salisbury threw us over. Count Gleichen (Commanding 37th Division) came over to see us.'

Wilkinson sent a postcard, which is undated, giving his new address and saying he is 'quite fit and well under canvas'. Young managed a quick hopeful note to his mother:

'Dear Mother, Today we have moved to a little village called Ludgershall near Andover and are now in tents.

'I expect you are rather surprised at this. So are we but I think we shall like it fairly well.'

On 8th Sharp recorded that there was a change in disposition of officers in the battalion:

'Boileau takes temporary 2nd in command. I take B Company.

'Friday 9: A clear but very cold morning. Parade at 6:45am. Battalion route march with Colonel through Collingbourne Wood, about twelve miles. Paid Company in forty minutes in afternoon, and got it right. Walk with Burnett over hill.

'Saturday 10: Everyone away. Practised drill and cleaned tents in the morning. Inspection by Gleichen at 3pm, I had B Company. He was very pleased.

'Sunday 11: I took church parade under Keppel. Walk with Maxwell, Campbell and Delbos to Sidbury Hill and back, tea together.'

Changes in personnel were common during the period in training. Experienced officers were needed to take over new formations. Inexperienced young officers were very much on probation with White and some names appeared in the monthly Army List during the early months in Colchester but disappear after two or three editions. A few were transferred to other battalions and one appears to have served through the whole war holding the rank of second lieutenant in four different battalions. There were many in the ranks with aspirations to be commissioned.

Roland Mountfort's voice now joins the group sending home messages from the camp. A member of C Company, he was born in Coventry in 1890, the son of a bank cashier and his wife. He attended the city's grammar school and on leaving moved to join the Prudential Insurance Company living in lodgings in Balham, south west London. He shared the lodging with his brother Bernard, two years his senior, and Ernest Pickering, who also joined 10RF.

In the first letter saved in his collection he commented on potential officers:

'I hear from Morris [a friend in the Prudential] that one of the juniors in the solicitors department - an absolutely hopeless idiot whom I have anathematised to his face times without number when endeavouring to knock information into his stupid head - a stupid, conceited effeminate boy of twenty-one - is obtaining a commission in this Battalion'.

Wilkinson wrote a short letter to his mother on Friday 9. He began by explaining that his leave from Friday to Sunday had been cancelled at the last minute and continued:

'Letter writing is difficult now, as we are ten men to a tent and at present have no recreation tent. We moved quite suddenly from our billets in Andover and are now on Salisbury Plain with thousands of other troops under canvas. The wind has been blowing ever since; we are nearly blown to pieces.'

He evidently had a bit of time on Sunday 11 to write in more detail to his sister:

'Dear Rene, I have no doubt my recent scrappy communications have given rise to a good deal of speculation at home so I will try to piece whole together in a more understandable manner.

'On Easter morning we were informed that we were to leave our billets on Wednesday and proceed to camp on Salisbury Plain. I went on guard at 6pm Monday until 6pm on Tuesday doing two hours on and four hours off during the night and spending the whole of Tuesday in the guardroom collecting passes of chaps returning from leave. The guardroom was an empty corn chandlers shop and filthy, the windows were plastered with adverts for birdseed etc and were dirty like the rest of the place. We slept on shutters in front of the fire when off duty during the night.

'Parnell was sent off with the advance party at 7:15am on Tuesday morning in the

pouring rain and had a very wet time erecting tents during the day. About midday when standing outside the guardroom watching traffic I was surprised to see Mr and Mrs Parnell. Mr Parnell had a day's holiday and had come to spend it with his son. They were very disappointed when I told them how matters stood and eventually they lunched in Andover and Mrs P returned home while Mr P went on and found Parnell and all in a horrible drizzle.

'I was naturally very tired when I came off guard at 6 o'clock and after tea I gathered together my kit which resisted my efforts to squeeze it into my kit bag for about two hours and then I went to bed about 9 o'clock. Wednesday was fine and at midday all Andover turned out to see us march away. We bought Mrs Noyes a work basket in remembrance of her kindness and she was delighted.

'After seven miles march in bright sunshine we arrived at our camp which is 600 feet above sea level (Andover is only 200 feet). That's about all I remember of the first two days WIND blooming, blowing, windy, WIND. I know we struggled through some drill on Thursday morning and did a twelve mile march across Salisbury Plain on Friday. By this time we were all "fffed up" (Three f's for emphasis). What with the everlasting wind, leaving comfortable billets and good food and being instead quartered ten in a tent and fed on army food (breakfast, bread, fat and tea) and being dumped down miles from anywhere or anything except the dirty hole called Ludgershall we were positively fed up. There nothing whatever to do here except walk, read and sleep. No picture palace or theatre and no library and memories of Mrs Noyes' puddings were still fresh in our minds to make our lot seem harder by contrast.

'The wind has dropped and on Saturday the weather was ideal. We are now more contented and are settling down to camp life quite quickly. On Saturday morning we were inspected by General Count Gleichen.'

Wilkinson's disappointment at the suddenness of the move and the poor weather supports Maxwell's observation that the 10RF were not a happy group of men. Maxwell had been quiet all the time the battalion was at Andover. His much loved mother died early in 1915 and he later wrote:

'The early months of 1915 were made dreadful to me by the death of my mother. With my grief mingled a most bitter remorse for the separation that I had made her suffer in this last year of her life.'

He summarised his views on the move from Andover:

'Then, in early April, we went out into camp again – this time on Salisbury Plain. The training had gone on without cessation. It became harder and harder all the time. I think myself that it was quite unnecessarily severe on the men, more especially such eager, willing young people as ours. Further the authorities seem to be reinforcing a very depressing lesson, that even with the most frenzied efforts, they could never hope to achieve all that would be demanded of them. Their spirits sank perceptibly.'

Young's next letter, written on the Monday after the move, 12 April, reflected the general depression with the camp.

'Darling Mother and Father, You are no doubt wondering why I have not written for so long but when I tell you the conditions under which we are existing you will understand.

'As I scribbled on that letter card last Wednesday we have now left our comfortable and in many ways delightful billet for the almost intolerable discomfort of camp life.

'As you can imagine the anti-climax is perfectly awful. No longer does our landlady knock at our door and politely inform us that dinner is ready but instead the beastly bugle blows and we go to the cookhouse for some miserable stew or something.

'Altogether the discomfort of camp life is too awful and we are not at all pleased with the change.

'Yesterday as a pleasant diversion after church parade I went to Weyhill to lunch and tea with the Smiths and immensely enjoyed the afternoon. If we are likely to be here very long I shall have to ask you to send my flannels and tennis racket [sic] down as they have three ripping courts here. I am awfully sorry that my friend Dudley has had to go to the depot in Kingston on account of his not being absolutely fit for active service. I am terribly cut up about it especially as we have been trying to get commissions together. However things may turn out well even yet and we hope to get together again sometime.

'Well I hope you are well at home. I got your letter Dad for which many thanks. As we are getting such atrocious food a cake or something would be immensely welcome.'

Maxwell's thoughts and Young's letter illustrate two issues which faced Colonel White. The battalion was composed of mainly well-educated, confident young men many of whom were capable of looking for commissions. The expected quick transfer to the Front, which had encouraged them to join as enlisted men, was not forthcoming. Many public school and university men had obtained Certificate A in the school cadet force or Certificate B with the University OTC which covered a syllabus to prepare them for service in the event of war, and reduced the amount of time to be spent in training before being commissioned. Others like Wilkinson, Parnell and Young applied for commissions but were not considered suitable. This was probably because although well educated, Parnell had a degree in chemistry, they had not spent time in the Cadets or OTC. Those who failed to demonstrate adequate levels of competence and fitness were returned to the Depot for reassignment and further training.

Sharp continued to log each day's events:

'April: Monday 12: Again have Company. Lecture by Bonnett in morning and Company drill. Judging distances in the afternoon.
'13: Battalion route march to Buttermere. Go over Chute Causeway and over country to Fosbury Camp. March back 3pm and arrived 6:30pm having done 22 and a half miles as well as cross country. Lost 2/6d at bridge.
'14: Company training. Do saluting and bayonet fighting. Another lecture by Bonnett. Company drill.

'15: B Company under me attack D Company under Shapley(?) at Sidbury Hill doing outposts. A very interesting morning indeed.
'16: Field Day at Amport. No 6 [platoon] and myself the enemy. Breakfast 6:30am, start 7:45 Arrive 9:30. The rest of the battalion attacked.'

The weather improved as the month progressed. White recorded his impression of the Field Day:

'Friday, 16 April: A lovely day. Battalion Field Day. Attacked both sides of Pillhill Brook from Thruxton to Amport. Cobbold in command. Dinners at Amport. Home at 3:30pm.'

After a weekend at home on leave Sharp returned to find the scale of training moved up a level.

'Monday, 19 April: First Day's Divisional Training. Attack on Pickpit Hill... Do same with Company sections in the afternoon. Night operation, Boileau and Birley attack. Got back easily by 10pm.
'20: Field Day outposts at Collingbourne. Boileau and I go to Court Martial of 13th Rifles.
'21: Flank and advance guard. Then rapid firing and bayonet fighting by platoons.
'22: I take Company out and defend Sidbury Hill against D Company and Shurey. Colonel comes out – very pleased. Bayonet fighting with No 6 and Bevis in afternoon. Brigade concert very good.
'23: Battalion route march to Netheravon over Salisbury Plain. B Company forms flank guard. March back by Companies and get in about 1:15pm. Pay Company at 2:30 in three-quarters of an hour.'

On 21 April Wilkinson wrote home to plan what might be his last leave before France:

'Dear Mother, I am glad to say I shall be home on Sunday for four days leave so that I shall be able to go to the display. I shall arrive at Waterloo at 12:04pm and will no doubt have a good appetite for dinner. Will you please get me a 1/6d ticket for the Display and one for Dad if he is going.
'This is our official "last leave" which means that when we have had it we may be popped off without further leave although we shall have weekend leave until we do go.
'I have had a lovely cushy job today minding the tents while the others were out and have had one or two naps out on the grass in the sun.'

On April 22 Young wrote to his brother:

'Dear Charlie, as I have the time and inclination to write letters I am just writing a few uninteresting lines to you.
'There is scarcely anything to tell you about the life of a soldier in camp except an incessant wail of complaint.

'Last night I sang at a concert in Andover given by the Band. The hall was packed but it wasn't a very excellent concert. An Officer from the Army Service Corps drove me there in his car and brought me back afterwards so it wasn't so bad.

'Tonight there is a Brigade Concert here which is to be a rather big affair. The General and about 150 officers as well as about 800 men are coming so I shall have to sing well.

'I hope you are getting on well and making plenty of money. I hope to be able to get home on Saturday but am not yet certain.'

The last week of April continued with regular marches, drills and other training. As Sharp recorded:

'Saturday 24 April: Three platoons and I did one hours drill at the miniature range. Bayonet fighting and rapid firing. In afternoon motor to Andover and have bath and tea at Herbert's.

'Monday 26: Bayonet fighting and rapid firing for all platoons. No afternoon parades. 7 [platoon] goes to Boileau for young officers[17], 8 to Pike for demolition. Birley and I take 5 and 6 and do night outposts.

'27: My first field day as O/C B Company. Rearguard and convoy under Fleming at Everley. Lunch at Lower Everley. Keppel brings us back by 5:30pm. Bridge after dinner as usual.

'28: Kit inspection and cleaning of tents. All subalterns to Trench Drill under Linton at Sidbury Hall. Mess meeting all afternoon. Company drill under Rowbottom.

'29: I took the whole Company for trench drill at Sidbury Hill. In afternoon did bayonet fighting and I took 6 in rapid firing.

'30: Very dull field day under the Colonel. Route march with flanking guards via Everley to Littlecot Down.'

Company Sergeant Major Rowbotham, aged 47 in 1914 with fifteen years military service, twelve in The Grenadier Guards and three in The Irish Guards, was probably the man taking company drill. In civilian life a hall porter, living in Kensington and married with four children. He rejoined the army from the reserve in August 1914. He was promoted to Company Sergeant Major in January 1915 and Regimental Sergeant Major in February 1916, awarded the DCM in February 1917 'for conspicuous gallantry and devotion to duty'. He became ill and returned home in June 1918, leaving the Army in April 1919.

Towards the end of April Arthur Parnell, Wilkinson's great friend and fellow Scout, married at the age of 25. Typical of many young couples, the decision was made to marry before he went to France. Born in Shepherds Bush the son of a port clerk, who in 1911 was living in Acton, Parnell was a chemistry graduate, his sister a typist. He married Annie Thompson, a native of Sunderland.

The happy couple went to Folkestone for their honeymoon, a strange choice of venue given that they would be seeing the daily passage of soldiers going to France. While there he sent an upbeat message on a postcard of The Leys to Wilkinson:

'Folkestone 28 April 1915: Dear Wilkie, Just a line from this place to taunt you. Think of me enjoying peaceful walks and excursions every day. Basking in the sun and feeding to

*my heart's content and other joys not for postcards. I shudder to think of Sunday. Yours
A.P.P.'*

Marriage was also mentioned in Young's next letter home to his sister on 3 May 1915. His response to the life of a soldier was a contrasting one to that presented by Wilkinson:

'Dear Florrie, I am just writing this note to ask if you would get two songs for me from Selfridges.... Well dear Florrie I suppose you are getting feverishly excited by now. I am so awfully glad that you have decided to get married and I am sure that everything will go well. There is nothing to tell you about our life here it is all so monotonous.'

He had spent the day on fatigue as a line orderly, looking after the tents; he took the opportunity to write to his mother, starting in a reflective mood:

'Life here is moving on more or less in the same monotonous fashion and I suppose we must not grumble as the weather is so beautiful. The country round here is very lovely and I think that even as a soldier this life is preferable to a city office especially on these glorious spring days. Next Thursday the band are giving a concert and Dudley is coming down from Kingston to play. The Bandmaster is talking of a recruiting week in London and one night during the week he is going to give a concert at the Queen's Hall and I hope to sing there. If so you must come and hear me.

Will you please send down my tennis things by next Saturday if possible? I will get the shoes if you will buy a pair of white socks.'

The routine of training continued into May. For the first week bayonet fighting, trench drill and marches filled the days, along with the regular kit inspections and tidying of tents each Wednesday. The pace of life was reflected in the letters, even Wilkinson, usually a voluble writer, found difficulties:

'5 May Wednesday: Dear Mother, You will be surprised to hear that I have been so busy I have hardly had an opportunity to write. Yesterday we marched out at 7:20am and arrived back in the evening at 6:10pm. I have put in a pass for this weekend and will most probably be home. If I get to Waterloo at 2:17pm as I expect I shall come home and then go off to Somerset House to see the Scouts. If I am later I shall probably go direct from Waterloo in which case I shall wire you.'

Mountfort wrote home:

'I enclose for you a PC of C Company marching through Andover. We wore white hat bands as we were the enemy that day. You see me enjoying the uncoveted honour of Commanding Officer's Orderly, on his left. He (Colonel White) is the old boy with white bands around his arms. The other, our ex-Adjutant, Captain Egerton Warburton is now at the front.'

Some of the men undertook an extended march, White wrote in his diary for 8 May:

'Thirty three men of D Co who had marched most of the way from Andover, which they had left at 6pm on May 6 reached the Stock Exchange at 11:20am. Great reception. Taylor[18] in command, inspected by the Lord Mayor.'

Early May saw both Young and Wilkinson enjoying some leave. Young spent a week with his friend Dudley at Westergate, near Bognor, Sussex. He wrote to his mother:

'Dearest Mother,
'Just a line to let you know that I have arrived safely if not too happily back in camp again after a most enjoyable week.
'I got down to Westergate at about 10 o'clock on Wednesday evening and found that Dudley had gone down there. He got my telegram but there was some confusion about it. However I was more than pleased to find him down at the farm. From then on we had a most excellent time, bathing in the sea at Bognor, having music after dinner, and in many other ways making the most of our time.
'Only those who are in the army under such conditions as ours can appreciate fully the joy of 5 days leave from camp.
'I went to Selfridges and saw Florrie for a few minutes on Wednesday evening and gave her your various messages.
'I think there is nothing else just at the present so will conclude.'

On 12 May Wilkinson wrote to his mother:

'I've had more luck! I drew second for leave and to oblige Williams who drew first I have changed with him and will be home this coming weekend about same time as last week.
'I arrived here from home about 2:30am on Monday morning, got up at 6am breakfasted at 6:15am marched to the ranges for firing at 7:15am arrived back at 8:30pm. I repeated this yesterday but today I am doing nothing whatever except keep out of the way in case I get put on fatigue. I had plenty of sleep in the ranges which made up in some measure for the lack of recreation in the evenings.'

After a frustrating weekend Mountfort had returned on the same train as Wilkinson as he too arrived back in camp at 2am on the Monday morning. In his letter to his mother on 15 May the indignation shone through:

'I had an awful job to get my leave pass. No. 9 platoon was for duty on Friday and I took it for granted I should be on fatigue. When I discovered I had escaped that, I put in my pass, only to be informed later that I couldn't go, as they hadn't got a sufficient number for Church Parade, if you please, on Sunday morning.
'Church Parade here lasts half an hour. Five battalions participate forming 3 sides of a square and the chaplain takes post in the centre. No one can hear a word except those in the front rank and the ranks in rear have to amuse themselves as best they can, and

their amusement, since there is no one to watch them, usually takes the form of playing pitch and toss[19], grousing about the army and a variety of similar things not usually associated with a divine service. For an institution of this description they had every intention of stopping, in our platoon alone, six men's weekend leave. And what, do you imagine, is the explanation of their keenness? The welfare of the souls of men who are going to endanger their bodies of course you reply. Wrong. The Chaplain is paid according to the number of men he preaches to...'

The 13th May saw an incident in the battalion which was perhaps the result of rising frustration among the men, and was triggered by the inefficiency and bullying of an NCO. White and Mountfort both record and comment on the incident with different levels of detail.

White's diary 13 May:

'Companies turned out late on parade. Spoke to NCOs.'

Mountfort, a member of C Company, in his letter home on 15 May described events:

'The Sergeant Major was due to wake the Company as at that hour they don't blow reveille. The night before, he got beastly drunk; and when the sentry woke him promptly went back to sleep again. A 4 o'clock he was again roused by the Cook Sergeant who had got our breakfast ready. This time he got up and called up the Company.

'Parade was at 4:15 which gave us exactly a quarter of an hour to dress, have breakfast, see to our rifles and get on parade. The result was of course that before we were dressed they served out breakfast; and before we could touch that they were yelling out "Come on Parade". It was raining in torrents and no one was in the best of tempers. Some stopped to snatch a mouthful of bread and butter, some didn't have time to do that, but anyway, at 4:15am the only men out were the four officers and the Sergeant Major and the whole Coy was reported as being late on parade. The same thing happened in D Company.

'We got away about 4:30am. It rained hard all day – a heavy and bitterly cold rain – I daresay you had it last Thursday. There was no shelter and by 6am we were drenched. We finished firing at 2:30pm, having been out ten hours. The only relief in the monotony was a visit from the Colonel and our Company Commander – the Major's successor – when the latter made a little speech about things. He said the Company had disgraced itself; he was once proud to command us, now he wasn't; and he was considering what steps would be taken as to punishment. As we considered an injury had been done to us in bringing us out at all his speech didn't make him very popular. Four other Battalions were due to shoot that day and we were the only one that turned out. Fourteen men who went to a portable coffee stall without permission had their names taken and were subsequently given three days CB [confined to barracks]. Our Company Commander referred to us once during the day as "this rotten Company". By the end of the day, when we got back to our tents with everything soaked through and the water squelching in our boots we were pretty fed up.

'The next morning twenty-six men of C Company and thirty-six of D went sick. At the sick parade everybody cheered them. When the CO heard of it he went round and had out the Medical Officer and told him he considered most of the men to be perfectly fit and he was to show no leniency. I don't know what happened; but at any rate the CO spoke to the Doctor in such a way before the men that the Doctor promptly resigned and went off the same night. By the afternoon the spirit in both C and D Company's was perfectly mutinous.

'The fourteen men who got CB insisted on being taken up to the CO to protest. The Sergeant Major tried to excuse himself by throwing the blame at the Orderly Sergeant, who immediately started to tell him what he thought about him. The knot of spectators took the part of the Orderly Sergeant so vigorously that one was marched off to the guard-room. The orderly Sergeant's reputation being at stake, he insisted on being taken up to the CO. The NCOs of the Company consulted together and decided to make the Company Commander apologise for the way he addressed us, or they would resign in a body.

'All afternoon knots of men stood about in the camp in the way men will when things are fermenting and I'm sure it only wanted one spark of insult from anyone in authority to set the whole situation ablaze. But the CO with greater wisdom than he knew, promised to go into the case on Monday and the Company Commander when the NCOs sought him out had rushed off on leave with a note to the second in command (a very decent sort) to "handle the situation", & the Sergeant Major got into a dickens of a funk and appealed to the NCOs "for God's sake to keep the men under control". No one can quarrel with a man in a funk; so everything is standing over; and to stand over, in a case of this description, is to simmer down and generally settle, so I doubt if there will be any great excitement on Monday – especially as we shall be out of camp for five days.'

Mountfort reflected that because the battalion was comprised of men who are clerks, not miners or dockers 'they do not have not a tradition of union and concerted action, so do not know how to gain redress for their complaints'.

This letter containing the details of the church parade and of the events surrounding the late arrival on parade incident must have given Mountfort's family some pause for thought as to what he was enduring in the army. His letters differ in style and are more open than those of Wilkinson and Young. Wilkinson does complain occasionally, but either laughs it off or changes to a more positive subject before the end of the letter. He gives the impression of an enthusiastic young man, keen to participate in and enjoy all that life has to throw at him. Young's moods swing and he can sound quite depressed and frequently comments on finding life tedious and a bore, perhaps writing in a style he believes to be that expected of young men of quality.

The reference in Montfort's letter to being out of camp for five days covered what Sharp refers to as the 'brigade trek'. This was the first experience for the battalion of what would become commonplace in France, long route marches, overnights bivouacking or in very temporary billets and barns, and occasional skirmishes.

As White recorded on 17 May:

'Very wet morning. Paraded at 9am. Whole brigade in marching order. 10RF did not wear greatcoats. Marched by Shaw Hill, Winscombe to Barton Court and Avington,

about two and a half miles E of Hungerford on the Kennet. Barton Court an empty house belonging to Sir R. Sutton. I slept at caretaker's lodge.'

The domestic arrangements for Sharp were a little more basic:

'Marched to Barton Court, billeted in lavatory, slept in linen cupboard. Conference in evening in CO's quarters, slept soundly.'

Typically Wilkinson gave a detailed account of the events, and was probably more comfortable than Sharp:

'We are billeted in an empty country mansion. It is a grand place about 500 men are quartered in the house and outhouses. There are ten men in our section's quarters in a fine bedroom larger than our sitting room at home. It is in splendid condition, white enamel, marble, etc etc and we have just collected a lot of wood from the shrubbery and lighted a fire so we can dry our clothes. It is past 6 o'clock and we are patiently waiting for our dinner. The parade was cancelled and the battalion sheltered in the house for the morning. The band played on one of the landings and the men joined in with singing in their rooms.'

Wilkinson read in his room and described the grounds as 'being like Kew Gardens running down to the River Kennet'. The rain eventually stopped and the men were allowed out. A trip into Kintbury allowed Wilkinson to enjoy two hot Chelsea buns and ginger beer and to purchase some new bread and Gorgonzola cheese which was taken back to the billet. The card he sent home that day just said 'having a good time in a splendid billet'.

The battalion paraded in the evening and marched at 9:30pm to Milton Lilbourne. Wilkinson spent the night with his platoon in an isolated barn. Again the daylight hours were spent tidying up and cleaning kit. He wrote about frying up some meat that he had hacked off a huge joint and 'was surprised to find it sweet and tender'. Some men went into the church and sang, accompanying themselves on the organ. The band played in the village street for an hour.

Leaving the barn on Thursday morning the battalion practised covering the retirement of 60 Rifle Brigade. They performed successfully and returned to the billets in Milton Lilbourne. The return to Ludgershall on Friday, 21 May involved the battalion acting as an advance guard to the brigade and supported General Barnes in pushing 110 Brigade, the enemy for the day, off the road.

Wilkinson ended his long letter describing the week:

'We fought our way back to camp at Ludgershall arriving at 3:30pm. We are now back in our camp again quite fit and well and understand that we are to have two or three days rest, whatever that may mean.'

After his return Young took five days to find time to write home. He played tennis on Saturday and Bank Holiday Monday and went for a long walk with a friend on the

Sunday. He made no mention of the previous week's trek but described the Sunday walk and the beauty of the countryside in some detail and referred to playing tennis with a Captain Henshaw and his wife on 'their very nice court and altogether I enjoyed myself immensely'. He ended:

'I do not tell you of the awful conditions, the disgusting food, the bombastic behaviour of the sergeants etc, and generally the whole atmosphere of the place, which is virtually putrid.'

On 24 May Wilkinson wrote about his weekend with Parnell and Richard Cordingley, the 20-year-old son of a newspaper proprietor. They visited Mrs Noyes, their landlady in Andover and spent an enjoyable day laughing and joking with her family, including her son Fred who was on a week's leave from searchlight duty on Gibraltar. Having got there on a brewer's lorry with thirty-three others, all of whom paid sixpence for the lift, they had to walk the eight miles back to camp at 9 o'clock at night.

At the end of May Sharp wrote the last entries in his diary. He had begun riding lessons at home in Reading, probably because his responsibilities as adjutant included the need to parade on horseback. He had his first two lessons on 26th and 27th, the final entry on 28th records:

'Third riding lesson in the afternoon. Still didn't fall off.'

Training continued through June. Wilkinson spent three hours filling in the trenches he'd spent six days digging earlier in the year. He also enjoyed his first experience of field firing where:

'Five hundred of us advanced in line shoulder to shoulder with fixed bayonets and on the command from our officer discharged ten rounds of real ball ammunition at some targets. We followed this up with a 'charge' bugles blowing and men cheering and luckily we came out of the affair unhurt.'

A precursor of the horrors to be experienced by troops in the following year, the advance in extended order was seen as being the way to get partly trained men to bring maximum fire power to bear which would be effective against enemy soldiers in trenches straight ahead but not when they had machine guns dug in to provide enfilade fire from the flank or side.

Maxwell had been having a difficult time training his transport section. He knew about horses and carriages but had little experience of carts and wagons. He had for some months been training his men to sit on the wagon and use the long-rein to control the horses. He was then told that in France only ride and drive was used, where the driver rode on one of the horses and controlled everything from there. These limbered wagons were more flexible in use and could go across country as well as on roads. He changed the training to take account of this but complained about the time lost.

Some of the battalion were looking for commissions. Wilkinson mentioned that both Cordingley and Hulford were hoping to be commissioned in the regiment; neither was successful. Parnell wrote to a friend of his who was a colonel to see if there were opportunities with him but received a reply within a week to say he had no vacancies for junior officers. A different avenue opened for Parnell and Wilkinson when they were asked if they were still interested in joining the Lewis Gun section; they had volunteered in February but their applications had not been forwarded in time by their officer, Lieutenant Roberts. On 31 May they paraded in front of the adjutant, probably Sharp who had recorded in his diary for 24 May that he was acting adjutant:

'The Adjutant catechised each of us individually as to our keenness, eyesight, health etc explaining that it was a compliment to be recommended and that we should take it as an honour to belong to the section which was composed of picked men and had most important duties to perform. He rejected a few men and told the rest of us that we were taken on as probationers, that there would be some weeding out and that we were to compete for the honour of remaining in the section. I start the special training tomorrow and will let you know soon how I like it; in the meantime I do no more dirty fatigue work and am someone of consequence. The Adjutant said "I consider a machine gunner more important than an ordinary section commander"!!!'

Uncertainty led to speculation about the future of the battalion. Early in June Mountfort wrote:

'There are rumours again about the front in three weeks etc, but there's nothing to show there's anything in them.'

Young wrote on 12 June:

'The latest rumour is that we are to be turned into an Officers Training Corps.'

He celebrated his twenty-first birthday in the middle of June but was unable to get home to celebrate with his family as it wasn't his turn for leave. He spent most of the month, when he wasn't training, in playing tennis. He was doing few concerts although he did sing for the Army Chaplain in the Church of England tent one evening.

On 13 June Egerton-Warburton, the former adjutant who had done much to create the battalion and its spirit, paid a visit. White had recorded in May that Warburton had been slightly wounded at Richebourg-L'Avoue and wrote in his diary for the day of the visit that 'he got a great reception from the battalion', Wilkinson wrote home and said of Warburton 'he is a sad wreck and walks with crutches through being wounded at the front with the Scots Guards'.

The end of June saw an inspection of the division by the King. It was a hot, dusty day. Young had not been convinced that the King would actually arrive; he wrote. 'Whether he comes or not is another matter'. Wilkinson described the event as a 'mobilisation inspection' and said 'it went off very well and must have been an impressive sight to the few onlookers. To us it was hard work, terribly dusty and hot of pack carrying at the 'shun'. Sharp was mounted for the parade; he wrote that he was just visible 'in the dust'.

The King inspecting 37 Division at Andover 25 June 1915. Sharp Collection IWM

Wilkinson wrote of the heat and discomfort in the dust. Sharp Collection IWM

Roberts, Boileau riding nearest the camera, Sharp just visible on horseback in the dust. Sharp Collection IWM

Although the men were keen to get to France there were still, in the minds of some other people, doubts about the wisdom of sending a group of such well-educated men, who would be capable officers, to serve in the ranks. On July 9 Hansard records that Mr Herbert Nield, MP for Ealing, asked the Under Secretary of State for War, Mr Harold Tennant, to consider whether, because nearly 200 of the battalion's volunteers had already received commissions, the rest of the battalion should be considered as a source of officers as 'socially and in all other respects they are of the class from which the best officers are obtained... the interests of the country will be better served by offering commissions to such of the rank and file of this battalion as are desirous of accepting them, and so distributing them over various regiments rather than sacrificing these men as a unit to the exigencies of service in the field?' In his view there were a further 600 men capable of holding a commission.

The under secretary replied that the commanding officer of the battalion was still putting forward names for consideration and it was up to the CO to continue to recommend men as long as it did not impair the efficiency of the battalion. Although a steady trickle of men continued to leave to take commissions the battalion did not suffer the fate of some others which were disbanded when a large proportion of their number took this route.

Training continued through July, men went home on leave and it was clear that a move was imminent. Mountfort wrote home in early July:

> 'All leave is stopped after Sunday week and preparations are being made to leave here are of such a nature as to leave no doubt we are going to the front. The Col says the date of embarkation has been fixed and he knows it but isn't at liberty to disclose it.
>
> 'Meanwhile 30 per cent of the battalion are going to have three days leave in batches concluding Sunday week. I don't suppose I shall get it but if I do I shall have my teeth seen to in London and then come down to Coventry.

Young writing on the 20th gave more news:

> 'As far as we can tell the day of departure is fixed for next Tuesday or Wednesday but we do not know for certain what day it will be. There is to be a final concert here on Saturday which will be rather a big affair. Maggie Teyte, Phyllis Dare[20] and Paul Rubens are coming down so it ought to be good.'

Individuals were making preparations for going to France. Wilkinson's company commander, Captain Roberts, had presented the men with a pair of clippers and they were putting them to good use cropping their hair. Wilkinson said 'I am putting off the evil day, can't in fact screw up the courage'. The following day he wrote that they had been issued with Service Pay Books, jack knives, with tin opener, Kitchener's message, can of rifle oil etc. In addition Captain Roberts's sister gave each man a phial of iodine and someone else gave them a pair of plimsolls for wearing in billets in France.

Wilkinson and Young sent books, spare clothes and other items home in parcels. Young's tennis equipment and music he left with Miss Bannerman in Andover. On the back of his letter Wilkinson listed every item he had to pack in his kit bag and haversack.[21]

Young wrote home on 28th in heroic mode:

Maggie Teyte.

'When you receive this letter I and my fellow Fusiliers of this battalion will be "en route" for the front.

'At last after all this bother and deferred hope we arrived at the time and tomorrow morning we shall move from Andover and all its pleasant associations and say 'goodbye' to the motherland for a little time at any rate.

'We are all very glad that we are going and naturally rather excited. However, when we get there rest assured we shall do our utmost for the cause of what we believe to be right and good.

'The thing is I am sure to take it all very calmly and to believe that whatever is going to happen to us will happen and that is all. I spent my last evening in Andover last night when I said goodbye to Miss Bannerman. They have become great friends while we have been here and are, I think, very fond of me. I have had some very good tennis with them and shall always hope to be associated with them.'

White addressed the men about the arrangements for travel and other preparations. He had opened a fund for tobacco and other comforts at Lloyds Bank, Temple Bar. Oliver and Williams of Victoria Street were the agents appointed to provide information and give support to the men and their families. Both Young and Wilkinson gave both the addresses to their families. Wilkinson also gave a list of addresses of people to be contacted 'in case anything happens to me'. He reminded his parents to contact the Hearts of Oak and Prudential Insurance Companies, as he said 'one has to remember these things you know'; his army pay was to be paid to his father. Maxwell was still depressed following the death of his mother, and had expressed the view that the men were being over trained, and were dull and listless. He reflected Young's view that they were keen to get moving:

'Suddenly when our spirits were at their lowest point, we received orders for France. We went to Southampton and across to Havre.[22] In every mile of this journey we became happier and easier. In this I am confirming what others have confirmed to me as their own experience. It was an immeasurable relief to be done with all that training. Peace sank into our hearts as we approached the War. What lay before us might be very bad, but it could not be so bad as what we were leaving behind. The Germans might kill us but they wouldn't nag at us.'

Chapter 5

Introduction to France:
July and August 1915

The 10RF advance party arrived in France on 30 July, with most of the remainder joining them the following day; a small number crossed the Channel later on 14 August. Apart from a short period in 1916 and a few days in 1917 the battalion was part of 111th Brigade, in the 37th Division of the Third Army. The writers of diaries and letters were clearly busy in the few days before the move and more detailed accounts were written after landing in France.

In his first letter from France Wilkinson described the events in camp on the evening before their departure:

'We had an enormous bonfire the night before we left England and finished up by rushing round it yelling like madmen, some of the Officers joined in for a few minutes, including the Chaplain who was afterwards carried shoulder high by the men. He is immensely popular.'

The chaplain was the 30-year-old Reverend Ellis Foster Edge Partington who had joined 10RF during the stay in Andover. Educated at Felstead School in Essex, a graduate of Trinity College, Cambridge and Ridley Hall Theological College; he played hockey for the university and for England in 1909.

Wilkinson, keen to keep his family informed of his whereabouts, managed to send two cards on the journey; the first.

'Friday afternoon 30/7/15 Just off, in train, George.'

The second, a field postcard from Army Post Office 3, marked as passed by censor:

'I am quite well. Letter follows at first opportunity, George 31/7/15.'

Revd Ellis Edge Partington with MO, possibly Dr Turner. Sharp Collection IWM

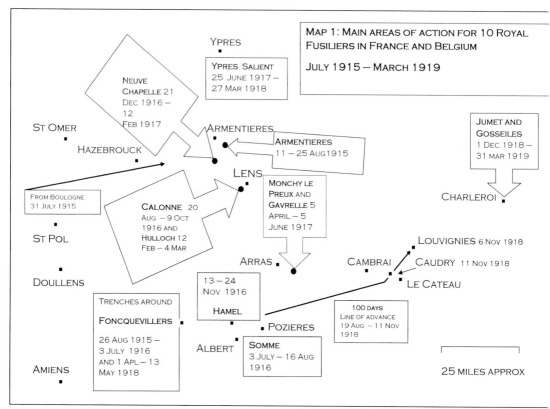

MAP 1: MAIN AREAS OF ACTION FOR 10 ROYAL FUSILIERS IN FRANCE AND BELGIUM

JULY 1915 – MARCH 1919

YPRES

YPRES SALIENT 25 JUNE 1917 – 27 MAR 1918

NEUVE CHAPELLE 21 DEC 1916 – 12 FEB 1917

ST OMER

HAZEBROUCK

ARMENTIERES

ARMENTIERES 11 – 25 AUG 1915

JUMET AND GOSSEILES 1 DEC 1918 – 31 MAR 1919

LENS

FROM BOULOGNE 31 JULY 1915

CALONNE 20 AUG – 9 OCT 1916 AND HULLOCH 12 FEB – 4 MAR

MONCHY LE PREUX AND GAVRELLE 5 APRIL – 5 JUNE 1917

CHARLEROI

ST POL

ARRAS

CAMBRAI

LOUVIGNIES 6 NOV 1918

CAUDRY 11 NOV 1918

LE CATEAU

DOULLENS

TRENCHES AROUND

FONCQUEVILLERS

26 AUG 1915 – 3 JULY 1916 AND 1 APL – 13 MAY 1918

13 – 24 NOV 1916

HAMEL

POZIERES

100 DAYS LINE OF ADVANCE 19 AUG – 11 NOV 1918

AMIENS

ALBERT

SOMME 3 JULY – 16 AUG 1916

25 MILES APPROX

White covered both days of the move in his diary entry dated 30 July:

> '*At 3:39pm the Headquarters of the Battalion, D Company and about half of the Battalion paraded at the telegraph and post office on Windmill Hill and marched to Lugdershall Station behind the band of 9th Lancers which had come over for that purpose from Tidworth. During our stay at Windmill Hill (April 7 – July 30) the 10RF and 9th Battalion, Lancers (Reserve Regt) had formed a great friendship.*
>
> '*A special train was provided to convey the Battalion and 111 Brigade HQ. The train travelled by Andover and Redhill to Folkestone. A lovely summer evening; the whole country bathed in sunshine. Arrived at Folkestone about 8pm when the other half of the Battalion joined us. We went on board a special steamer and crossed to Boulogne with all lights extinguished and escorted by a Government Destroyer. Arrived at Boulogne about 10pm.*'

The opening entry in the Battalion War Diary, recording the daily movements and action of a battalion on active service, was made on 30 July 1915. Battalion diaries vary in detail and that of 10RF gives a basic picture of key events and identifies places they pass through. This has been used to locate the position of letter writers as at the time they were not allowed to say where they were.

Battalion Diary 30 July 1915:

'Boulogne: Battalion less Advanced Party Disembarked. Proceeded to rest camp.'

White wrote of the events after disembarking:

'The GOC went with his staff to the Hotel de Louvre while the battalion was marched up through the town about two miles to an excellent standing rest camp. There were plenty of tents, water laid on, a YMCA and Salvation Army Restaurant.'

The following morning the battalion began its move towards the fighting, as White recorded:

'A beautiful morning. After breakfast the battalion paraded and having been inspected by the Colonel in charge of the camp we marched off with the band playing through French villages some five miles south-east of Boulogne to Pont de Briques. On our way we passed a great number of camps in which were base details, Artillery, ASC, Flying Corps, and Cavalry remounts etc.

'At Pont de Briques we waited for above three hours and got excellent coffee and rolls at the local estaminet; the men were formed up in the vicinity of the station and ate their haversack rations. At 1pm the transport train arrived from Havre bringing Cobbold, Maxwell (transport) and Delbos (Machine Guns).

'We embarked and proceeded past Boulogne and Calais to Watten where we disembarked. A very hot and dusty march, which distressed the men very much, now ensued. About 5pm we reached Bayengham and Monnecove. A Co billeted near the St Omer – Calais road, B Co near the Windmill, C and D near Campagne. My HQ in a farm of the usual type (large manure heap in a central yard, living house on one side, byres and hen sheds etc on either flank). Captain Waters (Adjutant), Rev Edge Partington (Chaplain), Dr Wilson (MO), Delbos (M.G. Officer), Groube (7th Fusiliers, Signaller) all slept in the central room. I had a small box bedroom looking out into the garden at the rear.'

Wilkinson's letter of 1 August began with the account of the bonfire at Ludgershall. He continued with the experience of being in France:

'I am billeted at present in a barn and sleep splendidly at night in straw. Our neighbours, the pigs, do not seem to resent our sitting about in their field and paid us a return visit when we were out and ate half a loaf.

'It was very amusing when we first arrived at our billet. Although several of our chaps spoke French they had great difficulty in understanding the proprietor who was showing us to our quarters. He spoke in a country dialect something like a Yorkshireman speaks English, and the old woman, who seems to be about 100 years old, is stone deaf.

'We have great fun while shopping in the village and are getting on splendidly with the French language, not to mention the French money. Good tobacco can be bought for one penny per ounce and most things are equally cheap.

'This morning [Monday] we marched to a river for a bathing parade. We had a good

dip and were just getting out when a thunder storm caught us and soaked us through. This afternoon we are sitting in the sun with our clothes spread out around us to dry. The sun is scorching.

'I have seen no one here the worse for drink, the wine and beer are cheap and have in them a much smaller percentage of alcohol. On the whole it is a very good change from Ludgershall. About the only thing I want is a newspaper. Will you please send me the weekly "Daily Mirror"?'

'I am not allowed to head my letters with my address so please let my friends know the address I gave you, when you see them. Parnell, Cordingley and I are still together with our old tent mates but Hulford, who is now in the transport, is billeted elsewhere.

'The food out here is quite good and consists almost entirely of tea, jam, hard biscuits and tinned meat. The cooks make quite a decent stew from tinned meat and desiccated vegetables.

'It seems ages since I was with you. I am quite used to this life and although we can sometimes hear the guns it is not exciting. Perhaps I shall feel differently when I get into the firing line!'

Writing on the same day Young was less enthusiastic:

'Dearest Mother, It is impossible for me to write at length to you at present as one's impression is at first necessarily confused.

'The superb callousness of the French people, the dull, drab monotony of the surrounding countryside and the whole experience make it extremely difficult to realise our situation.

'I shall be glad if you could send me some money as the army apparently are not paying us at present.'

He showed signs of becoming a little more positive in a letter to his sister and her husband the following day:

'Dear Florrie and Frank, I write to you jointly because we are only allowed to write one letter a day and also because I do not have enough time to write separately.

'I am feeling very well indeed although the French farm in which we are billeted has certain discomforts which cannot be associated with an August Bank Holiday in England.'

On the 3 August Colonel White was taken to see the Machine Gun School at Wisques. The introduction of the machine gun was a major development in the First World War. Beginning as a mobile weapon, described by some as an automatic rifle, the 28lb weight Lewis gun was used during an advance to increase fire power, providing an equivalent fire rate of 550 rounds a minute from its 4.5lb magazine which carried 47 bullets. It was realised, particularly by the Germans, that digging machine guns into fixed positions and targeting their fire enabled them to control large areas of the battle, especially no man's land, efficiently and very effectively.

They were at first used in the British Army by infantry men, like Wilkinson and Parnell, who were trained to use the Lewis gun in support of their own platoon and company. In

1915 there were four in each battalion but by July 1916 the allocation was increased to eight per battalion. In 1916 the Machine Gun Corps (MGC) was formed, which used the larger Vickers machine gun. At first men from Lewis gun sections remained with their battalions, some training to use the more powerful Vickers machine gun. As the war progressed volunteers transferred to the MGC, and others were enlisted directly as it became a specialist arm, complementing the artillery by barrage firing[23] in the attack as well as providing covering defensive fire in the retreat. The Machine Gun School at Wisques trained specialist officers, NCOs and men, as well as providing courses for infantry officers to make them aware of the potential and most effective ways to use the weapon. The Lewis gun remained an important weapon in infantry battalions, being allocated two to each platoon by 1918 when it was used primarily as an automatic rifle to cover rapid advances and movement.

The battalion moved nearer the fighting. On 4 August they marched to Campagne-lès-Wardrecques, a distance of about 13 miles, on the 5th a march of a similar distance saw them in Saint-Sylvestre-Cappel.

Mountfort described the events of the week in a long letter home on August 10, although the dates and locations are not included in the original letter:

'Wednesday [August 4] We left the village and marched fifteen miles. It doesn't sound much but when you think of the heat of the day, the weight of our packs and the state of French roads you will understand it was an enormous strain on our endurance.... The French roads are horrible. Through every village and for a mile or two each side they are composed of great rough cobble stones about eight inches square and not over carefully laid. Apart from their unevenness there is the difficulty that the nails in our boots slip on them as on ice.... Our packs I cannot find words to describe. It is a cruel unnatural weight no man should be called upon to carry. You get a pain in your shoulders like acute rheumatism after a few miles. The original Regulars and Territorials never carried such packs; we have asked both and they were surprised when we described ours. They came over with all their spare kit in a kit-bag; but that has been abolished and we carry it all on our back.

'Wednesday [5 August] We reached in the evening a small village on the banks of a canal [Canal de Neufosse]. We had a swim in the canal and slept in a barn where there was too much straw. Having had experience of both I prefer too little straw to too much.

'Thursday [6 August] At 6:30am still tired and sore footed we started off again. This day I suppose we marched eleven or twelve miles and I really don't know how we did it. The sun was blazing hot and the road was cobbled all the way. Every step was painful and packs felt simply crushing. To feel hopelessly exhausted and to know you must go on for hours more is not a comforting sensation. The men showed wonderful spirit and when on the point of collapse started singing like old boots – which they never do at any other time. We finished at a mere crawl. Only twelve men fell out, most of them going on till they fainted and several of these rejoined us at a subsequent halt. Unfortunately, of the Battalion in front so many fell out that the Brigade got more or less into hot water. We finished up at another village [Saint-Sylvestre-Cappel] and my company were all in one large barn at a very prosperous farm house. I understand the Germans made it their

head-quarters last September. The barn was not rat-less and insects were plentiful but it was pretty comfortable.'

White was clearly of the view that the problems of men falling out were due to the order of march which placed the Rifle Brigade in the lead, their rate of marching at 140 paces per minute was higher than that of the infantry. When the next move began two days later he took action:

'I put the 10RF in front and made the pace 110 to the minute. Halted every forty-five minutes for fifteen minutes. Allowed no water drinking for the first two hours, no one to fall out, no presents from inhabitants etc. Arrived without mishap no men having fallen out.'

Young was sounding more positive in a letter to his father written on 6 August. He asked for tobacco, this time looking for Players Medium Navy Cut at five pence an ounce. He requested half a pound or a pound, with his father to take the money from his next cheque. His mood had improved for later in the same letter he said:

'As for myself I am feeling very well indeed and quite enjoying the experience. One feels that at last life out here is very real as when we lie down at night we can easily hear the guns being fired.'

The battalion was following a route trodden by many of their predecessors. Most of the fighting in early 1915 had taken place around the Belgian border, places like Armentières, Houplines and Ypres forming focal points for action. By August 1915 the lines near Armentières had become stalemated and both sides established strong trench systems, so troops there, apart from experiencing raids and artillery barrages, were seeing little fighting. These areas were ideal to show new battalions what trench life was like, to ensure officers knew how to look after their men and give experience of moving up to take over a trench and standing sentry while in relative safety. More trenches were dug and the existing ones extended and fresh troops were used to give impetus to this process.

The Battalion War Diary recorded that on 9 August 500 men went to Armentières to dig trenches with the 12th Division. They stayed there until joined by the remainder of the battalion on 17 August.

The first entry in Alfred Mills' diary recorded their arrival in Armentières.

'Monday, 9 August, Armentières
'Armentières looked grey, even in the late morning sunshine, and my feet were starting to become a bit sore. Marching nine miles or so from Bailleul this morning on rough cobbled roads was beginning to take its toll.
  'Skinny was really labouring alongside me and despite all the training and route marches; he still seemed as fat as the day we met in the bell tent nearly a year ago. "It's my fate in life" and "God wanted me this way" were constant mantras, but he was a good sort and always up for a laugh. Skinny was from Swansea and a devout Chapel goer.

'We marched passed the Town Hall and turned into Rue de Lille before turning into a dark side street and halting outside a factory.

'The factory had been a used for weaving and looked pretty grubby."Right, dump your packs and find a cosy place to spread your blankets. This is your new home, there's running water and privies, and hot baths around the corner," yelled Sgt Clapp[24]. "Get smartened up and assemble out 'ere in fifteen minutes so we can go and get inspected outside the Town Hall" he intoned. This was the only time we actually prepared for an inspection at the end of a march.

'A colonel I didn't know, inspected us and he sat very still and resplendent on his charger as we marched past and then we stood in line along with some fellas from the Yorkshire Regiment.

'The colonel informed us that we all had an important job to do and this sector was very critical to the campaign. I immediately tensed with excitement. This was what we had been waiting for. A chance to have a go at the Hun. I was to hear those same words many times over in the next few years, by which time I had grown a little weary of them. But, standing in that square, I felt proud and set to do my best.

Alfred Mills photograph taken prior to departure for France. Graham Morley

'That night, about 9pm, we marched out following a railway line to a place called Houplines, where an assembled mound of picks and shovels awaited us. We worked all night digging trenches. Our efforts were sparked by a constant stream of machine gun fire from somewhere to the east of us. In the gloom all we saw were flashes but it induced us to dig deeper and faster. The sub-soil was wet and heavy and marching back to our billet in the morning just as dawn was breaking, we all looked a right bunch of ragamuffins. We used the baths around the corner from our billet in an old brewery. Some vats had been converted for bathing.

'By the time I had cleaned my kit it was gone 10am and I just collapsed onto my blanket and fell sound asleep.'

Work continued the next day, first enlivened by a preliminary exploration of his new surroundings.

'Tuesday, 10 August, Armentières

'I awoke about 4pm feeling a bit stiff and hungry. I reached into my pack for a couple of ration biscuits before rising and seeing to my ablutions. Shaving in cold water freshened me up and I set about tidying my kit up before seeking out the canteen to have a brew and a bite.

Mail arrived with letters from Ma, Winnie, and Dot (Winnie's sister).

'I and Skinny had a look around the town but were cautious as we had been warned not to speak to the locals, not that we could as they spoke French and we spoke English. All we saw were old women with huge wicker baskets and loads of fellas from other Regiments.

We popped into something called an estaminet but didn't fancy a drink, so left.

'That night, it was back to Houplines for more trench digging. Jerry had us taped.

Alfred Mills wrote to his family showing a view of Armentières where 10RF first went into the trenches. Graham Morley

This time they had searchlights and strafed us along the railway line we had to follow outside Houplines, causing us to duck and weave before we jumped into the trench we had dug the night before.

'By the morning, the parapet was up and various communication trenches had been created and we felt like hardened veterans, even though not one of us had fired a shot at the enemy yet.

'The morning was a repeat of the previous one. Get cleaned up and collapse on my blanket.'

Mountfort too was digging trenches. They were billeted in a house in Bailleul and he described a bombardment heard in the early morning as 'somewhat resembling a steam trolley always coming up the road without getting any nearer'.

Of Monday, 9 August he wrote:

'We spent the morning lounging about the town. The cathedral was rather fine, and we heard mass and a burial service. The organ was good and the singing, though queer, being all male voices in unison, sounded very well... In the afternoon we marched – or struggled - another nine miles and are now right up against the firing line. We are in a large town rather north of where Dormor[25] is and where our destination was rumoured to be, as I mentioned before we left England.

'Tuesday 10:

'Half the crowd are digging in the day time and half at night – I am with the latter – greatly to my disadvantage, as we get collared for things in the day time and then have to dig at night. This morning after a general fatigue clearing the place up we went into the town. The estaminets are closed to troops until 12, there is nothing that takes the

*place of the English teashop and there was precious little to do. I changed some notes
at the Credit Lyonnais (open for a few hours each day, the floor a mass of sand bags
and everything heavily barred) and got only 25 Francs apiece, a precious low rate.
Later I had steak and chips – the exact antithesis of a similar English dish, for whereas
over there the steak is plentiful and rich and juicy, while the potatoes are pitifully few,
here the steak was a flimsy piece of gristle, but I could not get through one half of the
potatoes.'*

Young was also in the trench digging detail and he wrote on the 13th to his mother:

*'As we have been constantly on the move for the last week or more I have been unable to
write many letters, but now that we are settled, at least for a while, I have time to write
and tell you I am feeling very fit indeed and in many respects quite enjoying my new
experience.*

*'I must tell you that we are now quite close to the firing line and every night we have
to dig trenches not far from the German lines, but we do it very cheerfully and there is
not much fear of us being shot, although of course there is always the possibility. But I
am very glad that for a time we have not had much marching to do for the pack is very
heavy indeed and very tiring.'*

The next day Wilkinson wrote home to his sister Rene:

*'Thanks as usual for the letter and promise of a parcel. We have heaps of hard work but
it makes the short spells of rest all the sweeter. I am getting quite expert at washing socks
and shirts, the only difficulty is to get a bucket and as for speaking French I can ask for
a cup of coffee or a slice of buttered bread quite easily.*

*'I find that I am only allowed to write two letters per week[26] but of course I can receive
as many as you'd like to send. Please keep the pot aboiling. I will promise to send one
home every week and sometimes both.'*

Mills wrote of the dangers facing him as he moved up to his digging duties in the
trenches:

Thursday 12 August Armentières
*'Getting into a routine now and I'm starting to think I'll be digging bleeding trenches for
the rest of the war.*

*'Mail arrived in the afternoon with letters and cigarettes from Dot and Emily.... Also
I had cigarettes and baccy from Dad.*

*'Night time and running the gauntlet along the railway line was becoming second
nature. There was more chance of being struck by all the picks and shovels flying around
as we hit the deck than the machine gun bullets that came whistling over our heads.'*

Between 17 and 25 August the battalion was attached to the 8RF for instruction in trench
warfare. This was the routine process of getting new soldiers and, probably more

importantly, young officers, used to the routines of trench life in a fairly quiet area. The improved morale is shown by the excited tone and casual bravery shown in all the letters and diaries. It shows the enthusiasm of the men as the battalion are at last facing the enemy across the no man's land. White is quite lyrical in describing in his diary entry of 19 August the position of the headquarters in a house by the River Lys, a slow flowing fairly shallow river banked by trees.

> 'Colonel Annesley's HQ is in a charming spot. The particular house he lives in is in a sheltered position hidden from view and practically untouched although the rest of the Houplines suburb is riddled with shell. The bridge is broken in half either by a gun cotton charge or shell fire and a mass of weeds and timber have formed a barrage on which the moorhen and waterfowl have built. The cattle stand knee deep in water and the whole scene is so entirely peaceful it is difficult to realise what is taking place within 1200 yards. Working parties are active in these farms and are shelled with great precision. Nothing, however, seems to teach caution to our men who expose themselves quite needlessly. Every now and then little processions of stretcher bearers from the various farms bear witness to the accuracy of the German shell fire and the carelessness of our working parties.'

Mills recorded his first turn in a trench when he wrote his diary on 19 August:

> 'Late evening, went into the trenches we had dug and thanked God we had done a good job. Fired a few rounds off but not knowing if they hit anybody. At least there was no danger of being hit by a flying shovel as we negotiated the railway line to get up to the front line.
>
> 'Snipers were particularly worrisome and although none of us were seriously wounded, or killed, a few picked up some nasty scratches or 'glory wounds' as we called them. The enemy trenches were about 100 yards away, close enough to occasionally see helmets bobbing about in the moonlight. The machine guns were a nuisance and many a plan was hatched on how to deal with them, from mass rifle fire (which we did a couple of times), to building a Trebuchet to throw a bucket of bombs at them (which of course, we never did).'

In his usual optimistic style Wilkinson described his first trench experience in a letter of 20 August:

> 'I am having a dose of simple life and am, writing this in a dug out in the firing line which Parnell and I are sharing. It is quite a cosy little affair dug in clay and has a little fireplace with chimney at which we cook our own food in mess tins. We even have a pair of fire tongs hanging by the fire and a shelf for food and nails to hang our mugs on. I have not seen anything very dreadful but have seen aeroplane duels, houses on fire, shells exploding etc, etc not to mention ruined houses and churches without number. We do the journey with our trousers rolled up and empty our boots at the end of the journey.
>
> 'I am only here for a short spell and shall return soon to our billet in a large town.'

On the same day Young wrote to his father in a similar positive vein recording his experience in a letter headed 'Trenches 20 August':

> 'As you can see by the above I am now in the trenches, the front line of trenches with the Germans about 400 yards away. You no doubt by now have a very fair conception of what trenches are like. I can assure you that it is almost unrealisable that the enemies [sic] trenches are so near. The fear of danger that you might imagine was present all the time has already vanished entirely. Men have their little fires in the dug outs where they cook their steak or bacon, just as if they were on holiday camping. I would much rather remain in the firing line here than be in the town where our billets are, for it is far safer.'

Mountfort's experiences were similar to those of the other two but he wrote of a little more action, beginning with the days of trench digging which got them used to being near firing and shells:

> 'We dug trenches for about eight nights, including Sunday, starting out about 7:30pm and digging till midnight or later. There was very little excitement about it. Stray bullets were pretty plentiful and made you jump at first and a sniper or two wasted a good deal of ammunition. A shell only came near us once, but in one spot where the road crossed a railway a machine gun used to open up at intervals which livened things up a little. We had two shells in our billets on different days when they were shelling the town but neither exploded. You hear a shell coming and it is a thrill better than looping the loop at the Crystal Palace waiting to see where it is going to explode.
>
> 'On Wednesday evening [18th August] half the battalion went into the firing line for twenty-four hours. I went with this half so now I have been in the trenches and fired a shot at the Germans (Their trenches were here about 75 yards away). The communication trench was in a pretty bad state – nearly to your knees if you stepped into a hole.
>
> 'We had a pretty quiet time in the trenches as far as the Germans were concerned, for the amount of work makes trench life anything but quiet. A good deal of firing goes on at night, but little by day, as you daren't put your head above the parapet. At night parties go out in front repairing the wire, listening etc. You are awake all night, resting when you can between 10am and 3pm. We return to the trenches tonight which is why I have so little time.'

Billets were often in damaged houses and factories. Wilkinson in his letter of 21 August described his billet and work in the trenches:

> 'It is a small empty house with most of its windows blown in. I sleep on a wooden shutter on the stone floor and am not very uncomfortable. In my last letter I told you what a muddy journey we have through the communication trench. I have since had the job of taking up the floorboards and digging a deep gully underneath and it poured with rain while I was at work.'

It seems that the battalion had a fairly gentle introduction to trench life. There was a shared view that the trench was a safer place than the billet. Confidence had grown and the fear of what the trenches would be like had reduced. Both Young and Wilkinson refer to the relative safety and their belief that casualties would not be high. However, even during this relatively safe baptism of fire there were casualties. Wilkinson mentioned one man slightly wounded; in the Battalion War Diary it was recorded that one man was killed and five wounded during this week.

Colonel White attended the funeral of the first member of the battalion killed, though for some reason he did not record this event as being killed in action. Private John Harris, Stk1002, aged 33, was born in Truro, Cornwall and was living with his grandfather in Towcester, Northamptonshire at the time of his enlistment.

Writing after the war Guy Chapman of 13RF who was introduced to the trenches in the same area and at the same time as the 10RF summed up his training:

'Our term of finishing school over, [we were] nominally trained soldiers. It was very little. We could put up wire, keep ourselves clean. We knew something about ration parties and other fatigues, and we had learned how to build sandbags into a wall which looked strong, a seductive art, too seductive as we were soon to learn.'

Maxwell reviewed the first days in the trenches and subsequent movement:

'We were put into the line first of all at Armentières. It was a specially chosen quiet sector, and was being used for instructional purposes, and, in fact, we had only one or two casualties while we were there. Then we moved southward to take over from the French.'

Chapter 6

In the Trenches:
August to September 1915

The battalion moved south overnight on 25 and 26 August; they left the Grand Place, Bailleul at 10:45pm, marched for just over two hours to the station at Godewaersvelde and were put on a train at 1:30am. Arriving at Doullens at 11am they marched five miles to Grenas in the area held by the French. The French wanted the British to take more responsibility for manning the line to release their troops for service elsewhere.

Wilkinson described travelling by troop train:

'You climb in with your pack and rifle into a sort of 'milk van' labelled forty-four men or eight horses, and when your forty-three pals are inside you wish you were a horse!! With a certain amount of planning arms and legs can be interlocked and you can squat on the floor. Then follows several hours jolting during which you doze, waking at intervals to restore circulation to some distant limb which has 'pins and needles'. Absolute indifference should be paid to intervening heads, arms, necks, etc and to remarks of the owners thereof as soothing replies, threats and promises are of no use.'

White described the area and deployment of his men around the village of Grenas:

'Here we had the HQ of the battalion in the house of the mayor. He has a beautiful formal garden. A rather melancholy feature is the tomb of his ancestors ten yards from the front door. We take our meals out on his beautiful gazon [lawn] of the front garden. The Brigade HQ is in a fine old Chateau: the owner has been killed in Champagne. Good barns for the Company billets. All this day we were among the French troops who thronged the Arras Road and all the villages. A fine smart-looking lot of men, very cheery and pleasant. A Co were bivouacked in the open on the fields near Pommera. They afterwards got very wet when the rain came on.'

White accompanied General Barnes in an ambulance to Foncquevillers, passing through villages held by French troops, to view the trenches. White was impressed by the French defences around Foncquevillers, describing the trenches and fortifications as 'excellent'. The following day, 29 August, he returned with his company commanders and showed them around the trenches. The machine gun officer, Second Lieutenant Delbos, the

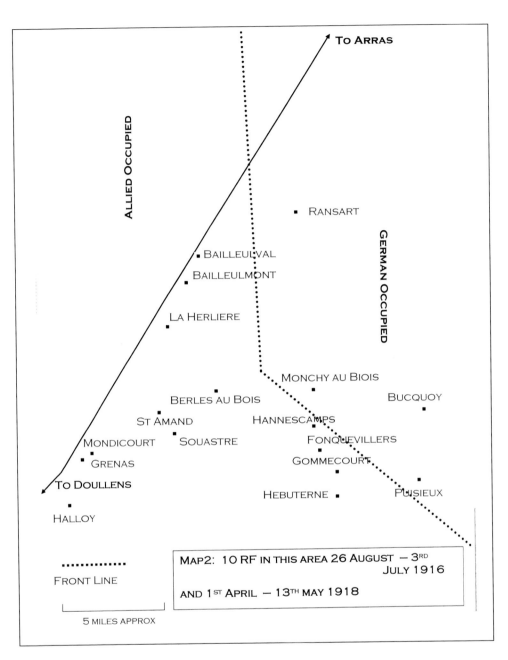

To Arras

ALLIED OCCUPIED

GERMAN OCCUPIED

- RANSART

- BAILLEUL VAL
- BAILLEULMONT

LA HERLIERE

- MONCHY AU BIOIS

BERLES AU BOIS

BUCQUOY

ST AMAND

HANNESCAMPS

MONDICOURT SOUASTRE

FONQUEVILLERS

GRENAS

GOMMECOURT

To Doullens

HEBUTERNE

PUISIEUX

HALLOY

....
FRONT LINE

MAP2: 10 RF IN THIS AREA 26 AUGUST — 3RD
JULY 1916
AND 1ST APRIL — 13TH MAY 1918

5 MILES APPROX

signaller, Lieutenant Groube, and medical officer, Dr Wilson, were also briefed by their French opposite number.

The brigade was inspected on the following day by General Sir Charles Munro, commanding the Third Army. Also in attendance was Lord Newton, Assistant Under-Secretary of State for Foreign Affairs, with responsibility for foreign propaganda and also for prisoners of war. He was the father-in-law of Captain Egerton-Warburton, who had been adjutant to 10RF. Lord Newton told White that he had to return to England urgently because Egerton-Warburton was very ill in hospital in Manchester. White added a note later to his diary 'John died that night at Manchester'.

Egerton-Warburton had septicaemia through dirt entering his wound. At that time the only treatment available was amputation, if this was feasible, to stop the spread of the poisoning. Before antibiotics if the condition spread to the organs it was fatal and it was this that led to his death, three months after he was 'slightly wounded'. Buried in Great Budworth, Cheshire, he left a widow, Lettice. His second daughter, Priscilla, was born three months later.

Wilkinson updated his family in his letter on 31 August. He began by praising the speed of the postal system, a letter taking only a couple of days to reach him from England, unless the battalion was on the move when it 'takes a little longer'. The importance of letters and parcels to the men isolated in France comes through the writing of all the authors and the delays when they occurred were the topic of loud complaint. Wilkinson in one of his letters said, 'Letter writing and letter receiving form almost our only recreation'. It was even worse when the letters written by the men failed to get home and the panic this could cause was reflected in a letter from Wilkinson to his parents in which he says he is sorry that Mrs Parnell had to come round to find out what was going on as she hadn't received a letter from her son. He commented that no doubt his mother has at some time gone to see Mrs Parnell for the same reason, but hasn't told him in her letters to him.

The hospitality shown to White by the French contrasts with the problems of the men of the battalion who had some difficulty in obtaining rations because of the move. Colonel White recorded in his diary entry of Friday 3 September:

'In the morning rode with Major Giles RE to Foncquevillers and went round the trenches with French Staff Officer. We lunched with Colonel Carrera and his officers. He gave us quite an excellent lunch, hors d'oeuvre, omelette, soup, excellent fillet de boeuf, caneton de Rouen, apple tart, Gruyere cheese, good coffee and liqueurs, within 1500 yards of the German line. His cook is a Paris restaurateur.'

Wilkinson's culinary experience on the same day was very different to that of Colonel White; as he wrote in a letter home a couple of days later:

'Thank you so much for the parcel. It arrived perfectly safely on Friday morning [3 September]. There are about twelve of us in our dugout and we should have had nothing to drink at tea time that day on account of a 'moving job' but for the tin of cafe au lait. The cakes were in fine condition and the pickles helped down our bully beef a treat. In fact we had quite an enjoyable meal instead of mere bully beef and bread.'

He went on to describe his new surroundings:

'You would be quite interested to see our present 'dug out'. It has eight sleeping bunks made of wire netting on a wooden frame. We have a tremendous thickness of logs and clay overhead. We possess a small table, four chairs and a form, a glass window, front

95

and back door (the front door has a spring which automatically closes it) and a washing bowl on a stand outside the door on a landing halfway between the floor of the dug out and the ground surface, wire clothes line and shelves for food. I might also mention that there are numbers of fruit trees overhanging the trench.'

After returning to St Amand the battalion paraded in pouring rain at 11:15pm and marched through Souastre to Foncquevillers. Here they were met by French officers who escorted them into the trenches and remained with them until daybreak.

Young wrote home on 6 September.

'Yesterday was Sunday and I was wondering what you were doing. We are now definitely in the trenches and are likely to stay for 18 days at a time, so you can imagine we get fairly dirty by the end of that time.

'There are several things that it will be absolutely essential for me to have now that we are really here. I have made a list of things I want chiefly so that from time to time you might send some of them.

'The trenches we are in are in fairly good condition and naturally when one has to live in them for three weeks at a stretch one wants to be as comfortable as possible.

'List: A few more handkerchiefs, a woollen balaclava helmet, a pair of woollen gloves with gauntlets combined, stick of shaving soap, Cadbury's "Mexican" chocolate; two or three pairs of good thick socks; one or two thick khaki shirts; steel looking glass; one tin tooth powder; soap; cakes are always acceptable. I want most of these things rather badly so that I shall be obliged if you will send them as soon as possible. Do what you think best with the remainder of the money but don't forget to take the money for these.'

The first spell in the trenches was recorded in the Battalion Diary:

'3 September 1915: Arrived Foncquevillers without incident and took over trenches 50 to 55 from the 355th Infantry Regiment French Army. Weather very wet. Trenches in good order. D Company held Reserve Trenches and billeted with HQ in dug outs in the village which had been almost entirely destroyed by shell fire.

'4 September: C Coy withdrawn from the 1st line trenches to reserve in village with D Company.

'Work of improving and strengthening trenches commenced. Good road but second half of journey exposed to shell fire. 9 September: C & D Companies relieved A & B in the trenches. 10 – 15 September: Companies in and out of the trenches worked almost continuously strengthening defences and improving sanitary arrangements in the village which are in bad order.

'15 September: Battalion relieved by 8th Battalion, East Lancashire Regiment and marched by Companies to rest billets in St Amand. The 111 Brigade becoming the Brigade in Reserve.'

This pattern is at variance with Young's statement that he will be in the trenches for eighteen days. At worst the battalion could be described as being in the trenches for twelve days and each company was actually in the front line trenches for six days. Those in reserve would have spent time in the trenches improving defences, but not for the eighteen days stated by Young. The battalion diary also records that during this period one man was killed and four wounded on 6 September and on 7 September Second Lieutenant Knox was wounded and one other rank (OR) was killed. The first man killed here was Stk40 William Bradley of A Company a 30-year-old stockbroker's clerk and son of a Methodist minister. He was killed when looking through a loophole, is buried in Foncquevillers and listed in the Stock Exchange Memorial. White records the death in his diary as being that of the first man of 10RF to be killed in action. Alfred Mills had been more fortunate a couple of days earlier when as a member of B Company he had gone into the front line trenches.

Saturday 4 September, Foncquevillers
'Moved up to the front line just before dawn. Shells were whistling overhead and the now familiar machine gun bullets whined above us. I found a comfy fire step and poked my rifle through a small hole in the parapet, a bit too far, for suddenly a hail of machine gun bullets descended on the parapet kicking up clods of earth. I retracted it hastily as everyone ducked down even further into the trench. Using a bit more caution, we found suitable key holes to use unobtrusively and under orders fired at a large wood over in front of us and slightly to the right. This I was told was Gommecourt Wood.'

Random death recorded in White's diary, 'a man of Knox's platoon was killed by the explosion of a 5.3 shell'. Author

The first man from 10RF killed in action is buried at Foncquevillers. Author

Twenty-year-old Stk152 Wallace Lees, died on 7 September. He had been born in Peckham but lived in Ilfracombe with his parents, his father a retired Congregational Church minister. Like Bradley a member of A Company, according to White's diary he was killed by the explosion of a 5.9 shell on the trench. He too is buried in Foncquevillers Military Cemetery. It would appear from White's entry that Second Lieutenant Philip Knox, the officer leading Lee's platoon, was wounded in the same incident. Mountfort gives more details of the incident leading to Knox's injuries in a letter of 1 October.[27]

Another of those wounded in this incident was Stk415 Sidney Greenhill who had served as groom/valet to Colonel White. He was wounded when a shell landed near a dugout he was occupying, burying him and injuring his spine and one of his hands. He was also shell shocked by the experience. After time in the hospital at Etaples, he was transferred on 21 October to a hospital in England. After recovering he was commissioned in the Notts and Derby Regiment (Sherwood Foresters) in January 1916 and survived the war.

Sidney Greenhill Stk415, groom valet to Colonel White. Steven Booth

Working out where loved ones were was difficult for those left behind in England. Writing on 7 September Mountfort gave clues as to his location:

> *'You have read in the newspapers that the British line has been extended. Now you can guess what has happened to us. You know mother's first name. Reverse the letters then knock off the first one. You have the name of the place (almost), we are three times as many miles S of there as are there are letters.[28]'*

He continued by describing the village:

> *'There isn't a civilian in it or a house that isn't a complete ruin. I haven't seen more than 3 houses possessing more than the outside walls and perhaps something of a roof. Walking through it now you would think that except for a soldier or two it was deserted. I can't tell you how many troops there are here, first because I have no idea and secondly the censor wouldn't pass it if I had – so you can imagine as many as you like (I don't suppose you'll over estimate it); and every man lives underground. It is a village of human rats. In cellars under the ruins and proper dug outs live – as many men as I didn't mention. There is a barricade every fifty yards and communications trenches run off each side and all over the place. I don't mean that we have to stay underneath. Within certain limits we can walk about, the main street is safe and many parts of the village are invisible to the enemy; but everyone must sleep underground and when an aeroplane comes anywhere near all the rats scuttle into their holes.'*

Sharp's postcard from Foncquevillers showing his family the route taken into the communications trench. Sharp Collection IWM

Every house in the village was damaged. Sharp Collection IWM

Mairie after shelling, the files were still on the shelves. Graham Morley

The ruined village church was visited by both Mountfort and Sharp. Both expressed surprise that a crucifix within the church was undamaged.

Between 15 and 24 September the battalion was 'resting' in St Amand. The Battalion Diary describes the accommodation as 'limited and generally bad'; Mountfort would agree with the description. Passing through St Amand on the way to Foncquevillers, the battalion had already passed a night there. In his letter of 7 September he described the experience:

> 'The place at which we spent one night in a barn before coming over here was the most disgusting I ever struck. All French farms are constructed on the same principle a square, one side of which is the house, the other 3 being barns and outhouses. The whole of the centre, save for the pavement all round, is a heap of straw, manure and general rubbish. However prosperous the farm, it is still so. It doesn't seem the most sanitary arrangement possible but it is the invariable one. On the muck heap the pigs, fowls and ducks all wander about together. At the place I am speaking of the central morass was particularly offensive, about it wandered dismally a handful of decayed poultry, several of which were featherless in places and kept falling over from sheer old age.'

The undamanged crucifix in Foncquevillers church surpr both Sharp and Mountfort. Sharp Collection IWM

Young, on sentry duty one night, also reflected on the situation:

> 'It is very curious to be standing alone outside one's billet with fixed bayonet listening to the guns in the distance. The night has been perfect the moon high and full, the sky cloudless. Inside the billet one's friends and comrades are sleeping absolutely impervious to the army, to the war, to everything. Absolutely unconscious. In a few hours they are awake again and the numbing routine of life has commenced again. It is all very curious thousands of England's finest men dumped down in a handful of French farmhouses. Filthy farmhouses they are, filthy peasants with positively no sense of cleanliness at all. I marvel that disease does not claim them all, so foul are their homes. One wants, like Hercules, to turn the course of a river through their farms to cleanse them out.
>
> Ever so many thanks my dear Dad for sending such a good parcel. Just the things I wanted so badly. You might when writing next enclose a toothbrush as I have mislaid mine somewhere.'

On 22 September there was a fire in a barn used by 10RF, Wilkinson described the event in a letter written a couple of days later:

'A few nights ago we had just turned in to a good clean barn when I heard a deal of shouting and a motor horn being sounded. A barn had caught fire close by and was blazing away as though it meant to burn the whole village. Luckily there was no wind or I'm afraid the best part of the village would have been burnt. As it was it spread to the next building. Working parties were soon on the roof of the adjoining barns ripping off the wood from the roofs with picks and arms and trying to demolish the whole structure. It was very exciting watching the blaze and wondering if the Germans would see it and drop a shell or two over. It was still burning when I got up in the morning.

In fact the barn that burned down was rather more important than Wilkinson suggested. Mills in his diary was more specific, probably because he wasn't subject to having his document checked by the censor:

'Wednesday 22 September St Amand
'Brigade HQ burned down during the night and we were called to help man the pumps. The odd shell was still whistling overhead and Jerry would know we would try and put it out and we're expecting a shower from him at any time, so heart in mouth time.'

On the evening of 24 September the battalion was ordered to move to La Cauchie, a couple of miles to the north. They were allocated the task of acting as reserve to the French 10th Army who were attacking the area south of Lens as part of the 'big push' Battle of Loos. It was a hurried move as Mountford reported:

'Yesterday we went out behind the village to practise a new scheme of attack and were just in the middle of it when orders were received that the Battalion was to be ready to move in half an hour. We were rushed back and packed our kit for dear life. At the end of the half hour nothing happened and presently rumours of the great things, which no doubt you know all about by now, began to come through and we were told to stand by ready to move at any time. We slept fully dressed and now it is Sunday morning [27th September] and we are still here. The official news was read out to us this morning.'

White kept a record of the three days the battalion was in La Cauchie, particularly noting the events of the Battle of Loos and the French attack in Champagne:

'25 September: British Army attacked 6:30am. Took Loos. French cavalry passing through, wounded etc.
'26 September: Sunday, service in orchard. I practised attack with the battalion. French fell back from Wailly Blairville position. 1st Army captured four guns and 2000 prisoners. French south of Arras took 8000 prisoners. 10th French army took Souchez and advanced on Givenchy. Watched very heavy shelling around Arras.
'27 September: French advance in Champagne continued. 1st British Army held ground taken near Loos.'

Writing later Lieutenant Maurice Sharp recalled:

'From 23 to 27 September we were constantly on the move in case we were required in the Battle of Loos. This was only a limited success so we were not needed and came back to Foncquevillers.'

The battalion was fortunate in not being more involved in the battle. The total British losses were over 61,000 of which 7,766 were killed. Other New Army battalions were involved and suffered huge casualties, but they were able to show that in spite of their lack of experience they were capable of taking the fight to the enemy. The 10RF waited in La Cauchie for two days, initially at half an hour's notice to move, later extended to one hour by day and one and a half hours at night. They spent the time practising trench attacks and company drills.

Mills was grateful that the battalion wasn't called into the battle:

'Sunday 26 September, La Cauchie
'Played football and cards, after Church service. Good news from the front. The French advanced and then fell back, so we're not needed. I think it's a bit of a wash-out, though according to rumour, our lads gained ground at Loos, but with a great cost of life, but we haven't any casualty numbers. They were like us, some of Kitchener's new army divisions and new to trench warfare. We are lucky to be south behind the French and not a few divisions north on the Loos front.'

Chapter 7

Winter 1915
October to December 1915

At the start of October the battalion settled into the routine of spending six days in the trenches, six in reserve and twelve at 'rest', and then starting it all again. The trench reliefs with 8 East Lancs all went without any difficulties. There were occasional trench raids to gain information and two men, Stk385 Lance Corporal Albert Duligall, age 24, the son of a saddler living in Hornsey, London and Private Neville Abrams, born in Natal, South Africa, the son of a retired sugar planter, were awarded Green Cards by the GOC for killing a German officer who had been leading a patrol across no man's land. Green and Red Cards were presented to men whose actions, although worthy of recognition, were not at a level to warrant the award of a medal.

The letters home deal with similar issues, living in Foncquevillers, domestic routine and attempts to describe the surroundings and conditions to those at home. Because the battalion is stationary for the first time for months the writers have time to get to grips with their surroundings, and are also looking for things to write about. Mountfort's letter of 1 October, written in Foncquevillers while resting, gave details to his family about domestic matters, and also commented on the losses suffered in September:

'Very many thanks for the parcel which arrived yesterday. The socks will do admirably, though if there is anything thicker on the market you needn't be afraid of getting them too thick. I have a pack of cards, thanks and don't need any soap. I generally have one mugful to clean my teeth, wash and shave in. We had an officer wounded the other night. He was out in front and they ran against a German sap head: one of the Germans got up to stretch himself and the officer shot him – foolishly, because the rest immediately opened rapid fire. A man who was with him is missing. The last time we were up here another of our officers[29] went back with a nervous breakdown. A man in the machine gun section was blown to bits by a shell just outside his (the officer's) dugout and the shock upset him.'

Young's letter of 5 September, headed as 'in the trenches' was written in Foncquevillers after A Company had been relieved on 3 September:

'My dearest Father and Mother, At last some encouraging news has reached you both from the British and French Fronts and although our battalion was not actually in the

fight we were not very far away. At present we are again in support of the firing line living in underground dugouts near that orchard.'

Wilkinson writing on 4 October described the village to his family and, like Mountfort, dealt with matters of hygiene:

'Dear Mother and Dad, Imagine a long straggling village of shattered white stone houses such as I pictured in my sketch; orchards entirely surrounding it and screening it from the view of the enemy and a few hundred yards away, deep wide trenches curling in and out among the trees, mazelike; breastworks thrown across the road at intervals, whisps of smoke issuing from crevices of masonry from the bomb proof shelters below. Picture also the ancient and picturesque wells, labelled UNFIT FOR DRINKING, also put into that picture all that you know of the war: rifle bullets occasionally whizzing overhead etc etc. Remember too that the village was once an exceedingly pretty one (and still is) and was peopled by families who have now gone elsewhere. Put into the scene a few sentries and groups of men in khaki and you will have an idea of my present abode.

'Yesterday at 2 o'clock when the sun had succeeded in making the air warm and pleasant our section had the astounding news that we were to have a warm bath! Two copper boilers had been fixed up in a stable without a roof. Hot water was poured into the stone food trough where we thoroughly soaped ourselves and another lot of water was poured in a canvas bath in which we rinsed. Each man before entering had to "draw" two petrol cans full of water to replenish the coppers and all had to "get a move on".

'On a previous occasion I had a bath in a quart[30] of water and it is no unusual sight to see a chap washing in a mug.

'Life here consists of fatigues. We in the village have to do all the work and carry up all the food, ammunition etc to the party in the fire trench. Starting before having our own meals two of us carry a pole on our shoulders with a Dixie of tea or stew slung in the middle. The journey up the slippery communications trench known as —- Avenue is about a mile and until we had replaced the French signboards with English it was most difficult to find one's way. The names given to the dugouts are quite interesting and some are very suggestive, "Itchycoo Villa" is a good example while "Lyceum" is I think quite subtle.

'Just at this moment a rude German machine gun sent a spurt of bullets along the village. We promptly sent back a shell. Bang!!

'I don't think I can write more just now as Parnell and I are going up to the front line with full water bottles for the chaps there. After that we are to be paid. We get our money in a lump every two or three weeks and when we are in inhabited towns we sometimes have some nice little teas.'

The final sentence in this letter shows how society in England was changing in response to the increasing numbers of men going to war:

'I do hope you are all quite well, that dad is now used to lady clerks.'

Life continued in its routine of days in the line based on Foncquevillers and at rest in Souastre. Training classes in machine guns and bombing were held. There were route marches and drills, practice attacks and working parties to strengthen the defences of the village. There were baths in Pas-en-Artois involving a march of four miles to get there, five minutes to undress, ten in the bath and fifteen to get dressed again before marching back. The letters reflect the routine nature of life. Mountfort wrote on 25 October:

'I have practically no news for you this time. Tomorrow night we go up into the trenches. We usually have a pretty comfortable time (considering) in this place, but this time it has been a bit of a nightmare – rotten weather and hard work from morning till night, Sunday included; so that I have had little inclination for letter writing.'

Those in command were concerned that troops in rest would become bored and that morale would suffer in consequence. At both local and divisional levels attempts were made to provide entertainment. Sporting competitions were held in football and rugby and a concert party was put together using performers from men in the division.
    White recorded in his diary on 16 October:

'Forty men under Harley worked on village defences. Visited bombing instruction in the morning. In the afternoon officers of 10 RF (self included) played 111 Brigade (including GOC) at football. French interpreter was sick on the ground.'

Wilkinson witnessed the match and was clearly impressed and entertained as he reported in his letter of 19 October:

'Last Saturday afternoon we had a treat. Just before the match started we heard the Divisional Band in the distance. It marched solemnly out of headquarters playing a march followed by a mounted officer carrying a flag and dressed in pale blue pyjamas. He was followed by our Colonel and several of our senior officers in various hued pyjamas and two stretcher bearers with a stretcher brought up the rear. On reaching the football ground through an almost hysterical crowd of men they helped one another out of their gaudy outer coverings and played a short match with the Brigadier General and his staff. The General was in one goal and our Colonel in the other.
    'In the evening about 150 of us crammed into the village schoolroom and enjoyed a sing-song. Our Chaplain (popularly known as Charlie Chaplin) had found a piano somewhere and installed it there for our benefit.'

November began back in the trenches having again relieved 8 East Lancs. There was sporadic shelling, with two deaths and seven men wounded on 2 November. One of the wounded, Stk173 Sergeant Charles May, age 30, was later discharged from the army. A merchant from Norfolk who had served for two years in the Norfolk Volunteers and then for six years with the Southern Rhodesian Volunteers, his experience was recognised with promotion up the ranks of NCOs between October 1914, when he was promoted lance corporal, and to sergeant before the battalion left for France. He had been in charge of a

Lord Gleichen.

Stk677 James Farrar seated in centre of the group showing their goatskin coats. Sir Julian Horn-Smith

party working in a communication trench when he was wounded by shell fire. His injury resulted in nerve damage which weakened his right arm and although he was released for agricultural service to bring in the harvest in July 1916 his arm did not recover sufficiently to return to the army and he was discharged with a pension in August 1916.

On 8 November Wilkinson wrote to his mother about the steps taken to avoid trench foot, now more prevalent because of worsening weather:

> *'I am in receipt of your parcel containing the American cloth puttees[31]. You could make a fortune if you put them on the market. I shall wear them next time we go in the trenches and I'll let you know how they work. The army is taking tremendous care to see that we don't get frostbite. We are to rub our feet once or twice a day with whale oil, wear two pairs of socks in large boots and have one pair drying round the brazier.*
>
> *'We've now got furry coats over which we are to wear mackintoshes in addition to two body belts, a thick vest, woollen shirt, cardigan and tunic.*
>
> *'I should like you to see my fur jacket: grey goatskin with brown left sleeve and piebald right sleeve, hair outside. It is lovely and warm.'*

Lord Gleichen, the Divisional Commander, was concerned that men at rest with nothing to do become bored and he proposed the formation of a permanent concert party to

106

remain in the rest camp and provide morale boosting entertainment for the men when out of the trenches. Staff officers were charged with trawling the brigades and battalions to find officers and men capable of forming the core of the party. Young wrote home on 9 November:

'A few weeks ago while we were having our twelve days rest from the trenches Rubens and I had orders to report to the headquarters of a certain battalion a few miles away. When we arrived we were met by several officers and staff officers who asked us if we would be willing to take part in a Divisional Entertainment Party when we should be free of all military duties. The idea is to provide concerts for different battalions when they come out of the trenches. However I am afraid I shall not stay here long as it is more a comic party than anything else and they want us to dress as Pierrots or something, which of course, I am not going to do. However I shall stay here for a little while and see what happens. I expect soon I shall go back to the 10th. It is certainly quite a good idea, but I could not dress as a Pierrot. After all one came out here to fight as a soldier, not to sing in a concert party.'

Auditions held towards the end of October resulted in nine men being selected to form the basis of the party under the leadership of a 'talented pianist', Lieutenant Haines, or Haynes. The founder members from 10RF were Stk731 John Kortright, Stk219 Herbert Rubens, Stk293 George Young, and Stk1003 John Hawley. *The Golden Horseshoe*, the bulletin of 37th Division, reported that 'the most popular turn of the early days was George Young, a baritone singer of fine power, extensive repertoire and sympathetic rendering'.

On 18 November, Young wrote to his father:

'I write to acknowledge your letter dated 16th and am glad to hear you think I am doing the right thing in accepting this new position. I hope you clearly understand what the position is. It is the General's opinion that in doing this we are being more helpful than if we were in the trenches. You see when the troops come out of the trenches there is absolutely nothing for them to do in the villages in which they are billeted and in the fierce winter evenings a concert hall decently done up with a good concert party is just the thing to cheer them up.'

The weather continued to deteriorate and White described a trip round the trenches:

'In the afternoon up to Roberts quarters then back by 55A. Here the liquid mud was three inches above my knees and the men in very bad conditions but most cheerful. This part of the trenches falling in in many places. Three of the communication trenches quite impassable. Got gum boots for about 180 men.'

The bad weather with days of rain, or mist, or frost began to wear down the good humour of the troops in the trenches and in rest. Digging drainage sumps and clearing trenches of mud were regular tasks. Mountford described working in a forest near Pas-en-Artois felling trees, cutting stakes, making hurdles and burning charcoal. This was a task taken on by one company each time they were in 'rest'. As Mountfort described in his letter of 30 November there wasn't much relaxation:

> 'We are having a rotten time here. We parade at 7:30am and don't get back till 4:15pm and then we have dinner. Lights out is 8:30pm. You see we only get those few minutes leisure in the whole day, there are always things to do such as mending and cleaning. The weather has changed completely. It poured hard the whole day yesterday and we got soaked. Imagine woods in drenching rain. I dried my clothes in the obvious way – sleeping in them. Today has been fine.'

Routine work could sometimes be seen to have a humorous tinge, particularly when the story is recounted by Wilkinson who continued to see the funny side of life. On 2 December, having expected a relatively leisurely breakfast and a parade before going on a route march, he was told that men from his company were to draw lots to get together a party to go digging for the day:

> 'Cards were produced and Parnell and I together with several others drew the unlucky spots. We rushed through our breakfast and with groundsheets round our shoulders hurried to headquarters about half a mile away. Arriving there we were put into a party of 25 men and marched off to a battered village three miles away to report to the Royal Engineers for digging. After a dismal hour's trudge we marched into the RE headquarters and our sergeant was just reporting twenty-five men for work when another twenty-five men and a sergeant from a different regiment hove in sight from the opposite direction. The REs were only expecting 25 so our sergeant agreed to toss with the other to decide who should do the work. The coin went up; we called 'heads' and the coin dropped into the mud. A second time it was spun with the same result. We called 'heads' a third time and breathlessly waited for the coin to be uncovered; 'heads it is!'. We yelled a cheer and then hushed one another up for fear of attracting attention and having more labour thrust upon us, then we formed fours and set out through the drizzle, which had started, back to our billets.

> 'Result 6 miles marched by each man   25 x 6 = 150 miles
> 'Work done by one man = 0
> '" " " 25 men = 0 x 25 = 0

> 'Someone had blundered, jolly good job we won the toss though.'

Relief was short lived for the following day he and the same group were called out to work again. Fortunately another member of the company looked after their interests:

> '5 December: Dear Mother… The very next day I had to parade at 7:30am, march four miles, shovel mud out of a trench for four or five hours and then march back dripping with rain. Luckily 'Porky' had arranged a grand dinner of pork cutlet, chip potatoes and

beans at 6pm in the local estaminet so we finished the day off in the best of spirits – I should say 'coffee'. Porky is the familiar name for Hurst, a member of our team who is a perfect gem in the trenches as far as 'eats' are concerned.'

Throughout December Young, now permanently in Souastre with the Barn Owls, showed a reflective mood in his letters to his mother and sister perhaps added to by an element of homesickness and depression in the bad weather:

'3 December 1916. Dear Mother, As I sit down to write to you tonight at a table the untidiness of which would make you shudder (for there is on it a residuum of an evening meal composed of tinned food of every conceivable description). I cannot help thinking as I think a thousand times during the day, of what you are doing at home, and of the upheaval which has made the last sixteen or seventeen months so abnormal and so separated from my previous life before the war. If it were possible, I know it will not be so, but if it were possible I should like to think that when it is all over I could return to England and take up life as if no war had ever been. That of course is a rather an absurd wish seeing that it will affect for years to come every possible branch of life and experience. But everybody and everything is so saturated with khaki (both metaphorically and otherwise) that it really would be most refreshing if one could exist without that dreaded colour and never again hear the word WAR mentioned again even in a reminiscent manner.

'5 December. Dear Doris, By the time you receive this letter your debate upon poetry v music will, I expect, be almost forgotten but I should be very interested to hear what your opening remarks were and which of the two you championed. Of course you must remember that both poetry and music are only expressions of art and are in themselves only technical. All true art emanates from the soul and without that vital and eternal something which men call art no man or woman can possibly appreciate either music or poetry. A Beethoven concerto although beautiful in itself is really nothing disassociated from the soul of the great composer. Similarly beautiful poems like 'The revolt of Islam' by Shelley or Tennyson's 'In Memoriam' could never have been created by a person who was not an artist.'

The Battalion Diary noted that on 10 December three snipers took a notice about the Peace Demonstration in Berlin, fixed it to a board and placed it on the wire by the German trenches. The Germans took it into their trenches shortly afterwards, the Battalion Diary recorded this as 'the enemy having removed this as desired' so the message was delivered. On the 14th four snipers left the trenches at 6:30am and took up position outside the German wire. As dawn broke they fired twenty-five shots on German soldiers walking along the parados, hitting five men. As they returned one sniper was wounded, but after sheltering in a shell hole they all got back successfully.

The weather continued to be atrocious with a wind from the north-west and rain. To avoid the risk of exposure and illness the GOC agreed to the battalions in the trenches reducing to half companies of four platoons and rotating the half companies every twenty-four hours. The half company in support bivouacked midway between the front line and the village. Companies in Reserve moved forward every forty-eight hours to change places with those in the front line. The weather and attention from artillery necessitated the regular repair of trenches but it was not only 10RF having difficulties. On 13 December the Battalion Diary noted that:

'The Germans have also been busy and a considerable amount of pumping heard from their trenches.'

On the same day Young wrote to his father:

'For many days past it has been raining incessantly but today the weather has changed and the sun is shining brilliantly. It is pleasant to see the sun for it makes one feel much happier in the worst conditions. At the present time I am not very busy. Last Wednesday the boys went back from their billets to the trenches. It is no exaggeration to say that most of the time they are waist deep in mud. So that I suppose I ought to be very thankful that for a few weeks I am not there. Well, honestly I am not glad about it for although I am out of the trenches and have a comparatively easy time I miss the associations of the 10th enormously and so does Rubens. In fact we are both thinking seriously of going back.
  'You probably have no idea how well known the 10th has become out here in France. Everybody seems to speak well of the battalion. It is indeed unique.'

In his letter of 15 December Wilkinson, untypically, mentioned an incident that happened in the trenches, but was probably intended to reassure those at home:

'You won't be frightened if I tell you will you? Parnell had a shell burst about three yards from him which knocked him over, but except for a shaking he was unhurt. Wasn't that a bit of luck? Don't tell his people in case he hasn't mentioned it. I thought this little tit bit of excitement in my letter would be interesting and it really shows how many chances there are against us getting hurt when one can be undamaged although within three yards of a bursting shell.'

On 17 December White recorded in his diary:

'Two officers, Lieutenant Lutyens and Lieutenant Taylor with Corporal Lelen and Private Curtis crawled under the German wire, bombed a sentry and brought away chevaux-de-frise'[32] [which White put up with a label outside the Battalion HQ in Foncquevillers]. Other actions were carried out to harass the Germans.'

Young in his letter of 17 December to his brother Charlie, remained philosophical:

'My dear Charlie, What I desire is beauty. The soul and beauty of nature, the wonder of the undying sun, the might of the restless sea, the beauty of human life above all. Only some annoying circumstances prevent me being at home. The heart of man was barbaric

Chevaux de frise.

and vile and it conceived a war, and in due course the war was proclaimed and I am only one of the most insignificant details of its huge mechanism. I wish people would think a little less seriously of the war. I admit that its ultimate effect will be of enormous influence but if you understand my dear Charlie what I mean, the lives of people, their existence, their manners are so saturated with war that sometimes I think that the things which count most in life receive very small consideration.

'How beautiful it is for me to think of the jewel stained windows, the sweet, sad music, the constant flame before the shrine. War cannot affect the vital things of life.

'I expect before long to be back in the trenches as I had much rather be there, but I will let you know when I go back.'

Christmas approached with the troops looking forward to receiving parcels from home. Young continued his letter to Charlie:

'I was very pleased with the parcel especially the Christmas pudding and the diary.... Well my dear Charlie I reciprocate your Christmas wishes and will drink to your jolly good health in a glass of "vin blanc".'

Mist for a few days in the middle of December meant that artillery and aerial activity was limited. This would no doubt be greeted by the troops in the trenches with some relief as

Sharp visited Amiens and commented on the normal life there. Sharp Collection IWM

in the previous month Mountfort had complained at the actions of the allied artillery:

> '*Incidentally I may say we haven't any affection for artillery. Everything is nice and peaceful and we are just beginning to settle down and make the best of our bad conditions, when the RFA, coming leisurely out of the safe and comfortable quarters away back somewhere, decide to have a little strafe. So they fire a lot of shells at the Germans. The Germans say, "well look here we're not going to stand this; we want to be quiet but if they want a noise we'll see who can make most". So they go and fire a lot of shells back. But do they fire at the disturbers of the peace and try and smash up their safe and comfortable quarters away back somewhere? No fear: they fire at the poor wretch in the trenches, increase the burden of his life; knock down his parapet, which he must laboriously renew, break up his wire, which he will risk his life to mend and make his leaky dug out leakier still.*'

Wilkinson wrote home on 21 December:

> '*My Dear Mother, You're a darling you really are. When I arrived here yesterday after a tiring march I was handed your parcel of cakes, home made ones too!! Please thank Aunt Emily for the ginger cakes, they were fine. The marmalade has gone into our 'doings bag' as we call it. Miss Mulford sent me a nice parcel and Mr Shott sent me 25Ffr and says a parcel is on the way from Stanley Works. We have booked one of the village estaminets for Christmas Day dinner for the MG section and are looking forward to a jolly time.*'

He described a walk through the town. Sharp Collection IWM

Changes brought about by promotion, illness, injury or changes in role affected the battalion at all levels. Mountfort writing home at the end of December referred to a photograph his parents have of his section in training:

'You remember you have a photograph of the original section - some eighteen men, of whom six remain. I don't mean all have become casualties; they went sick or took over special jobs and so forth. It gives you some idea of the wastage of a battalion fighting strength though.'

Among the officers there were changes as White recorded on 22 December:

'Cobbold[33] appointed to command 10th Battalion, Loyal, North Lancashire Regiment.'

Maxwell described Major Cobbold's departure in his autobiography:

'Cobbold left us to take command of a battalion in another brigade. Francis Popham[34] went with him. Popham, a charming and refined man with delicate taste, later on covered with himself in glory as the colonel of still another battalion.'

White had arranged Christmas with some care:

'We had a great day. Had sent the QM and NCOs from each company to Amiens to purchase supplies and we had a real good blow out. I went round the dinners and had a very kind reception from the men.'

GHQ had not forgotten the fraternisation of the previous Christmas and orders were given forbidding any contact with the enemy. To reinforce this the Battalion Diary recorded a telegram from GHQ which:

'Warned the troops to stay alert and not to relax vigilance as there were indications that the enemy might take advantage of the day to launch an attack but nothing of this nature occurred and the artillery of both sides were quieter than usual.'

Maxwell described it as his happiest Christmas:

'We had a Christmas tree and presents for the children of the village; Company dinners with English turkeys and sausages at which we officers stood up and made speeches and drank toasts; and later on our own mess dinners, and further speeches (sitting) and more toasts. We cracked old jokes and rather stale walnuts, told tales that were not new to Noah, confessed with pride that apes humility that we took no credit for it, but our battalion was the best in the Army.'

White in his diary for 29 December recorded the children's party:

'In the afternoon at the Mairie we entertained eighty-four children of Souastre and St Amand. Bran pie and Christmas tree and all sorts of Christmas fun. It was a delightful oasis in their dreary young lives. The men had good quarters on the whole in big barns and farms. The cost of the entertainment was 200 Ffr.'

In a footnote to the published version of his diary White says that when he returned in the 1920s those who had been children at the party still remembered the event.

Young was busily engaged with the Barn Owls; in a letter to his parents on 29 December he described the events:

> 'On Saturday (Christmas Day) we gave a concert in the evening and the General commanding the whole Division was there and enjoyed it immensely. There is now a new programme and the last part of the concert takes the form of a burlesque of the celebrated play called "The Whip". It really is a great success and every evening the hall (which is really a huge barn converted into a theatre) is packed with soldiers out from the trenches.'

The performance of 'Pull through Derby', as the skit on 'The Whip' was called, was an unscripted and spontaneous piece directed by Herbert Rubens. It was described in the *Golden Horseshoe*, the bulletin of 37 Division, as a 'great success and for broad comedy one of the 'Barn Owls' greatest successes'.

Wilkinson writing home in early January referred back to the celebrations around Christmas, clearly a satisfied patron of the Barn Owls:

> '3 January, Dear Mother, I went to the Divisional Theatre again while back in billets and so thoroughly enjoyed the show that I went back again the night after and saw the same show a second time. They had a fine art review called 'The Whip'. The rescue of the horse from the train and the chase were screamingly funny.'

Alfred Mills was also out of the trenches and recorded that he had received a wonderful pair of brown leather boots, waterproof to twelve inches. Having spent Boxing Day digging in the stone quarry at Henu he had a break on 27 December which was a bank holiday. The passing of the year was quiet; as Mills noted in his diary on Thursday 31 December with just two words:

> 'No celebrations.'

Chapter 8

Winter into Spring
1916

Returning to the trenches on 1 January 1916 the battalion regrouped for the New Year. White in his diary for 2 January and Mountfort in a letter written on the 3rd both record the arrival of a personage White described as a visitor; Mountfort identified him as the new second-in-command taking over from Cobbold.

Mountfort's letter:

'I have not received the parcel you speak of, nor the Citizen's[35], nor Hilda S's cigarettes, nor some I am expecting from Morris. We hear there are parcels back in S[ouastre] which they won't bring up. We can't imagine why unless the transport is busy bringing up our new Second in Command's hats. He arrived last night his predecessor being appointed to a Battalion. He is rather well known and as I am not sure whether one is supposed to mention these things I will guardedly say that it is Major W..st.n Ch..ch.l .'

White's diary:

'In the afternoon Winston Churchill came over and spent several hours going round my front line trenches with me and Reggie Barnes. He had tea at my headquarters at Foncquevillers and then we walked back to Brigade HQ at Bienvillers and talked till 10pm. I then walked back. He was most interesting and rash exposing himself on the parapet.'

Winston Churchill had resigned from the Government in November 1915 after failing to be appointed to the War Committee. In December 1915 he had been posted to the 2nd Battalion Grenadier Guards, which had been involved in the Battle of Loos, for a month's training. He arrived with the 10RF as a major on 2 January but three days later, on 5 January, he was appointed temporary lieutenant colonel and given the command of 6th Battalion, Royal Scots Fusiliers. Whether his visit to the 10RF really was a preliminary to his taking over as second-in-command, or a familiarisation visit prior to taking over his own battalion is not clear, although from the tone of White's entry it would appear that the latter was more likely, certainly in White's mind.

Life in the trenches went on. Lieutenant John Dexter, who had arrived in early December, was wounded on 5 January and returned to England. White says he was wounded in Sniper Square when they were watching aeroplanes. The Battalion Diary recorded that:

Captain Roberts, a big game hunter and Fellow of the Royal Geographical Society. Sharp Collection IWM

'A German battle plane accompanied by a Scout plane hovered over our lines for some time this morning and received particular attention from our anti-aircraft guns. Lt J E Dexter wounded by a fragment of aircraft shell as he was lying down in his shelter.'

There were occasional forays to observe what was happening in the German trenches. The Battalion Diary on 4 January reported that it was thought that the Germans were not manning their front line trenches as heavily as before. A group of Germans approached within 20 yards of the 10RF trenches at 5am on 6th but were driven off by B Company opening rapid fire. To prevent the Germans picking up casualties intermittent fire was continued, but a later search found nothing. Artillery fire was exchanged, the Germans sent up a fixed observation balloon which directed fire on trench 50.

One of the first big actions involving some of the battalion took place early on the morning of 13 January. A strong patrol of fifty-six men of B Company under Captain Russell Roberts set out to make use of a gap in the German wire that had been spotted the previous evening. According to the Battalion Diary the night was moonless, the raid carefully planned, and the men's faces blackened to give camouflage. Men with wire cutters began to carefully make a new gap, but as they were working they heard German voices and were immediately fired on from close range. Captain Roberts was badly wounded by the first shot and three other men wounded by a bomb. Maxwell told of the event in his autobiography:

Ectos Maffuniades, front centre, and tent mates at Colchester 1914. Paul Reed

War Illustrated 18 March 1916, 'Fusilier rescues wounded Captain under fire'. Sharp Collection IWM

'Roberts, although hit by bullets in several places, picked up one of the enemy's live bombs and tried to save his men by carrying it away. Anybody else would have been killed two or three times but Fred was so much harder than ordinary nails that he survived. While he lay at a Field Ambulance, General Gleichen pinned the Military Cross upon his bandaged chest.'

Alexis Ectos Maffuniades, a 20-year-old private in B Company, was a member of the raiding party. Employed by his father, a Turkish immigrant, in the family printing business in Tottenham he had joined 10RF early on, enlisted with the number Stk466. Another member of the raiding party wrote later to Maffuniades' parents:

'Although suffering great agony the Captain uttered no sound which would reveal the position of the bombing party, and Private Maffuniades was struck on the head by a bomb, which fortunately did not explode, and only stunned him for a few minutes. On coming to he resumed his crawl, and discovered Captain Roberts lying so badly wounded that he was unable to move. The others of the party were some distance off by this time and it was impossible for Private Maffuniades to attract their attention without shouting, so under a hail of rifle-fire bombs he half carried and half dragged the Captain back towards the British lines; a minute or two later, when firing died down the Germans came out, hoping to secure prisoners, but Maffuniades with the captain on his back managed to evade them, and eventually reached the British lines in an exhausted condition.[35]'

White recorded that Roberts received a total of nine wounds but because he hadn't said he was wounded had been left behind by the main party. His wounds were dressed and he was sent to the Casualty Clearing Station at Hem. Maffuniades, like Roberts, survived the event and was awarded the Distinguished Conduct Medal, (DCM). His citation in *The London Gazette* of 15 March 1916 referred to two incidents:

'For conspicuous gallantry in carrying a wounded comrade, at great personal risk, into a place of safety. On a previous occasion he remained out alone with his Captain, who was wounded, dragged him a distance of 100 yards into a place of comparative safety, and remained with him till stretcher-bearers arrived.'

The Battalion Diary for 29 January recorded additional awards. Red Cards were awarded to Second Lieutenant Heathcote, Stk309 Sergeant C.F. Allen and Stk319 Sergeant R. Bambridge. Wilkinson added to the story in his letter home of 3 March in which he referred to the incident:

'Pleased to hear that you read about Captain Russell Roberts or 'Rusty Bob' as we call him and Maffy. Both of them are in my old platoon photo you have on the wall at home. The bombing stunt was quite elaborately planned and was postponed two nights running because the weather was too fine and unsuitable for surprise visits. I was on duty with our gun and several others three nights running at a specially selected position from

Souastre, a postcard sent by Alfred Mills. Graham Morley

Souastre now. Author

which we could send a perfect hail of bullets from the several guns onto a particular part of the German trenches in case our bombing party wanted covering fire.'

The Lord Mayor of London, as Honorary Colonel to the battalion received letters from Colonel White giving him information on events involving the battalion. One such, quoted in *The City Press* published on 11 March, gave information on the state of the battalion, the poor weather being experienced and that although some men had been killed and wounded so far the battalion had been comparatively lucky. The men are 'quite wonderful, always willing and cheerful and willing to stick it out. Excellent recruits are arriving from the two reserve companies but the drain of men gaining commissions, although a credit to the battalion, is making for difficulties.' White's letter continued: 'I am sorry to say Captain Roberts has lost his legs. This is a dreadful business as he is an active man and one of the most gallant officers but I am glad to say he got the MC. Maffuniades got the DCM of which he is naturally very proud. He distinguished himself very much and is a great credit to the battalion.' The newspaper report concluded by saying that the Lord Mayor was to send Maffuniades a memento of his gallant action; an article later in the month said that he was sent a silver pocket watch.

Young was still with the concert party and to judge by his letter to his mother on 12 January more positive and aware of the benefits the party was bringing to the troops:

'I am still with the concert party and for the present have decided to stay here. Every evening from 400 to 500 soldiers come to see the show and I am certain that it is doing a tremendous amount of good. A lot of men say it is just like being at home it is so comfortable and cheery in the place.

'A friend of mine from the concert party a man named Kortright[37] is going on leave in a few days and will call to see you. I imagine he will call in the evening. He is a short stumpy man with dark hair but he is quite charming. He will tell you heaps of things that would be impossible for me to write about.'

For the remainder of January the battalion moved between the trenches, reserve positions in Foncquevillers and rest in Souastre. They maintained the half company system to avoid illness and hypothermia. The letters return to the familiar themes of wet, mud, cold, rations, parcels received or not received, letters and vermin. Mountfort described a fairly typical scene in his letter of 15 January:

'Strangely enough we are troubled a lot more by vermin now than we were in the hot weather. I am not so bad but some fellows are in a shocking state. A couple of them on sentry post in the trenches the other day disrobed to enjoy the pleasures of the chase. They had slain about fifty apiece when a shell just missed our shelter and smothered them in earth. They abandoned the pursuit.'

On the same day Wilkinson welcomed the arrival of a pair of waders which, because they were marked as 'urgent', were taken straight to him in the trench. He wrote of the chances of leave:

'I have one chance in 47 every fortnight. If I draw first next time I shall be home in about a week; if I fail to draw first 47 times I shall be home in about 2 years time. Officers' servants go first!!'

He also mentioned that he and his great friend Parnell have been separated into different gun teams, both a number two so carrying out similar duties. He asked for some special clothing:

'Will you please send me an under vest of cheese muslin. Mrs Parnell Jnr sent one out for Parnell, she soaked it in an anti-louse solution which, however, has proved ineffectual and they promenade as usual. The advantage of the muslin vest is that it can be held up to the light and cleared of any unwelcome guests in a few minutes, whereas with a wool vest it is very difficult to find the beggars, short sleeves are best.'

The end of the month saw an increase in German artillery and machine gun activity with shells landing on the rest billets in Souastre, and machine guns becoming more active. Towards the end of the month 20-year-old Stk473 Clarence Mitchell died having received a head wound from a sniper's bullet. The Battalion Diary notes 'he was wearing a steel helmet at the time'. This was noteworthy as the Brodie Steel Helmet had been introduced in late 1915 and only in early 1916 was it becoming more available, though they were kept in the trenches and issued to men, usually snipers, who were thought to be at greater risk of injury. It was only later in 1916 that supplies were sufficient to issue one to each man at the front.

Alfred Mills on 30 January suffered from the increase in artillery activity from the enemy:

'Out wiring in no man's land this morning between 2am and 6am. Hell of an artillery strafe and had to knock off for a while. Heavy mist in afternoon and went back out wiring. Found a few souvenirs from the morning strafe. Wrote to Ma.'

Later that week he was in the audience to see Young perform in the Barn Owls concert in Souastre.

In a letter to his sister on 2 February Young told of the other side of home leave:

'I expect that you heard from mother that one of my friends [Kortright] called to see her when on leave. He told us that the return to France from England is dreadful.'

On 6 February, having suffered the annoyance of increased German shelling and machine gunning, the battalion moved from trenches to Souastre for the last time. After five days in rest they set off to march a few miles north to Bailleulval where they took over trenches from the French. Headquarters, stores and transport were based in Bailleulval, and the trenches were about a mile and a half away on a ridge. Rations were cooked in Bellacourt and carried up to the trenches from there. As before there was occasional shelling and men were wounded and killed by shrapnel. Having spent the winter sharing work with

Bailleuval. Author

Route to the front from Bailleuval. Author

the 8th East Lancashires the 10RF were now manning the trenches in turn with 13th Battalion, Kings Royal Rifle Corps.

Mountfort in his letter of 11 February gloomily described the move north:

'I don't like writing other than cheerful letters, but if I could compose one now I should be one of the most deserving VC heroes of the war. We worked very hard on our old trenches to get them in a fit state for handing over, inspired by the thought that we might be going to get a rest. Last Friday having been out of the trenches only five days (we usually get twelve) we marched ten miles and straight into new trenches seven or eight miles north of our old ones. After five months in the trenches ten miles was a stiff proposition with full kit; and we arrived exhausted. It had snowed all night and it rained all day – so wet is a mild term to apply to our state. A few leaky dugouts, capable of holding about half the men at a time seemed to be the only excuse for a jump from twenty-four hours [in the trenches] to six days. In the summer we only spent one quarter of our time [six days in twenty-four] in the front line trenches. Now, in mid-winter, after six months continuous duty we are to spend half.

'It blew great guns, it snowed until the wet ground was covered three inches deep; it rained again and washed it away. In the morning the trenches fell about our ears. We struggled out somehow and crawled to a village about three miles back, the rain still coming down in bucketsful.'

The continuation of this letter, written the next day, was more positive, possibly because the weather had improved, and they weren't back in the trenches. Letters like this show the resilience of the men who, only eighteen months before had been living comfortable lives as professional and business men, with their families in relative luxury, and in a few cases extreme luxury, mostly in London and the surrounding counties.

The trenches at Bailleulval were wet, but there was little activity apart from occasional artillery shots, machine guns and raids across no man's land. The battalion continued to suffer from random casualties; Stk266 Jack Walters and Stk1401 Arthur Sermans were killed together by a shell in a trench on the 12 February. A machine gun team was hit on the 21st and two stockbrokers' clerks killed. Stk215 Leonard Roddis, the 22-year-old son of a member of the Exchange who is listed in the Stock Exchange memorial and Samuel Ellis Levy, Stk458, who had enlisted under the alias of William Mack. Aged 24, he had lived in East Ham with his family, his father was a traveller for wines and spirits. Three others, the remainder of the team, were wounded.

During March George Young's letters are all short and keep referring to his boredom, the desolation of his billet and the hope of getting home sometime. The highlights are the arrival of letters and, especially, parcels. He has little information about what is happening outside his little world:

'Attached 6th Bedford's Transport, 8 March 1916, Dear Florrie and Frank, You will understand that it is difficult to write many letters out here, so that I write jointly to you. I was delighted to receive your letters and also the excellent parcel which came yesterday. I was glad to hear that you are both very well.'

Bairnsfather cartoon popular with the troops.

The Barn Owls were not the only source of entertainment. A publication called *The Bystander* published a cartoon by Bairnsfather in the edition of November 1915. Both Mountfort and Wilkinson make reference to Bairnsfather in letters in March 1916. Wilkinson said in a letter to his mother on 3rd:

'Have you seen Captain Bruce Bairnsfather's humorous sketches in The 'Bystander'? They are absolutely 'it'. I like the one depicting 2 Tommies in a shell hole, shells bursting

all around and one is saying to the other, "well Bill if you know of a better 'ole you'd better go to it".'

Mountford was similarly impressed in a letter written on the 8th :

'Do you see Bairnsfather's pictures in the Bystander? A lot of them are collected in an issue called "Fragments from France" and are well worth looking at. The small details are always meticulously accurate.'

The Germans facing the battalion at Bailleulval showed little enthusiasm for a fight. On 5 March the Battalion Diary reported:

'The German gunners have spent a restful day and our artillery has made several attempts to liven them up but without results. Many Germans observed walking about in Ransart.'

White went to see a new weapon which was being developed for use in the trenches. Flame throwers which shot jets of burning oil across no man's land had been used in trench warfare from October 1914. With a range of at best 40 metres and a narrow spread, with just 40 seconds of fuel, they were of limited effectiveness, and of great danger to the men carrying them who were very obvious and a prime target for rifles, machine guns or any other weapon to hand. The British were trying to develop more powerful flame throwers but White was not impressed by the version he saw at La Cauchie on 16 March. He wrote in his diary that, '[The flame throwers] showed complete harmlessness'.

On 18 March the battalion was relieved by 2nd Battalion, Duke of Wellington's Regiment and commenced a march to a new area. The companies and transport arrived safely at La Herlière, formed up again and set off through Mondicourt and Grenas to Halloy, where they stayed for the night in specially constructed canvas huts intended as temporary cover for troops on the march. They moved on the next day to the training area around Mezerolles. The training programme was planned, according to the Battalion Diary:

'With a view to getting the men steady under arms and generally improving discipline and incidentally to counteract the effects of the bad habits naturally acquired through a long spell in trenches.'

Since arriving in France seven and a half months earlier the battalion had spent most of the time in relatively quiet areas, Armentières, Foncquevillers and Bailleulval, but were nevertheless constantly in the sound and range of artillery, machine gun and rifle bullets. They had carried out exploratory raids, attempting to ascertain the nature and strength of the German forces facing them. They had suffered artillery bombardments and sporadic shelling, fire from machine guns and were overflown by scout and battle planes, one of which had bombed the road to their rear. They had learned that there was a regular pattern of action around the time they left the trenches to go into rest. This took the form of raids by the battalion leaving or artillery action by the Germans as a mark of farewell and during the period of handover, when more men were in the vicinity.

The battalion had arrived in Boulogne with a strength of about 1100 officers and men, by the time they arrived in Mezerolles there were about 850 on the roll. Eighteen men had been killed in action or died of wounds. From figures in the Battalion Diary a further twenty-nine were wounded or ill, and one, Stk1507 Private John O'Connor, had been sent back because he was under age.

O'Connor's papers show he first joined in October 1914 at Wimbledon volunteering to serve with the 5th Battalion (Reserve), East Surrey Regiment; he was tall enough at 5ft 7ins, declared his age to be 17 years and one month and was accepted for Territorial Service. He served with them for nine days between 12 and 21 October before he was discharged under Para 156(7) of the Territorial Force Regulations for falsifying information at his attestation, his real age being 15. He volunteered again on 21 July 1915 at Kingston-on-Thames, this time claiming his age to be 19 and he was again accepted. After travelling to France on the 19 November with the 5th Entrenching Battalion, which was a unit only permitted to operate on building defence lines in safe areas, he was transferred to 10RF on 15 December 1915.

His father wrote to the Fusiliers Depot at Hounslow, London, on 23 January and sent in his son's birth certificate, receiving a reply dated 31 January 1916 saying that the information would be passed to the Adjutant General of the BEF. On the same day a letter from the colonel in charge of records, Hounslow to Deputy Adjutant General stated: 'the correct age of J. O'Connor STK1507 according to his birth certificate is 16 years and 174 days'.

Messages were sent to 10RF at Foncquevillers and on 10 February the adjutant logged the departure of Private O'Connor in the Battalion Diary. The same day notification was sent from 37 Infantry Base Depot, Etaples to the Royal Fusiliers Depot, Hounslow, 'Ref J.E. O'Connor Stk1507: the above is being sent to you for the purpose of being transferred to Home Establishment as under age'. The final entry in the file on 21 February is a letter to the OC Depot Royal Fusiliers: '1507 Pte J. O'Conner (sic) being 17-years-of-age will be discharged'. He was discharged under Regulation 392 (VIa) on 26th February, a month after his father wrote to the regiment. Although entitled to his 1915 Star and Victory medal he probably never saw them as, having taken work as an electrician on the railway, he died of infected salivary glands in July 1920.

Chapter 9

Moving towards Battle:
March to June 1916

Colonel White recorded his delight at being away from the trenches; on 19 March 1916 he wrote:

> 'We marched round Doullens and had dinner in the town. At 4:30pm we reached Mezerolles a dilapidated village on the Abbeville road. George Keppel and I put up at the deserted chateau on the hill, the property of Monsieur de la Serre. Portraits of ancestors, Marie Adrienne de La Tour etc. No sounds of guns. Very strange after so many months in the front line.'

On the 20th:

> 'A day of complete rest for the men. They bathed in the Authie River and cleaned up. Keppel and I rode into Doullens and lunched. Table cloths and napkins!! 6pm conference for all officers.'

The battalion officers had to devise a training programme which met the requirements of the 37th Division training curriculum, intended to overcome the bad habits and less formal discipline of the trenches. On the first day, 21 March, the officers and sergeants were drilled by the adjutant and battalion sergeant major. The men were given a further three days of rest and on the 24th the programme began for the whole battalion. Each morning began with a half hour of running and physical drill for all ranks; every man was made to have a biscuit and cup of tea before going on parade. A session of drill lasted from 10am until work ended for the day at 12:15pm. A similar programme on the next two days included drills in saluting, squad and platoon drills, mass formations and column of route and arms drill, culminating in practices of the march past. These basic drills were intended to get consistency and a sense of belonging back into the squads, platoons, companies and the battalion as a whole. Time spent in the trenches working in small squad groups or at the largest the platoon, the lack of route marches, other than when moving from place to place and little opportunity for discipline in dress had resulted in a lowering of the desired standards. It was also necessary to get the men who arrived in the drafts integrated into their companies.

The briefing provided in orders presumed that the battalion would be out of the trenches for six weeks. The syllabus to be covered included bayonet work, grenade work, attack over open country and through woods, defensive positions, route marches, drills and musketry. Specialists also had their own training in Lewis gunnery and bombing, runners were trained in the importance of keeping communication open between HQ and companies in the trenches and with Brigade HQ in the event of telephone lines being broken.

Wilkinson writing home on 21 March with the address, 'In a house, France' reported the change in living conditions:

'Dear Mother, I am now miles away from the firing line and have clean buttons and boots. Our Division has moved back for a rest of several weeks. A couple of weeks ago we were standing in the trenches in several inches of snow with feet like slabs of ice and now we are getting back into our 'shiny' habits, bugle calls, button cleaning, boot polishing etc.

'Our billet is the best we've had for a long time. I am now in an attic with twenty-four others, the roof is good and the floor is clean, it is swept daily. We mess at an improvised table in an old barn near by and wash in a river which runs at the foot of a meadow.

'We've never been gassed but have always had to carry our 'gas helmets'. These we have now discarded for a time. For a week or two before leaving we were working very hard on dug outs. Four shifts through the night and at 3:30am on the last night after getting down into the earth about eighteen feet several tons fell in. Luckily nobody was hurt. We are used to this waste of labour by now. I am feeling very fit and well and am enjoying the change. The country is hilly and very pretty.

'I am posting my waders in a day or two as I shan't want them (or hope not) until next winter. Perhaps there is hope of the war terminating before then, eh?

'I shall have to cut this letter a bit short as I am cleaning guns and ammunition at 2 o'clock and don't want to miss the post which goes at 4pm.'

Mountfort also wrote happily about the change in environment, the letter is dated 25 February but the content indicates it should probably be 25 March 1916:

'Dear Dad… I suppose we are now fifteen miles or more from the firing line and well off your map. The village lies in a valley and the slopes on either side are heavily wooded. A stream runs through it, coming down a weir just above the village bridge. It turned suddenly cold and we woke up yesterday to find four inches of wet slushy snow and it snowed nearly all day. Today, thank heaven, it is pure March warm sun with wonderful blue skies and white cloud and a high wind.

'We are spending our time at present by doing three-quarters of an hour at physical drill before breakfast and drilling all morning till 12:30pm when we finish for the day. At present it suits me very well.

'During our second day's march we skirted a large town [Doullens] from which we are now five miles or so. I got my first glimpse of civilisation for seven months and yesterday 300 of us were taken there by motor lorry in the evening to go to a concert. I

understand about twenty found their way to the concert, the remainder, of whom I was one, preferred to revel in the luxuries of streets and pavements and cafes with English beer and stout and suppers.'

Alfred Mills also went into Doullens that evening, and does not say he went to the concert. The following day his freedom, and that of the rest of his section, was curtailed after Stk666 Hubert Ellen[38], known as Gus, was taken away with measles. The Battalion Diary noted that the outbreak was limited to part of C Company by quickly quarantining the platoon to which the infected men belonged.

A rushed letter home from Wilkinson sent on the 25th gave good news, laced with his typical reserve:

*'Dear Mother, I am next for leave and if all goes well I shall be home in few days…
With best love, George'*

The battalion was inspected twice in two days by very senior officers. The first inspection on 29 March was carried out by Sir Douglas Haig and General Allenby (commanding Third Army). White was pleased to record in his diary that:

'The men were very steady and smart. Afterwards companies route marched.'

The second inspection was by Field Marshal Lord Kitchener on 31st., as White noted:

'He asked much about steel helmets and leather equipment. The men stood extraordinarily steady. Kitchener much impressed; spoke in very flattering terms about them. I told the men "Lord K says he never saw such a battalion". This was received with as much merriment as satisfaction.'

Alfred Mills noted the inspection in his diary, but perhaps regarded himself as fortunate because he was not involved, as he was still in quarantine.

Wilkinson writing on the same day provided an update on his forthcoming leave, and reported on the inspection:

'My dear Mother, No doubt you are wondering what sort of news this letter carries.
'I still hope to be home in a few days, possibly next Tuesday or Wednesday. Please have a complete change of underclothes waiting for me. We spent about three days practising the 'Present Arms' and hours and hours cleaning up our clothes and equipment so they were spotless. The great ceremony lasted about three and a half minutes.'

The Battalion Diary recorded the beginnings of a change in the structure of the army and the transition of the machine gunners from being members of individual battalions to the embryonic Machine Gun Corps (MGC). In 10RF this began with the movement of machine gunners from a specialist section back into the companies on 1 April. The MG officer was to remain with battalion HQ and retain responsibility for all matters pertaining to machine guns, pending the arrival of a new War Establishment Table.

The creation of the MGC was a political as well as logistical exercise. The corps, which had been created by Royal Warrant on 22 October 1915, was intended to make better use of the power of the Vickers machine gun and not leave it to an infantry officer who may not really know how to make best use of the guns at their disposal. The gunners at first remained members of their parent regiment but over the course of a few months were transferred to the MGC.

Another weapon, being used increasingly was gas in its various forms. As Wilkinson had said in his recent letter crude helmets were distributed and used, but opportunities were taken to let men see the effectiveness of the equipment in preventing injury. On 5 April White wrote:

'100 men and 12 NCOs marched to Lucheux to see smoke practices and lachrymatory bombs. Went through the trenches where the tear bombs are thrown. Very trying to the eyes but relieved at once by putting on "goggles".'

Individuals went off on courses. Between 10 and 16 April White attended a week long officers' course at Auxi-le-Chateau where he was lectured on house defence; physical drill; and use of the bayonet. This lecture was delivered by Major Campbell who had a fearsome reputation as an advocate of the weapon; later in the same month Sassoon was shocked by his lecture, and commented on it in his memoirs. Sir Henry Wilson lectured on the European position, General Rawlinson, Commander of Fourth Army and General Snow, Commander of VII Corps were present.

White put some of his lectures to immediate use when on his return to the battalion he lectured to the MG officers and men on the use of machine guns, and examined the battalion scouts who were under the command of Lieutenant John Haviland. The men in camp had diversions from training ready for the next stage of the war. Mills noted in his diary that on 13 and 14 April his C Company beat first D Company in the semi-final, and then HQ in the final, of the inter-company cup.

Also on 14th Wilkinson wrote home to thank his family for what he describes as 'the happiest week of my life'. He had got back from leave and spent the evening 'yarning' with Parnell and Cordingley about things back in England. He had been lucky to get home as leave was once more stopped. He ended the short letter by showing something of the emotion brought by the visit:

'I can't write tonight somehow. I've had a "loverly" time.'

April 15 was the day of battalion sports in a large meadow. Wilkinson and his colleagues in the MG Section were much amused when one of their number, Stk914 Spencer Maxwell Bradley, won the bomb throwing competition, to the chagrin of the specialist bombers. There was a hockey match against an Indian regiment on the Sunday, which was a draw at four goals each. Presumably the Reverend Edge Partington, the chaplain, a former England cap and Cambridge blue, was one of the 'several big hockey men who played for our team', reported by Wilkinson.

Stk 914 Max Bradley, the machine gunner who won a bombing competition at Mezerolles. World War One Photos

131

Wilkinson had hinted at homesickness in an earlier letter but on Monday, 17 April he noted in his diary letter:

> 'Dad's letter arrived. I have read it through several times. It seems to have cured my homesickness in a magical manner. I feel I could put up with anything now. Tuesday: Orderly today and have cleaned dixies. Fired the gun on the range and attended a lecture (or discussion as he preferred to call it) by the Colonel on the use of the gun. I have started learning French and have put in one and a half hours today and on each of the last two days. I hope to be able to report steady progress…. Wednesday: Practised stripping the gun blindfolded and afterwards had some gas helmet drill. Spent the afternoon polishing all our equipment leather with brown boot polish and the buckles with Soldiers' Friend. Washed our packs and haversacks in the river. After cleaning up I rubbed my trousers on the axle of a wagon and made a hugh [sic] greasy black mark thereon. Thursday: Fired the gun this morning on the range wearing gas helmet and have been on fatigues the rest of the day till 5:30pm cleaning gun, loading wagons etc. We move to another village tomorrow to continue the "rest".'

The battalion stayed in Mezerolles until the night of Thursday 20 April. During the four weeks there they had carried out some housekeeping and routine activities as well as training. The Battalion Diary recorded that the men had been re-inoculated and there had been church parades. An entry made on the 20th reflects positively on the fact that only eighty-nine men had been evacuated because of illness since the battalion arrived in France. The adjutant suggested two reasons for this:

> '1. During the period of training in England all the men who were immature or showed signs of weakness were promptly weeded out and posted to the Reserve Unit for more gradual training, their places being taken by later joined recruits of more robust constitution.
> '2. By the detention and treatment in the Regimental Aid Post of such men as require a short period of rest etc. This obviates the necessity of evacuating them and their consequent loss to the battalion for a lengthy period.'

On the same day Mountfort went to the Divisional School of Instruction at Lucheux. He wrote on the following Saturday afternoon to his mother:

> 'Thank God we're not in the trenches. As a matter of fact beyond knowing that we are not in the trenches I don't know where we are. That is to say I know where I am, but I don't know where the 10th Battalion is. I believe they moved yesterday from the village where we have been resting to some destination unknown, but I didn't move with them as I had moved already…
> 'The school is at a large (so-called) Hotel at Divisional Headquarters and we have a dormitory and a mess not to mention a private entrance to the bar. The mess is a large room at the front of the building with trestle tables and benches; and crockery with fatigue men to wash it up afterwards – some luxury for a lance-corporal on active service I think you will admit.

'On the other side of the picture we have severe discipline, unprecedented smartness of appearance and long days work. We commence at 8:45am with an inspection by the Commandant, work till 12noon and again from 2pm till 4pm and at 5:30pm there is a lecture which does not last less than an hour. The class consists of ten Officers and twenty-six NCOs. The Officers drill and work with us but have separate quarters in the same building.'

Mountfort was correct in suggesting the battalion was no longer where he left it as on 21 April 1915 the men had set off to march to Humbercamps breaking their journey for one night at the rest camp in Halloy. Wilkinson was less than impressed by the accommodation in Halloy.

'What a night we had last night. There's another man we want to meet after the war and that's the man who was responsible for the building of the huts we tried to sleep in. Roofs of sackcloths instead of canvas so the rain drops were broken up and came through in tiny particles which soon soaked everything uncovered. I was one of the few who did sleep.'

The Battalion Diary recorded that although it was wet on the march from Halloy the men arrived in their new billets in good spirits but the village was not looked on favourably by the adjutant:

'Humbercamps is an insanitary agricultural village ten miles east of Doullens. Manure heaps and pools of stagnant water comprise the external decoration of many homes. The water supply is bad and all water is brought by cart from Warlincourt three miles distant.'

Wilkinson found one redeeming feature:

'We reached our present barn and journey's end after a march of four hours. Heaps of mud but plenty of estaminets.'

While in Humbercamps for six days the battalion supplied working parties to dig and move stores for the Royal Engineers. Wilkinson approached the fatigues with his usual ironic comments:

'Easter Monday: Reveille at 6:00am, Breakfast 6:45, Parade 7:50 (everything polished) and another parade at 8:45. Stood still about half an hour, were inspected and marched off for a day's work. Arrived at trenches (behind the firing line) about an hour later. Sat about on the grass until 12 o'clock while Officer found something for us to do. Knocked off for lunch until 1:30. Repaired trenches and marched back about 4:30pm. I make no comment. Besides the Sergeant Major told us the other day that we must not think.'

Young had been with the Barn Owls for six months and often seemed unsure how much he wanted to stay with them. His letters contain some of his thoughts about war and his place in it. He was clearly torn between the safety of being back from the line, away from the mud, and the desire to be with his comrades in the 10RF. There is one unfinished letter in Young's collection which is placed with the ones written in August 1915, but the reference to Spring, and the fact that at the time it is said to have been written he is saying in other letters that he cannot form a view about the horribleness of France and its people, suggests that it was written in Spring 1916.

'Dear Dad, More than once this morning I have said to myself "I wish Father were here now". Only a few miles separate us at present and I know that the sun and the returning spring are making you feel an intolerable sickness of war… I am trying to forget how hideous it is. I am sitting upon a grassy bank. Below runs a very narrow brook as clear as any I have yet seen in France. Round the bend of the hill it runs quite silently over the waving grass. Here it murmurs incessantly over a few scattered stones. The country around is very beautiful and I have left the billet where only vulgarity and coarse laughter is heard, to come here and read.

'I have been reading William de Morgan's[39] autobiography. I have tried to imagine the dingy room in which he wrote and have tried to look back upon my short existence as one views a distant panorama. Really I do not know what to think. I have not commenced to live yet.'

He sent a letter to both his parents on Friday 28 April:

'A Company No3 Platoon 10 Royal Fusiliers.

'Dear Father and Mother, I imagine that you will be rather surprised to see by the above address that I have now returned to my battalion. I have not done so without a great deal of thought and consideration and I cannot help thinking I have done very wisely.

'The other position was intolerable, the associations perfectly odious and, when all is said and done I have had a very good rest from the trenches.

'The battalion is not in the trenches and may not see them again for a long while.

'The sausage rolls were delightful. The weather is perfect, and we are all very happy. Best love to you all, your affectionate son, George.'

Two days later on the evening of Sunday, 30 April the battalion received orders to move that night to Berles-au-Bois and take over billets from 2nd Battalion, Seaforth Highlanders, and to relieve 1st Battalion, Royal Irish Fusiliers in the trenches. They left Humbercamps at 8:15pm and arrived in Berles at 10pm. The village population had shrunk from about 800 in 1914 to 234, largely because houses had been damaged and destroyed in and on the edge of the village. Under the village large chalk pits, originally excavated in medieval times, had been extended to provide shell proof shelters for two battalions.

The following night they moved the final half-mile into the trenches. All four companies were in the trenches, each with one platoon in reserve a short distance behind the line. Almost immediately the attrition of trench warfare began. Shells passed over the trenches and landed on the edge of the village, causing no casualties; but there was a feeling that the bombardment of the villages behind the trench lines was intensifying. A trench mortar and artillery shells landed in some of the trenches, killing one man and wounding another. The Battalion Diary recorded the damage as 'slight'.

Still in the trenches on 3 May, the battalion suffered regular mortars and shells landing in or close to the trenches. The suspicion was that the Germans were registering fire onto the communication trenches. Another man was killed. Overnight, snipers reported hearing movement behind the enemy lines, including what they thought might be another trench mortar being moved up.

At 2:35am on the morning of 4 May 1916 the enemy opened a bombardment along the trench line being held by the battalion and the adjacent sector, which was held by 13KRRC. A number of guns of different sizes as well as trench mortars were used. After five minutes the assault on the 13 KRRC was lifted but was maintained on the10RF lines. The British artillery responded by bombarding the lines opposite, particularly concentrating on the area in front of 10RF. Ladders were seen in the German trenches which to those watching indicated an attack was imminent.

Wilkinson was in the reserve trenches and described the bombardment:

'Woke at 3am on account of a terrific bombardment. Went into a funk hole and trembled like a jelly until sent for a further supply of ammunition. I then felt as strong as a lion and ran as I've rarely run before to the magazine and drew a box of cartridges which, with the help of another chap, I carried to the required place. It was simply raining shells and we bent double as we ran. The noise was like a hugh [sic] continuous thunderclap. I was then ordered down the funk hole to be ready with rifle and bayonet should the Huns pay us a visit.'

The intensification of the British artillery bombardment onto the German front line seemed to discourage any attempt by the Germans to enter no man's land. The Battalion Diary and Wilkinson's letter both record that the men in the front line of trenches were disappointed that no enemy tried to come across as both sources record 10RF were 'ready for a scrap'. This was the most costly single action so far involving the battalion. Six men were killed, fifty-one were wounded of whom three later died.

George Knight Young was among those listed as being killed in action. It had been six days since his letter home suggesting that his parents would agree that he had done wisely to leave the concert party and return to the battalion. Later in that month a notice appeared in the Broomwood Wesleyan Church Magazine:

'We all received a great shock when we heard that George Young had been killed in action in France and our hearts go out to those who mourn his loss at home. Mr and Mrs Young have received many letters from France speaking in the highest tones of respect. George was honoured by men and officers alike.

'His chaplain writes: "He was killed in the trenches early yesterday morning (4th May) during an intense bombardment. You will be comforted to know he died for his country doing his duty".

'His officer wrote:"His death was absolutely instantaneous as a shell burst within a few feet of him. He died at his post as the good soldier that he was. At the time he was in an advanced post guarding the main trench."'

Although not wounded Alfred Mills was badly shaken by his experiences on 4 May:

The enemy bombarded us like hell at 2:30am. Absolutely like hell. I had just come off sentry watch and as usual had a walk along to get warmed up. I was talking to the chaps on the next post, and as I spoke, a red flare went up from the German trenches right opposite us and this was followed by red flares all along the line and immediately all hell was let loose along our front with shells landing everywhere. The piece of trench which our section held was subject to enfilade fire and we had to evacuate it during the shelling. It took us two hours crawling on our bellies to get along it. Sandbags were flying through the air along with all sorts of debris. I was struck on the head. We have about sixty casualties, but no one killed. I tried to stick it afterwards during the day but had to come down to the Aid Post in the evening suffering from dizziness and feeling sick. We were lucky not be wiped out on account of the intensity of the shelling.

Friday 5 May Berles

'Sent down to Berles village from the Aid Post behind the lines by the MO this evening. Shaking uncontrollably and I feel I cannot face going back to the trenches.

'Wrote to Dad and sent home two bulletins.

'I shut my eyes and feel as if I'm sinking into blackness.'

One of the wounded was 1316 Private Herbert Hope aged 24, a clerk employed in the City who had originally joined 17RF in September 1914 but was transferred to 10RF on 26 January 1915, presumably to replace one of those going for a commission, or judged unfit during basic training. The description of events and his wounds are recorded in the medical report accompanying his pension award:

'GSW [gun shot wound] right thigh caused by German shell when in sap 20 yards from German Lines opposite Monchy Wood, 4th May 1916 gangrene poisoning followed. Leg numbed and occasionally fails when walking. Posted Depot 16.5.16 Class W Army Res 15.8.16 employed at Waterlow & Sons, 26&27 Gt Winchester St London EC Class P 31.10.16 Married 3.3.17 Discharge 12.7.17'

His wound, described generically as a gunshot wound, was sufficient to move him in August 1916 into a category, which meant that he was fit to work, at Waterlow and Sons, but not fully fit to serve in the Army. However, he could be recalled if the situation demanded it. He would not receive payment from the army during the period of civilian employment. In October 1916 he was moved to category P which meant that he would receive any payments or pension due from the Army in addition to his employment salary. In most respects this was tantamount to having his service terminated, but this was not done finally until July 1917. Presumably feeling more secure regarding his future he married Lillian Gibbs on 3 March 1917 in Camberwell, London.

Another man wounded was 1513 Private Thomas Spicer, a 21-year-old who was apprenticed to a farmer in Kent. A shrapnel wound to his left ankle turned septic causing pieces of bone to become detached. His condition was at first described as serious but after a few days in the Canadian Hospital in Etaples his mother was informed that his wound was not life threatening. He returned to England on the Hospital Ship *Cambria* and had treatment in hospitals in Leicester and Bournemouth where he had pieces of bone removed from his leg in October. In April 1917 he was given a six month pension and reclassified as Category P.

Colonel White had been on leave in England between 26 April and 6 May 1916. On his return he wrote in his diary:

> *'The battalion had moved to Berles au Bois where I found them under George Keppel. On 4 May at 2:30am the Germans opened an intense bombardment on our trenches 95 and 96 and to the north. A and D Companies suffered severely with six men killed and fifty-one wounded, of these latter three have since died. Two days previously two men were killed and one wounded. Our men shouted to the Germans to come over. The men behaved splendidly.'*

Roland Mountfort was still training at divisional HQ, but had heard about the incident. In a letter to his mother written on the 7th he wrote:

> *'In a way I must congratulate myself on being here for the other night they had a wicked strafe. At the same time I feel that I should like to be with my pals if they have to go through it. I was sorry to hear that a fellow who was in the same tent, house and billet as I through all our English training, was killed. We had many a lively night together at Colchester and Andover and you probably have his photo in half a dozen of those I sent home. I am anxious to know how the rest of them are for we have only had the names of the killed and not the wounded.'*

Wilkinson and his friends reflected on the experience in the trench when they returned to Berles on Monday 8 May:

> *'Had a delightful day back in the village. Spring has made an enormous difference to the country in the last few days and the village looks beautiful. Saw Cheshire today and yarned with him about the strafe, also with many pals. Our escapes and feelings. Our pride in everyone's behaviour, especially the officers. Really a very happy day.'*

Having returned from leave in peaceful Hammersmith, Wilkinson was made aware of the different conditions under which the French soldiers' families were living.

> *'The farmer's son in whose barn we are billeted is home on a few days leave and while a few of us were in the house purchasing coffee the sister presented us with some pancakes as a "souvenir". It seems so strange for him to be here on leave among the ruins. His mother is cooking a fowl tonight in his honour.'*

One announcement which was greeted with great satisfaction in the Battalion Diary was that of the passing of the Second Military Service Bill which included provision for compulsory service for all men aged 18-41. Men who had volunteered, including Mountfort and Young, commented frequently in their letters at the frustration felt by those at the front towards those who were thought to be shirking their responsibilities. All through 1915 the army suffered from declining numbers of volunteers. In May 1915 Lord Derby was appointed as Director-General of Recruitment with the task of providing sufficient recruits to meet the demand. His solution, the Derby Scheme, allowed men to volunteer for service, to be called up only when needed and married men would only be called forward when all single men had been recruited. It also made provision for some occupations to be exempt from service. The scheme was judged a failure when only 350,000 men enrolled, rather than the one million required, and the scheme was abandoned in December 1915.

In January 1916 the Military Service Act was passed introducing conscription, but with some exceptions, for instance those who had been discharged from the military on the grounds of ill-health or termination of service. The Act of May 1916 removed most of the exceptions thereby making most males in the country liable for service if they were between 18 and 41 years of age. Those at the front thought this much fairer and were confident it should bring forward the 'shirkers'.

During the period in rest work continued as normal, with working parties and training. Artillery fire was constantly exchanged but caused little damage to the village. On 12 May a draft of fifty-four OR joined from the 18th (Public Schools) Battalion which had been disbanded after many of the men had taken commissions. Those who remained in the ranks were pleased to be transferred to a battalion with men of a similar background and went with them into the trenches on the following evening.

The exchange of artillery, howitzer and rifle grenade fire was maintained, but with no injuries recorded in the Battalion Diary. The divisional return of the number of admissions to hospitals due to sickness, published on 16 May, showed that the battalion continued to be healthy with few men being evacuated sick. The next healthiest battalion had had more than 100 admissions in excess of 10RF over the previous nine month period.

On 18 May Wilkinson was on duty sandbagging the front trench:

'Under a lovely sky, the guns were quiet but I could just hear D Company's gramophone playing some topping music a little way on my left. This is the first time I've heard music in the firing line. Our battalion has had letters of congratulation from the General, the battalion in support and the artillery on its behaviour during its great strafing.'

Coming out of the trenches on 19 May, relieved by 13KRRC, the battalion spent the next six days in reserve in Berles. Training, working parties and rest predominated. A further draft of twenty-six men arrived from the 37th Infantry Base Depot at Etaples; the men had all been in 31RF, one of the 10RF's reserve battalions which was based in Colchester.

Back in the trenches on 25 May the battalion began to suffer again from the attrition by wounds and deaths caused by random shells and bullets. On 26th two men were killed and three wounded in an artillery attack early in the morning; one of the wounded died the following day. On the 27th the battalion's snipers were effective in causing difficulties for the Germans, wounding one man, making one loophole close and destroying five periscopes.

On the following day, 28 May, a patrol discovered the bodies of twelve French soldiers apparently buried by a shell in the earlier part of the war. They were together in a sunken road in marching order as though caught by surprise. The 10RF continued to be a target this time for about seventeen shells were fired onto a section of the front line and communication trench but none of them exploded. One man of the 10RF was recorded as being killed on this day; he was Stk466 Ectos Maffuniades DCM, the hero who had rescued Captain Russell Roberts five months before. He was wounded and died shortly afterwards in the dressing station at Berles-au-Bois; he is buried in the village churchyard. White wrote in his diary 'Muffuniades [sic] (DCM) killed in B Company. A fine soldier'.

Mountford had returned to the battalion from his course and home leave finding them at Berles-au-Bois. Writing home on 25 May he reflected on the contrast between life in the trenches and in England:

Ectos Maffuniades is buried at Berles-au-Bois. Author

'The thing that strikes me most about it all now is the hopelessness of trying to realise or make anyone else realise exactly what trench life is like unless you are on the spot. I discovered during the last two nights that my efforts to picture trenches in winter from an armchair at home were about as successful as a blind man's to imagine Niagara. At the same time I was disappointed to find on returning here how little (comparatively with what I had many a weary time imagined) I had appreciated the luxuries of pyjamas, clean sheets, good food, England, home and beauty; having taken it all as a matter of course. From which two things I have arrived at the conclusion that the two modes of life are both natural to me in their place but like East and West, never the twain shall meet.'

Wilkinson's' next letter indicated further reorganisation of the Machine Gun Section and he and Parnell were again separated, each being in different teams within B Company. Wilkinson was in Lance Corporal Montague's[39] team, a man he described as being:

a 'very nice young chap who was at school with Ray Mobberley, [Wilkinson's friend in the scouts]. Porky is still with us and Park, who was at one time MG cook is now in the team. 'Tubby' Rutherford[41] is now with us. A Cambridge man and master at a public school, speaks French and German. He is a character. His home is at Torquay. All his old pals in the Battalion now have commissions and he is left behind. He hears news from *home that the local butcher's son is now an officer. Another man, a stockbroker, still a private in the MG section hears that his office boy is now an officer. The other two in the team are Hember[42] and Tutt[43] of whom perhaps you will hear something on a future occasion.'*

The Battalion Diary recorded on 29 May 'several Germans in dark blue uniforms with dark blue caps, shiny peaks, have been observed looking over their parapet and have been earmarked by our snipers for attention in due course'. Enemy working parties were disturbed by 10RF firing rifle grenades; there was a false gas alarm, but all men were quickly into helmets; a sniper from the battalion shot two Germans; artillery shells landed in and close to the trenches occupied by the 10RF, but 'a large percentage were duds' the adjutant noted in the Battalion Diary. The battalion left the trenches on 31 May, again being relieved by 13KRRC.

In rest in Berles in early June the battalion continued to provide working parties, and lost one or two men through wounds. An order received on 9 May required the battalion to mount a raid on the German trenches, which was finally carried out on 5 June. A group led by Second Lieutenant Arthur Rees accompanied by Second Lieutenant Frank Shutes and twenty-nine men practised for a week to cross no man's land to capture documents and gain other information about the troops facing them. The raid was planned in detail with the men divided into groups to carry out specific tasks. Two groups were to clear the trenches and dugouts with bayonet and bomb; the following groups had to search for documents. If they encountered a machine gun it was to be brought back. All efforts were made to disguise the identity of the battalion concerned. No badges or identity tags were worn; a cap bearing the name of another battalion was left behind in the German trench after the raid. Steel helmets were issued to the raiders; covered with sandbag sacking to avoid noise, they were described in the report as being responsible for saving casualties 'to judge from the marks on them'.

Scheduled to last seven minutes the raid was preceded by a bombardment from artillery and howitzer, which the report on the raid says was dangerous to the raiding party while they moved forward to the start point. It was suggested that some form of protection such as boarding or other splinter proofing should be put in place for future raids. The route to the parapet of the German trench was taped to show the direction and although both tape men were wounded they reached their objective. The bombardment had been successful in clearing the Germans from the trench and making access easier by breaking down the parapet. The raiders commented on the depth of some dugouts, suggesting that they may in fact be mine entrances.

The report included a section on 'other points to be taken into account when planning future raids'. These were significant, and would have a hollow echo in a few weeks time on the Somme. They noted particularly the benefit of an accurate barrage in clearing the trenches but as the entrances to the dugouts were undamaged any sentry at the top of the stairs could probably have escaped and by giving the alarm would have turned out the occupants before the raiding party made the trench. The Germans had practically no parapet, but a high parados, which if manned would make withdrawal difficult.

Other divisions wrote reports of raids and actions at this time making similar points about the depth of German dugouts and the way in which the men were sheltered from the effects of bombardment, able to emerge quickly once the shells stopped. The German machine gunners were trained and practised taking up their positions within three minutes of the end of the artillery barrage to be ready to deal with British troops advancing under cover of the shells.

The Battalion Diary report of the raid noted that 'losses were trifling' with nine wounded. It said that the raid had caused considerable damage to the Germans. Corporal Percy Pavey was awarded the DCM for his part in the raid. Listed in *The London Gazette* of 27 July his citation read:

> *'Stk/195 Cpl. P. Pavey, 10th Bn., R. Fus. For conspicuous daring and enterprise when with a raiding party. Although wounded and partially blinded, he remained at duty and finally, when his party had retired, remained in order to carry back a wounded comrade.'*

It is likely that his wounded comrade was Private Walter Grainger who was carried back to the trench and on to the casualty post at Doullens where he died of his wounds the same day. The 21-year-old insurance agent from Wimbledon was an only child. One of the others wounded was Stk247 Charlie Stroud, later to find fame as the battalion's cross country champion.

Other awards were announced on 5 June. Lieutenant Martin Heathcote was awarded the MC and Second Lieutenant Rupert C. Bambridge and Second Lieutenant Cyril J. Allen, who had transferred to 10 Loyals with Major Cobbold, were both awarded the Military Medal. It is probable that these three awards were in recognition of the raid carried out in January in which Russell Roberts was wounded. At the time of that raid both Bambridge (Stk320) and Allen (Stk309) were sergeants and so eligible for the MM rather than the MC. Both received their commissions just three months after the raid, on 18 March 1916. Lieutenant Heathcote's award also included recognition for a raid of 21 February 1916 when he and two men went into the German trenches and captured two prisoners.

Back into the trenches on June 6 the battalion, along with the rest of the Army, received the news on the 7th of the loss of HMS *Hampshire* which was carrying Lord Kitchener to Russia. The Battalion Diary recorded the loss with the words:

> *"As creator of the 'New Armies' of which this Battalion is part Lord Kitchener was regarded among the troops as 'Our General' and his untimely end has thrown all ranks into the deepest mourning. Although his loss is irreparable some consolation is derived from the knowledge that although the 'Great Engineer'[44] has gone he has left behind his machinery in good running order. He will ever be remembered as having brought into being the greatest voluntary army the world has ever known. RIP.'*

On the 8th the Germans were seen to be repairing the trenches which had been virtually destroyed in the barrage before the raid led by Rees and Shutes. There was some shelling from the German side which again resulted in casualties, one man killed and five wounded.

Captain Dallas Waters now the Adjutant of 10RF, noted somewhat wryly in the Battalion Diary entry of 9 June:

"Frequent reports are received that elderly Germans in dark blue uniforms and caps with shiny peaks have been seen opposite leading to the assumption that our opponents in this sector are principally men above middle age. If this is so then they indulge in bursts of rejuvenation not usually prevalent among the aged as the activity of their working parties and artillery retaliation bear witness. Of course it may have occurred to the enemy that a front line trench is an excellent place to exploit that elementary law of nature dealing with the preservation of the young and fit at the expense of the old and worn.'

On 10 June 1916 the Germans concentrated shell fire on the railhead at L'Arbret which supplied the trenches around Berles, and L'Herelière, where the battalion transport was based. Although about 125 shells landed in the villages and on the station, damage was minimal. The Germans had a plane flying above the targets directing the fire. More mortar fire on the trenches led to two further deaths and the wounding of three men. The battalion suffered from more shelling and mortars and a retaliatory raid by two officers and two men fired rifle grenades from just in front of the wire into the German trenches. One of the men wounded was 1598 Private Edward Branch who had arrived from Trinidad in 1915. He signed his attestation form on 9 September and after time in the 31st Training Battalion was posted to 10RF on 19 November 1915. His wound was to his little finger but he also suffered from shell shock. He spent time in hospital at Le Treport before returning to the battalion. Another man wounded rather more severely was 1432 Private Percy Harris, a native of Cardiff. He was wounded in the arms, stomach legs and face, losing his left eye. He was discharged from the army with a pension in August 1917.

A relief by 13KRRC was carried out without interference by the enemy and the pattern of rest resumed. Working parties were provided day and night for the Machine Gun Corps, Engineers and Signals; also for wiring and to operate the Berles tramway.

Men moved round in June. On 3rd Alfred Mills took up his new duties as clerk to the town major of Bailleulmont, about two miles from Berles. The town major was responsible for good order and discipline in occupied towns. Holding that position in Bailleulmont was 25-year-old Second Lieutenant Arthur Passenger, of 10RF, formerly a clerk from Brixton, commissioned on 31 March 1915. The appointment as clerk surprised Mills and he wondered how he had managed to be chosen for this post of which he said 'any of the boys would have given anything for this job. I can only surmise that someone got wind of my background or perhaps it is just my handwriting'.

On 13 June 1916 Stk131 Sergeant Edgar Johnson was sent back to England suffering from neurasthenia, nervous debility caused by shock, commonly called shell shock. Just married in March 1916 and aged 28, he had been a clerk before the war. He had served in the Surrey Yeomanry for two years before joining 10RF in August 1914. He was discharged with a six month pension in August 1916.

On the following day George Wilkinson wrote home to give his new address:

Alfred Mills, the photograph shows his battalion number on the collar. Graham Morley

'I am no longer in the Battalion, a startler for you!! My address in future will be Pte G A Wilkinson 575 111th Company, Machine Gun Corps, BEF. Please have this shouted at the street corners and proclaimed from the house tops or I shan't get any letters… Why did I leave? Well it was like this. They asked for six volunteers and forty-one out of forty-eight gave in their names. I am one of those chosen. Unfortunately Parnell isn't but we considered the matter before we both put in our names and decided to take the risk of being separated. I am not far from him… I was number one in the last team (that is the person who fires the gun and is responsible that it is kept in working order) and would have been next for a stripe. Now of course I shall have to learn all about the new gun.'

This was a result of the creation of the Machine Gun Corps. The MGC took over responsibility for the use of the Vickers gun which was more powerful and had a much larger magazine than the Lewis gun. It was less portable and generally used in a fixed position to give, in concert with other Vickers guns, cones and arcs of fire to support attacks and to cover retreats. The MGC was created in October 1915 but because of administrative delays and some opposition from infantry battalions the arrangements and transfer of men took a few months. The corps also wanted to ensure it was getting suitable recruits. The MGC did not have to accept those who volunteered or were put forward by their battalions. The entry criteria used was quite precise, men had to be:

- Intelligent and well supplied with common sense
- Fairly well educated
- Of good physique. Strong, healthy and able to carry heavy loads over bad ground while keeping pace with the infantry
- Mechanically inclined and of a logical turn of mind
- Possessed of plenty of 'guts', be resolute, brave and well disciplined as at times MGs have to be deliberately sacrificed e.g. rearguard or other desperate situation.

The gun was technically advanced, it was a powerful weapon which, when used well, could be instrumental in aiding an advance. The members of the MGC did not have to carry out the hundred and one little tasks given to the infantryman when in rest; the working parties, trench digging and repair and providing labour for the engineers. Life wasn't all cushy though as the gunners were still in the trenches as Wilkinson's next letter related:

> 'My hands are all greasy from the gun, my boots and puttees caked with mud and the odour of stale sump water offends my nostrils. A working party has been cleaning out the trench sump by throwing the water over the parapet. Thus some liquid ever obedient to nature's laws whether the result is convenient to man or no has drained down through a series of rat holes into this dug out.
> 'I am now in a team with Hember and two chaps who transferred from our battalion a couple of months ago, Hadlow and Smith, the latter was promoted yesterday to Lance Corporal. One member of the team is cooking all the stuff and well he does it. One young chap in the team, 'Jock' by name was at one time footman to the Duke of Wellington.'

At first the men retained their battalion numbers, but these were soon replaced by new MGC numbers. Of the six transferred Wilkinson became MGC 25428; Hember renumbered from Stk431 to 25424, Gerard Webber; Stk1446 transferred with the number 25245; Stk291 Joseph Whitehall, a sergeant, was number 25426, Alfred Treherne, Stk859 became 25427 and PS 5721 William Peeke became MGC 25429.

Returning to the trenches on 18 June the battalion found itself under intense scrutiny by both enemy aircraft and spotters who were standing with field glasses rather than periscopes. A plane from the British side managed to force two German planes to land behind their own lines, and a sniper shot one of the spotters. The enemy was active in putting out wire and moving equipment behind their lines at night. Artillery shells during the day hit both front line and communications trenches wounding four men on 19th.

One of the wounded was Stk988 Private Hugh Stroud Green, a former clerk at the London County and Westminster Bank, who received wounds to both legs, left arm and right foot. He was sent to hospital in England arriving in Exeter two weeks after he was wounded and then transferred to Moretonhampstead, on the edge of Dartmoor, where he remained until October. He was medically examined in February 1917 and discharged in September of the same year to return to his position in the bank. Unlike some of his fellow soldiers who added years to their age to enable them to enlist in August 1914, Hugh Green had subtracted eleven years from his age of 41. Although he had some experience in the Volunteer force he still had to meet the limit of 30 for those without military service as required by the regulation of 6 August 1914, and he would still have been 'too old' when the limit was raised to 35 at the end of that month.

A German patrol was discovered on the night of 21 June. Three men were spotted lying in front of the battalion wire by a returning patrol. There was an exchange of fire and one of the Germans got up to run back to his trench; he was shot and killed but the other members of the patrol escaped. The body was recovered and brought back to the battalion lines where he was found to be a 21-year-old Unter Offizier from Hamburg. The Battalion Diary was careful to identify the regiment he served with and the fact that he was well nourished, his equipment was in good condition and he had recently returned from leave. A couple of days later a German was seen wearing a steel helmet in the enemy's trench.

Allied artillery began to be more active after June 23. The Battalion Diary recorded that more shelling was heard 'on the right', in the direction of the Somme. The Germans were also firing shells and finding targets. On 24 June Stk1073 George Orford, aged 26 was wounded when a shell hit his post and he later died. Before the war he had been a lawyer's clerk living in Clapton, North London, and he was a bell ringer at St Matthew's Church and treasurer of the Ringers' Association. An entry in the *Bell News Magazine* reported:

'...wounded in the head by a shell a week to ten days ago. Operated on and survived a few days, but succumbed. Second ringer to die from this tower. Had been in France for about ten months, though had been home. A memorial service was held for him on 15 July followed by a muffled peal of the bells.'

On the 25 June the civilians behind the British lines were ordered to take what they could carry and leave the area. The Provost Marshal and Military Police ensured that any furniture left behind was locked away and large signs were erected prohibiting entry to seemingly abandoned properties. The army provided both lorries and interpreters to assist the move to more protected areas. Perhaps showing confidence that the forthcoming attack was going to be successful, a new laundry was opened in the village of Berles. This was recorded by the battalion diarist as being welcomed as it would enable the men to get clean clothing after each spell in the trenches. Training in the use of bayonet and attacking from trenches was carried out while the battalion was in rest.

A raid using gas and artillery was carried out on 27 June. The diarist wryly noted that the Germans in the trenches opposite responded to the advancing gas with rapid rifle fire 'which sensibly diminished as the gas cloud reached their trenches'. The cloud was seen to spread over the nearby village of Monchy-au-Bois and towards the north-east. The dangers of the use of gas to those releasing it was emphasised when a shell burst damaged a cylinder releasing gas which injured a number of men standing nearby. A further gas attack with artillery support was mounted in the evening.

Wilkinson spent his time in learning about the gun and keeping it clean. He wrote from an address given as MG Fort on 28 June:

> *'There is an accordion player making a din in part of the dugout, but I like to hear them enjoying themselves. I am learning about the gun, but it is difficult to keep it clean. How would you like to make a white silk dress sitting in a coal cellar in which several people kept their belongings, slept, cleaned rifles etc etc? This would be something like trying to clean a Machine Gun in a dugout, heartbreaking.'*

Increasingly frequent raids were being carried out all along the line; the men of 10RF observed a coordinated set of divisional raids involving the Leicester Regiment and KRRC on the morning of the 29th. The bombardment continued and although it declined in ferocity it never stopped. The Germans retaliated and landed shells around a 60-pdr battery behind the lines. Working parties were busy repairing front line and communication trenches but the Germans were targeting them with retaliatory barrages and caused further damage. On the evening of 30 June men from 10RF were engaged in carrying gas cylinders into the front line ready to release a gas cloud on the morning of 1st July.

Chapter 10

To the Somme:
July 1916

The Battalion Diary and other letters and diaries make no mention of the events planned for 1 July. Although security was imposed only to the extent of marking documents and maps as 'secret' it was evident from the amount of building, stocking of shells and guns and the preparation of aid posts and casualty clearing stations, that an attack was imminent.

For the men of 10RF the morning of 1 July 1916 opened with the release of a smoke cloud over the German trenches opposite. The German artillery opened fire in retaliation and hit some of the trenches in the sector. Over the next three days shells landing around the trenches, and shrapnel over the brigade HQ in Berles caused casualties. One man who died on 2 July was 25-year-old Stk1084 Private Arthur Penfold, a clerk in a newspaper office who had lived in Wandsworth with his parents and brother. The relative quietness of the sector was evident because on 3 July the battalion was ordered to withdraw from the trenches to be replaced by a battalion of the Staffordshires who had 'suffered severely' in a failed attack on Gommecourt.

The losses suffered by the British on 1 July led to reorganisation of divisions. This was partly to provide experienced reinforcements, but also to strengthen the recently arrived battalions by placing them in brigades with more experienced units. The 37th Division was split up and the 111 Brigade, of which 10RF was part, provided reinforcements for the 34th Division. This division had been in the attack of 1 July advancing from the Tara and Usna ridge, just south of La Boisselle. Their attack was preceded by the exploding of two huge mines, at what is now called Lochnagar and Y-Sap. Although these damaged the German trench system and caused many casualties they also served to give notice of the attack and up to 80 per cent of the men in the first advancing battalions were casualties. Just one day after being informed of their transfer, by 10pm on the 5th, the 10RF was on buses and travelling by way of Amiens towards Albert to join the queue of troops preparing to move into the battle lines.

They were put into a large barn in Bresle, just south-west of Albert, which had been equipped with shelves to serve as beds. The officers were taken by bus through Albert and up to the Usna-Tara ridge to look at the positions the battalion would be occupying. Back in Albert an accidental bomb explosion wounded six men. One of those involved, Stk326 Arthur Beauchamp, aged 23 died later at the Serre Road dressing station. He was

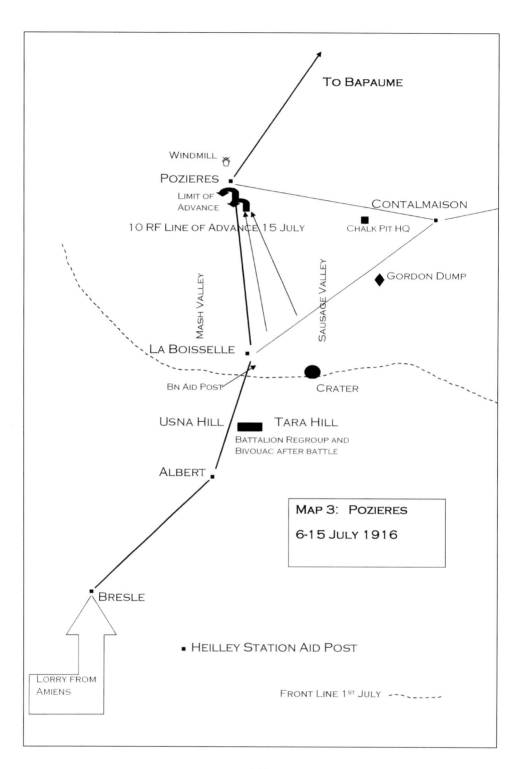

TO BAPAUME

WINDMILL

POZIERES

LIMIT OF
ADVANCE

10 RF LINE OF ADVANCE 15 JULY

CONTALMAISON

CHALK PIT HQ

MASH VALLEY

SAUSAGE VALLEY

GORDON DUMP

LA BOISSELLE

BN AID POST

CRATER

USNA HILL

TARA HILL

BATTALION REGROUP AND
BIVOUAC AFTER BATTLE

ALBERT

MAP 3: POZIERES

6-15 JULY 1916

BRESLE

HEILLEY STATION AID POST

LORRY FROM
AMIENS

FRONT LINE 1ST JULY

a clerk in a news agency who, had been living with his family in Thornton Heath, a suburb of Croydon in Surrey.

The battalion diarist recorded the next move forward on 7 July:

'Reveille 2am, the Battalion marched off at 4am, great coats and packs being left behind. In addition to ammunition each man carried two bombs. Baggage wagons left at Bresle.

'Bn marched about 3 miles where first line transport and cookers were left beside the track at D18 d (central). The Bn then took up their position on W side of railway 600 yards south of where the Amiens Road enters Albert. Here an intense bombardment took place on Ovillers and ground N of La Boiselle as far as Contalmaison. The 19th Division attacked between these two and reached its objective. About noon the 111th Brigade moved forward to the cemetery near Bellevue Farm where it bivouaced [sic] and billeted for the night. 500 German prisoners arrived at Bellevue Farm during the day in a very miserable and demoralised condition.'

Wilkinson found time to write a quick note home:

'Under canvas: Still going strong. Not much to tell you except that we've left the old place and have done a deal of marching. PS I saw Parnell today. He was quite fit.'

On 8 July Colonel White and the HQ staff moved forward to a road junction 250 yards from the church in La Boisselle. A report in the Battalion Diary recorded the situation:

'The trenches in about the village were full of German and British dead and the scene was one of devastation. Heavy shellfire was encountered during passage through the village from the direction of Contalmaison and Ovillers. On return journey down Sausage Valley large parties were met with who were engaged burying the dead which lay about in large numbers.'

Shelling of Albert caused more casualties the following morning. A shell landed in an ammunition dump where men of the battalion were among a group preparing bombs. The dump contained about 50,000 hand grenades and the explosions continued for much of the afternoon. The Battalion Diary recorded that one officer was wounded, one man killed and two others wounded.

The evening of the 9th saw the battalion move into support positions behind the 13th Battalion, Rifle Brigade which was in the old German trenches east of La Boisselle. The diary commented that not a single wall was left standing in the village. The trenches had been shelled and the men spent every available hour in deepening and clearing them to give cover from the enfilading artillery fire which was causing casualties, including Second Lieutenant Frank Shutes and a further twenty-eight men who were wounded.

Supplies were brought up Sausage Valley from Gordon Dump[45]. The War Diary recorded deaths on 10 July. Second Lieutenant James Hodding, a 17-year-old officer in A Company, was the son of a retired major in the Indian Army. He had been commissioned on 28 May 1915. The records show that he died of wounds at Heilly

Station on 10 July and was probably the officer wounded the previous day in the explosion in the ammunition dump. It is likely that the three men killed were Stk1090 Charles Read aged 27, a bank clerk born in Huntingdon; 1683 Thomas Roseveare, aged 17, born in Barrow in Furness, son of a railway storekeeper; and Stk34 Private Thomas Skilton Brown, aged 29, a member of A Company, a stockbroker's clerk living in Wimbledon.

Mountford wrote home on 9 July covering the events of the previous week. He described the barn at Bresle:

> *'At this village there was a gigantic hut with sorts of layers of shelves, like a warehouse into which they put 750 of us.'*

He told of the move up to the cemetery near Bellevue Farm and of an opportunity to go into Albert:

> *'I slept in a puddle with the rain coming in on me but slept nevertheless. The next day we stopped there all day and I am writing from there this morning, but now a hot sun is shining and things are happier. I believe this evening we go up but whether to the support or the front line (such as it is) I can't say. Many prisoners have been taken here and guns and all sorts of things come down. They say that up in front there's the deuce of a mess of dead bodies.*
>
> *'Yesterday afternoon they let us out into the town for two hours. It is rather badly knocked about, especially the big church – I don't think they call it a cathedral – which is a pitiful sight. At the top of the tower stood a gigantic gilded statue of the Virgin Mary holding the child above her head and this has fallen, but in a miraculous way the base has held fast or caught in something so that now the Lady is in the act of diving into the street. There are few civilians left and only two or three small shops.*
>
> *'We are surrounded by guns of the largest types and I am almost deaf. At night, besides the row there are flashes to admire. Sometimes the sky seems almost alight.*
>
> *'I went to communion this morning and knelt in the long grass beneath the blue sky. I preferred it to some places I have been to.*
>
> *'Please send a parcel by return with two thick pairs of socks, 100 cigarettes and as much else as you can get in. Also some of that Boots' Vermin stuff, which I will give another trial. The state of my body is appalling. I believe I could get a bag of three figures any old time with patience.*
>
> *'Please circulate this as much as possible. It's the only letter I've written for about three weeks and goodness knows when I shall write another.'*

On 10 July Wilkinson wrote home:

> *'My dear mother, For several days we have been on trek sleeping in the open with just our groundsheets for protection from damp. Last night we slept by a track through some corn and as the night was warm and dry we were quite comfy. Once or twice though I have had to sleep in wet clothes, a new experience for me. So far I have not been*

dangerously close to the shelling but I have seen some of our 'heavies' sending tons of stuff over to Fritz.

'It would amuse you to see how eagerly we read week old newspapers to get news of what is going on under our noses. You, at home, know sooner than we do what is happening. I shall have heaps to tell you when I come home about this affair; the Huns have been having a bad time.

'Thank you for the letter which arrived yesterday with Rene's. I got the Vickers book all right, thank you.'

The dangers faced by those caring for the wounded was underlined when the battalion diarist recorded the discovery of a large German medical post dug into the chalk near La Boisselle:

'At the bifurcation of the road we found a large German aid post with two storeys and five entrances, three of which were blocked. In this dug out were found many dead and some wounded Germans and also a few British. It continued to be heavily shelled, a large crater being formed by the constant shelling, and it was a post of extreme danger.'

Maxwell with his transport was engaged in carrying supplies forward from Albert and later Gordon Dump, to the battalion and others in the front line. In his autobiography he recalled incidents from this period. He was living under a transport wagon cover with the padre, the Reverend Edge Partington. He described the padre as 'an excellent companion':

'No words could exaggerate the extent of his goodness and tolerance. Although caring nothing himself for alcohol, but seeing that I was put about for want of my drink, he trudged into Albert through the miles of dust and glare and came back with a bottle of wine under each arm, running the gauntlet on the long return journey of the people in Staff cars and on lorries, who smiled and made merry at the sight of a chaplain thus laden.'

The 13th Rifle Brigade (13RB) attacked towards Pozières on 10 July using a tramway as their left flank marker. They made some progress over the trenches but faced intense machine gun fire and were forced to withdraw, their active numbers reduced to four officers and 400 men; a total of eighty-four men died. Two companies of 10RF, C and B, were moved up to take their places in the front trenches to allow the survivors to withdraw.

July 11 saw the battalion in reserve but, according to the note in the battalion diary, they 'lost considerably from heavy shelling'. The remaining companies, A and D were moved forward at 3pm to take over from the remnants of the 13RB in the support trenches. Six men were killed and twenty-nine wounded plus one was listed as missing. One very young man who died on this day, was 16-year-old Stk1655 Albert Bowl who succumbed to his wounds in a casualty clearing station at Puchevillers. He had been born in West Ham in 1900 and lived in Leyton, the son of a carpenter. Colonel White in his diary recorded:

'We lose many men today by constant heavy shelling, our position on the Contalmaison Road being practically without cover.'

On the 12th, having spent the morning digging to connect the front line trench to the Contalmaison road, the battalion was moved back to La Boisselle and occupied the trenches between a large crater, probably the one now called Lochnagar to the south of the village, and Gordon Dump.

Although not involved in any direct attacks the attrition of deaths and injuries continued. The battalion diary recorded that one man was killed and three wounded but the SDGW lists six men killed in action and two dying of wounds on this day. One of the dead was a close friend of George Wilkinson. Stk365 Private Richard Cordingley, aged 21 lived with his family in Homefield Road, Chiswick; his father was a newspaper proprietor. Sergeant Bambridge also died, aged 21, his brother was in the 10RF and they had joined on the same day, leaving behind their family in Clapham Common. Rupert Bambridge had received his commission in 10RF in March 1916.

Stk 320 Sergeant Frederick Bambridge killed near Albert J, 1916, his brother Rupert had t, number Stk 319 before being commissioned in the battalion. World War One Photos

White wrote in his diary:

'In the last 2 days we have lost 134 killed and wounded.'

On the 13 and 14 July the battalion was resting while XV Corps attacked towards High Wood and 25th Division moved towards Ovillers. There was general astonishment at the lack of damage done to the German dugouts by the allied artillery bombardment which had obliterated the trenches. The construction was described as demonstrating 'expert workmanship' with 'luxurious fittings' and 'in a number of cases electric light'. This reflects the report by the battalion earlier in the year when the raid at Berles-au-Bois on 3 June discovered that the dugouts in ruined trenches were virtually untouched.

The battalion moved closer to the action on 14 July. Percy Ray Zealley, a man transferred from the 18th (Public Schools) Battalion in May, was involved in the preparation and execution of the attack and wrote an account of his experience shortly afterwards.

Sergeant Bambridge, buried, Albert. Author

'Our position is in front of La Boiselle (N.E of Albert) and astride the Albert – Bapaume road. We have arrived at a German R.E Dump in a quarry where excellent dug outs exist. Alas it is not for us to occupy them for we have been given the grim task of burying the British and German dead which are lying about in the near vicinity. However we eventually occupy these dug outs where wine and cigars of German origin are appreciated. A conversation with a wounded German of 138th Saxon Regiment rather indicates their demoralised condition.

152

'From this position can be seen an attack in progress – open warfare – and Contalmaison is reported as taken.

'We are ordered forward to take up supplies, my personal load being two petrol cans of water in addition to fighting kit. We are heavily shelled and little cover is afforded – there are many casualties in consequence. The 13th Rifle Brigade attack and we support. When Standing-To it is imagined a counter-attack is forming but it merely turns out to be about 200 Bosche giving themselves up (and very demoralised they are too).

'The night passes with little fighting but great "WIND-UP" as is indicated by the numerous flares sent up by each line. Our meals for today are scanty (2 biscuits, one eighth of a tin of bully and half a cup of water per man) owing to the fact that our supplies the previous evening had in many cases remained behind with the dead and wounded.

'We are relieved by 13th Kings Royal Rifle Corps being peppered with shrapnel on our return to the Gordon Dump. A sleep in the trench, although it is raining, is appreciated and a rum issue is a necessity indeed.

'From 1 to 2am I am posted as "gas sentry" for on our right and left gas is liberated which is followed by an attack (2 Army Corps operating in each). In the centre, our front, there is a bombardment only, really a blind to distract the attention on our right and left. The news which follows is successful. The Indian Cavalry are pushing through and the 60 pounders are now forward in front of the German First Line. Orders are now received, we are to rest our feet and boots are to be taken off. It is significant that a long distance attack is imminent.'

10RF joined the battle on 15 July.

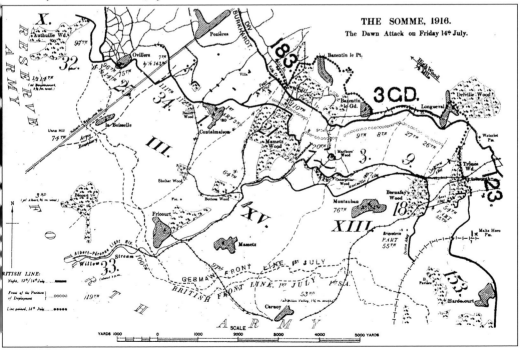

The view from the 10RF start line on 15 July. Their objective, Pozières, is beyond the white edifice that is the Pozières War Cemetery. Author

The morning of 15th July was looking to turn fine with early mist clearing during the morning. In the area between the Albert to Bapaume road and Longueval, about 6 miles to the east, a series of attacks was planned, starting with a dawn attack on Waterlot Farm and Longueval coordinated with the South African Brigade's attack on Delville Wood. At 9am other attacks began along the line, with 91 Brigade (7th Division) attacking High Wood with support from 100 Brigade (33rd Division) which attempted to clear the west side of the wood. No 2 Brigade in the form of the 1st Loyals gained 400 yards of German trench at the western edge of Bazentin-le-Petit Wood and with support from 2nd Battalion, Welsh Regiment eventually managed to establish a line of posts joining with 34th Division.

The 10RF moved forward at 9am to follow and support 112 Brigade as they attacked Pozières. The battalion's orders were to push through Pozières and establish a line from the Windmill [now the Australian War Memorial] on the north side of the Bapaume road to where the German line reached the tramway. Heading out in file up Sausage Valley with C Company in the lead followed by B, D and A, they reached the Contalmaison road, wheeled left and formed up along the front line trench with C and B companies in the lead. The advance was over 1300 yards of open ground up a gentle slope with Pozières at the crest.

Heavy machine gun fire held up the advance of 112 Brigade about 300 yards short of the village. The 10RF HQ was by now about 250 yards south of the chalk pit on the Bailiff Wood to Pozières road and they requested an artillery barrage to support their advance, which they hoped would re-energise the stalled attack. The Battalion Diary says that this barrage was agreed and the battalion advanced, as the diary recorded, 'in steady formation without any hesitation' until the small orchard to the south west of the village was seized by Lieutenant Taylor and members of D Company. Deadly German machine gun fire from well concealed positions caused a retreat to a line of trenches in the orchard, about 200-300 yards south of the village.

The battalion HQ, well established in the chalk pit was joined by the HQs of 10 Loyals and The Bedford Regiment. The commander of 34th Division, Major General Ingouville Williams arrived there at about 2pm and informed the officers present that there would be an artillery barrage at 5pm, followed an hour later by an advance of the remnants of the brigade to take Pozières. The remaining men of 10RF were to be joined to 112 Brigade and placed under the command of Brigadier General Robinson. Once the village had been taken 10RF would continue to advance to the windmill and German trenches, the objectives which they had been given in the morning.

Unfortunately when the barrage ended the rockets were not fired, because they were both damp. In consequence some troops began to advance, because it was 6pm, and others waited for the signal. The few minutes delay was decisive as it allowed the German machine gunners to resume their positions and begin an even more intense fire than the battalion had experienced in the morning. Again pinned down they sheltered in the same trenches they had occupied in the afternoon and were eventually relieved during the evening by 10 Loyals. The remnants of the battalion made their back to the Usna-Tara line; they arrived in scattered groups between 11:30pm and 2am, and bivouacked in the open.

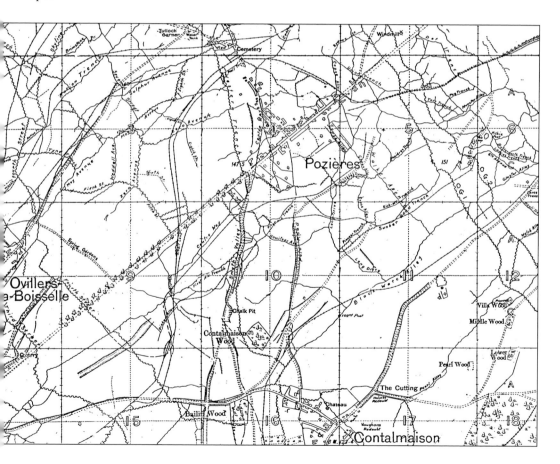

Chalk Pit.

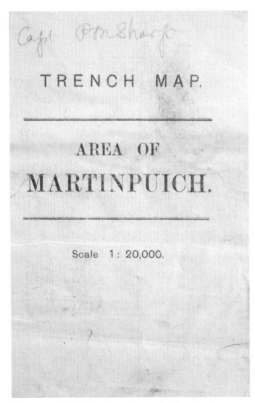

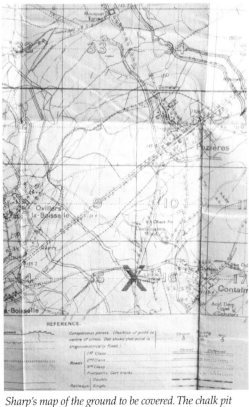

The cover of Captain Sharp's map for the attack on Pozières. Sharp Collection IWM

Sharp's map of the ground to be covered. The chalk pit was used as HQ by the battalion. Sharp Collection IWM

Ray Zealley described his experiences:

'On July 15 at 9am we move forward to attack the village of Pozières and the front line beyond it. Over open ground under shell and machine gun fire we advance taking cover when possible in shell holes. The distance is abnormal, a 1500 yard charge in fighting kit and carrying a spade for consolidation – many casualties result. We drop into a captured German trench over which we have to pass to our final objective now manned by the 6th Bedfords and East Lancs Regiment. There is scarcely room to take cover in it as it is so full with the dead of British and Bosche. A slight pause is taken here while our gunners bombard Pozières which is about 200 yards in front of our position. Several fall short and almost in our trench. On the flank out of a reconnoitring party of 40 Bedford Bommers [sic] only 3 return.

'Later we go over the top a distance of about 100 yards under the most intense machine gun and shell fire. Men are simply mown down but those that almost reach the objective are frustrated. We drop into what is called Orchard Trench just outside Pozières itself, a positive death trap. It is shallow and cannot be deepened on account of hurdles being placed on the ground.

'Enfiladed machine gun fire causes the order being given to retire when only a few yards from our objective. Equally bad is the retirement in the way of casualties and when relieved at 10pm the same evening by the Loyal North Lancs some 200 men return out of a battalion strength of about 1000 men.'

Maurice Sharp was in command of B Company, having taken over in January 1916 from Captain Fred Russell Roberts. He had been attending a course at the 3rd Army Infantry School at Auxi-le-Chateau and had raced back to rejoin 10RF in time for the attack. Writing after the war he recalled that the order they received was that as 112 Brigade had already occupied Pozières the task given to 10RF was to advance through the front line and attack the high ground to the east of Pozières to take the machine gun positions.

They quickly discovered that the intelligence was incorrect. His company was one of the leading pair and they took heavy casualties from what he described as 'withering machine gun fire'. He and Captain Henry Hall asked for artillery support but were told to continue without for the present. His batman, Stk489 Private William Peat, was wounded, his Company Sergeant Major Stk301 Frederick Hendry was killed beside him as the company ran forward towards Pozières. He continued 'suddenly I found myself on the ground feeling I had run into a brick wall I had not seen. When I tried to get up two others fell on top of me and I found I was pouring with blood. One of the others had a lung wound and I bound him up as well as I could with my left hand, I had been shot through the right elbow joint. I then got him to tie me up and we staggered down somehow to our First Aid Station. When I had my wound dressed I tried to return but fainted from loss of blood. That finished me off for the time being!'

Maxwell in his autobiography written in 1937 recalled the events and consequences of the day:

'The day came when our battalion moved into position for action. It was told to attack the village of Pozières and take it at all costs. At the appointed moment it plunged forward

eager and gallant, to show at last what it was made of. It was met by murderous machine gun fire. Wave after wave of it was mown down, and still it drove on. It reached the edge of the village and even penetrated it, but after a time it was compelled to yield its incomplete hold. Then they withdrew shattered. We had lost half the battalion in a useless and futile attempt that should never have been made. Our men had been set to do an impossible task. It was awful to think of all those gallant lives thrown away.

'That night, obeying Brigade orders, I had chosen a place of bivouac on the Usna Tara Ridge near the high road. There all that remained of the battalion would be brought to us. Between midnight and 2am we were there expecting them, with the Quartermaster and the Sergeant Major, the cookers and the hot stew, and the officers' mess cart with some straw on the floor as a bed for our Colonel. They arrived, a dribbling procession, with large intervals, of worn-out men. Five together announced that they were all that survived of A Company. Ten or twelve said that no more of B Company was left in existence. They believed this to be so, but in fact many more of each company came straggling after them. "Captain Hall?" "Wounded, sir[46]". "Captain Campbell?" " Dead, sir". "Captain Shurey?" "Dead". "Mr Beavir?" "Dead". "Captain Sharp?" "Wounded, sir." Lieutenants Taylor, Richards, Heathcote, Haviland, Hodding – all dead. A grievous tale. Last of all came dear Bobby White, the commanding officer.

"Oh, my Battalion," he moaned. "My splendid Battalion! And to think I had not the luck to get killed too." Then with an arm round my neck and his head against my shoulder he wept most bitterly. As soon as possible we got him down among the straw in the mess cart. And soon he slept. He was, of course, utterly worn out.'

The War Diary officially recorded the number of killed, wounded and missing as being 3 officers killed and 8 wounded, 39 other ranks killed and 175 wounded, with 24 other ranks missing. Maxwell merged the number of later deaths from wounds with those which occurred on the day. The records of Soldiers Died in the Great War show that 4 officers and 64 other ranks died on 15 July. There is no doubt that this attack, with the attrition of the previous days, resulted in a significant reduction in the numbers in the battalion, particularly in those who carried the history and traditions having been original 'Ditchers'.

Mountford, who had been wounded in the advance of C Company wrote a rather ironic letter from his hospital bed on the following day, the16th:

'Dear Mother, After having been up against the push since I wrote to you last and seen in 3 days more wonderful, more pitiful and more horrible sights than would suffice any ordinary mortal for 3 lifetimes, we tried a push ourselves yesterday morning. I hadn't pushed far before a machine gun pushed a bullet through my shoulder as I pushed up. Am in hospital at Rouen.'

Wilkinson on 17 July added a paragraph to the letter he had started on 10th:

'I am now in a rest camp with a sprained ankle which I got in the new front line!! Parnell is in another rest camp with a scratch on the face, I think.'

By the 20th Mountford had transferred to hospital in England and wrote from Ward H2 in the Mile End Military Hospital, Bancroft Road, London.

'I am afraid I have kept you rather long in suspense since my letter from Rouen, but I have only just settled down.

'We were attacking Pozières on Saturday morning when I was wounded. Machine guns simply swept our lines, and I was running forward, stooping, a bullet hit my right shoulder just at the top and came out several inches lower down my back, a nice clean flesh wound. I have had an absolutely negligible quantity of pain. I'm afraid the 10th will be practically non-existent. We had lost over 200 in the previous 3 days and this attack must have about finished them off.'

In 1927 Sharp's cup was returned. It had been found with the remains of a soldier at Pozières. Sharp thought the man could be Colonel White's runner who was delivering a message when Sharp was hit. Sharp Collection IWM

Captain Sharp, wounded in the elbow, arrived in a hospital in Rouen where he was told by a French surgeon that his right arm was to be amputated. That evening an order arrived to evacuate to England all those who could walk to make space for more wounded arriving from the Front. Sharp was sufficiently mobile to get off his bed and make the journey to England. He was sent to a hospital in Somerville College, Oxford where he was again told his arm would be amputated.

Sharp with Roberts, back left, outside the King of Portugal's Hospital in Brighton. Sharp Collection IWM

159

Through the intervention of Colonel White's friend, Lady Dudley, now Head of the Red Cross, he was able to move to another hospital, and selected the King of Portugal's hospital in Brighton, where Captain Russell-Roberts was recovering from his injuries. The surgeon at Brighton, Mr Nunnely, saw some movement in the fingers of Sharp's right hand and managed to save the limb, which gradually returned to working order. He remained in Brighton until the end of 1916 when he went home to Reading and was an outpatient until early 1917. Returning to the Royal Fusiliers he was sent first to the 5RF in Dover, which provided drafts, but was then ordered to 105 Training Battalion as its adjutant, first in Edinburgh and then in Catterick.

Wilkinson next wrote home on 21 July from 102 Field Ambulance in Franvillers, south-west of Albert to inform his parents of the deaths of many of his friends:

The King of Portugal's Hospital in Eastern Terrace was later part of Brighton Teacher Training College and is now a residence. Author

'I am sorry to tell you that Cordingley was killed about a week ago as were many of our old regiment. It's very sad but the work done by everyone lately has been magnificent.'

Between 16 and 19 July the battalion remained on the Usna – Tara Ridge above Albert. They saw the bombardment of the German lines about Pozières and across to Delville Wood. They also suffered the German counter shelling some of which landed on the reserve positions and Albert. The battalion reported casualties and noted in the diary that although every company commander, every CSM and the majority of sergeants had become casualties the administration of the battalion continued smoothly as usual. On the 19th the battalion withdrew to Bresle where, following what was described in the War Diary as 'a thorough inspection to check clothing, arms and equipment', it began to reorganise and await reinforcements so that as the diarist recorded 'it can be fit to return to the line at an early date'.

Chapter 11

Reflect, Recover, Retired, Regroup, Reallocated: July to September 1916

The Lewis gun teams had suffered particularly during the attack on Pozières and virtually all had to be replaced. Five replacement officers arrived and acting NCOs were appointed. On 23 July, the same day that the Australians took part of Pozières, the 10RF gathered to participate in a service of remembrance for their colleagues who did not survive the action. On the same day their Colonel also attended the funeral service of the divisional commander, Major General Ingouville Williams who had been killed by a shell in Mametz Wood. In his diary White recalled the General as being 'a fine officer, very daring'.

Also on 23rd, but in hospital in the East End of London, Mountford wrote a long letter to his mother recounting the events of the previous two weeks. He expressed the views and feelings of a serving soldier with such clarity and conviction that the bulk of the letter is reproduced here:

'We had left our packs behind a couple of days previously and our rig out from then onwards consisted of our equipment less pack, with our haversacks on our backs containing a towel and razor, a few odds and ends and the day's rations; a hand grenade in each breast pocket, two extra bandoliers of ammunition slung, a shovel and two sand bags. We set off at 8pm and went for two or three miles up a fairly good road over the ground where our old communications trenches used to be, through a wood and emerged into the open country, which had been devastated by the advance. There was little to be seen at first, but a mile further on, where trench after trench had been the scene of a conflict it was a wonderful spectacle. As far as you can see it is a wilderness of torn up soil intersected with ruined trenches, it is like a man's face after smallpox or a telescopic view of the moon. The shell holes overlap and run into each other; some are mere scratches, some would hide the average hay stack; here and there distorted posts form all that remains of a wire entanglement. But the most striking feature is the debris that is lying, scattered on the surface and thick in the trenches. Lots of equipment, rifles, bayonets, shovels, shrapnel helmets, respirators, shell cases, iron posts, overcoats, ground sheets, bombs (in hundreds) – I don't suppose there is a square yard without some relic

and reminder of the awful waste of war. More pleasant to behold is the stuff left by the Germans. In their old trenches you can get any mortal thing you fancy as a souvenir, from a sniper's rifle or a grey blanket, to a Prussian helmet or a clip of dum-dum cartridges. If you like you can have the battery that supplied electric light for a dug out; or the notice board from the one with all the bottles outside, marked "Larger Vorwalker", or the special cardboard case used for carrying explosive bullets. Or you may prefer to collect postcards to "mein lieber, lieber, Hans" from "Deine Elise". After I had seen dead bodies lying on all sides in the weird attitudes of sudden death, souvenirs seemed a bit paltry.

'Our guide lost us – it is not surprising – and we wandered about for a long time in the open with shells falling unpleasantly near at hand. Eventually we got into a narrow, shallow, little trench where we remained huddled up all night. This was the first support line. It ran alongside what had been a road into a low lying open space with German dug outs all round it. Owing to their great depth, some were still intact and one was used as our aid post. [La Boiselle] *In the morning [July 10] as soon as it was light we were started on burying the German dead who were lying all over the road and in the open square. I assisted with half a dozen – one we dragged up from a dug out, one from a shed full of German stores and materials of all sorts. The day was spent in deepening the trench. We were shelled often and had a good few casualties. In the afternoon we saw a fine sight on our right; the second and successful attack on Contalmaison. It was thrilling to see the lines of infantry advancing in extended order despite the shrapnel bursting all round them. They disappeared in the trees and presently we heard the attack had been very successful. Later appeared strings of German prisoners being taken back.*

'In the evening we got our first taste of fire in the open. The Rifle Brigade were holding our front line and we were under the impression we were to relieve them. The way up was over ground for a little way, then along some trenches, then up a light railway line for nearly half a mile, from which the trenches turned off to the left and right. Suddenly we saw that in front they were starting to run. What did happen is that the Rifle Brigade went over the top to the German trenches opposite them; we came running up the line past the trenches the Rifle Brigade had vacated and on towards the German lines. The Germans of course had got the tram line taped. Shrapnel was flying all over the place and a machine gun on the left caught us with the protection of a bank only about 3 feet high. Men were going down every minute and since there had been previously been bodies lying all the way the place began to look a bit rotten. The advance had been steady enough but I'm afraid the retirement was a bit of a scramble. It was not far though and then we turned, some to right and some left into what, as I had told you, had been the front line trenches. Our orders were to spread out and man the parapet, which we did. The trenches were being heavily shelled; we didn't know what was happening and consequently when we saw men advancing towards us fire was opened for a few moments until we saw that some were English. They proved to be RBs bringing back wounded and prisoners. Of the latter over 200 came or were brought in and some of them are supposed to have said that if we hadn't fired there was a whole battalion ready to come over and surrender.

'That night was rather horrible. We were shelled all night; but the rottenest part was the unsettled state of things. The RBs received the order to retire and they came back from the German trenches. (We heard the Germans return to it presently, chucking plenty of

bombs about by way of precaution). Then they wanted the RB on our left and we all moved to the right; then they took them away altogether and we were left with about 30 men to a couple of hundred yards of front line trench and had to spread out as best we could. Then they brought up our own B Company and mixed us up properly. This was about 2am, C Company ("my fighting Company" our old stockbroker Colonel used to say) having until then been quite alone. For some time I was in a bay with one wounded RB man lying on the floor, and a man wounded in the throat making gurgling noises sitting on the fire step. Then a shell burst on the parapet and half buried us all. I lost two men in my section and three from my old section, including Fredericks in whom Gwyneth was always interested. I saw him go down just in front of me in the run up the tram line but he was only wounded I think. (P.S In this little escapade, which ought never to have been made apparently, the RBs lost all their officers except one and most of the Battalion.)

'[July 11] As soon as it was light we started digging down. They then moved us right back to the left over the tram line to get B and C Companies sorted out and we started digging down again. Unfortunately in the bay where I was, a German trouser and boot protruding in one place rather put us off making it as deep as we should have liked.

'We held the front line for two days and were shelled almost continuously. There were three sorts of shell, a light one nobody minded, a 5.9 which fired either 'crumps' (a heavy shrapnel bursting in the air) or a high explosive which burst in the ground and gave you a very nasty jar, and a heavier beast which they turned on from time to time. When this dropped one near the trench it shook your very soul up inside you. Water and rations were brought up via the tram line at night. On the second night I was ordered to take three men out and try to get some wire up. On the third night [July 12] we were taken out, down the tram lines, which were being shelled of course, and back to a support line, behind the one we had previously occupied, which ran close to the village of La Boiselle. Here we were allowed to dig ourselves little cubby holes in the side and curled up like hedgehogs, go to sleep. It was the fourth night since we left Albert and our first sleep. We had lost over 200 men already.

'Before I leave the subject of the front line there is one little incident I want to recount. The trench to the left of the tramway ran into a communication trench, which led towards the Germans. A party under an officer was sent to explore it. About 500 yards along they found an advanced trench empty, and 20 men and an officer were sent to hold it, which they did until we were relieved. I wonder what the people at home who say "We will fight to our last drop of blood" would think if they were taken up that trench. For 500 yards it is paved with English dead. In places you must walk upon them for they lie in heaps. I went up with rations, and again to help carry down a casualty on a stretcher. I won't describe that trench until I have forgotten it a little.

'In that support line we stayed three nights and two days [July 13th -14th] and hadn't a great deal to do. The village of La Boiselle would amuse you. It was in pure chalk and all the posts and bits of wire and the whole ground for hundreds of yards around it were white as snow. We slept in our little excavations at the side of the trench and having no protection were moderately chilly. The man in the one next to mine tried to deepen his and struck sacking. Suspecting nothing he got as far as a blood stained cap; and then he went to dig a new hole. What the eye doesn't see etc.

'[July 15th] *In the morning we got "stand by ready to move off at an hour's notice". As we had been in the habit of standing by ready to move off at 5 minutes notice this looked well. Then at 8:30am we had orders to be ready by 9:30 and then suddenly at 9 o'clock "get dressed". (That means equipment of course). We moved off in platoons, overland towards the front line, jumped over the support lines and lay down just behind the front line. Then the crumps began and, what proved our undoing, machine guns crackled from the village. We advanced at the walk. We crossed over another trench with troops in it and about 200 yards further on I was running forward a little with my head well down I felt a punch on the shoulder and lay down in a shell hole to think things over. A man with a bullet through his leg shared the hole and after a while he went off back. Then a man with a bad wound in his back came in. After a while stretcher bearers, who behaved magnificently, I never admired anything more in my life, came along, dodging from man to man, patching them up with field dressings, helping them into shell holes and carrying on as though it was Hampstead Heath on manoeuvres days; while the whole time heavy lyddite shrapnel was bursting overhead and the machine guns were playing as freely as ever.*

'*I had been in the shell hole for about an hour and a half, but the attack was evidently hung up and the fourth line of our men had not long since passed over me. So, as several lumps had fallen near me, and I was getting pretty fed up, I took advantage of a slight lull to make my way back to the nearest trench, which proved to be continuation of the one I told you was full of dead – but here the dead were all German. I got safely down this and along our old front line on to the tram lines. Here again I had an anxious time, but nothing happened until I got near the end and there I ran into a spot where they were putting over gas shells - not lachrymatory but asphyxiating, and as I had no respirator got the wind up pretty badly. I had not much difficulty in finding a respirator lying about though and arrived at the open square where as I said we had made an aid post in a German dug out. Here they advised us if we could to walk further back, as they were awfully busy and the dug out was full of gas. So we went further back to the next, where they were busier still and to cut a long story short we eventually walked all the way back to the hospital at Albert. Here I had my wound dressed, got some tea and food and then was packed off in a motor lorry to some place about 10 miles away where we got onto some cattle trucks and went by rail to a place called Douras [sic]. This was a clearing station. We got more food and turned in on mattresses until about 6am the next morning when we went by hospital train to Rouen* [July 16].

'*Tram cars took us to the hospital situated in the centre of a race course. It was not really more than a clearing station; most of us got blighty tickets and after 2 days [July 18] were taken by train to Havre and went on board the Asturias*[47] *about 9pm. It was very crowded, no beds left and we slept on the mess room floor. At Southampton next morning I missed by a fluke a train going to Carlisle or some impossible place and the next one happened to be London. At Waterloo I was with the first party of 30 out of the train and they put us into private cars. I saw a nurse give the driver a card with Mile End on it and knew our fate. There was the fatheaded crowd, just as you read of, gawping and throwing cigarettes etc and the whole ride was most detestable – through the heart of London with me perched up in front, not quite in such a bad state as on reaching*

HMHS Asturias *on which Mountfort returned to England.*

Rouen but nevertheless with two days dirt and beard, hatless and dishevelled and a dangling sleeve.'

At the end of the letter he added three further reflections:

'1. I can remember now what a curious feeling it gave me to be leaving my equipment behind; even at that time and place. There was my rifle, on which for more than 12 months I have spent hours and hours of labour to keep it clean, looked after better than myself often; fixed bayonet, one cartridge in the chamber, cocked and safety catch on. My equipment I have greased and polished many a hundred times, my ammunition, all laboriously cleaned a few days before; iron rations, until then clung to like life itself; ground sheet, haversack, with razor from Hadden's, brush from Leytonstone years ago – and all my portable property that I had carried until it seemed almost part of me – chucked into a shell hole and left there to rot.

'2. I gather the attack was a failure. The latest I can be sure of is that we reached a trench just in front of the village and finding it useless to go on lay there until 6pm while the artillery had another go. This trench was so full that 9 and 12 platoons had to lie behind the parados. One man said he could only see 5 men of 9 platoon. At 6pm they advanced and I have met no one who knows what happened. But the papers never said a word about the affair so I gather it was a complete failure. One man thought we had

165

to retire right back to our original position. I trust it was not so or many wounded would have been left lying out. (The men who held the advanced trench I told you of said that at night you could hear the wounded out in front crying for help and water, but nothing could be done). Two brigades were employed and the dead and wounded were thick as peas. I have written to my platoon officer to know who is left.

'The failure seems to me to have been due to insufficient artillery preparation (why heaven only knows for we had enough in all conscience; Albert bristled with guns of all calibres) and a too lengthy advance. It was all too much to try. I must have gone 500 yards before I went down and the village still seemed a long way.

'3. The treatment we got in French hospital trains and hospitals was greatly superior to that over here; but of course we had a good deal more experience of them. This hospital and the journey here was all we saw of this side, but neither is anything to be proud of, after the way they do things over there.'

On the same day that Mountfort was writing home Stk519 Arthur Rimer died in the Kitchener Hospital in Brighton; aged 29, he had been a solicitor working in Kingston-on-Thames. A member of the prestigious Fell and Rock Club, his name was later added to the memorial erected by the club and which stands at the heart of a memorial service held each year on Great Gable in the Lake District.

Wilkinson spent nearly two weeks at the Field Ambulance and like Mountfort he lost much of his equipment. He returned to the battalion and wrote home on 1 August to describe his time in hospital:

'I arrived at the hospital with kit comprising a pair of field glasses and a pair of dirty socks! By the second day I had increased this by one empty butter tin out of which I ate my meals. I have now been almost entirely refitted but my French Grammar Dictionary, rubber shoes, soap dish, shaving soap etc, etc I shall see no more. Neither shall I have the fag of carrying them. I also lost my compass and cigarette case through holes in my pockets.

'I have seen Parnell again, he is now Lance Corporal. He was not sent to a rest camp. The information I sent to you in my last letter was incorrect. He is quite well.'

On 2 August Mountfort wrote to his mother to pass on bad news received from France:

'I have had some bad news today, though only such as I might have expected. The first letters have arrived from France and though they say very little about what I want to know, it seems that two of my best friends have not been heard of and are believed to have been killed. Of Pickering I can't hear a word. I am inclined to think from this that he is either killed or wounded, for I know he was the next for promotion, and the new NCOs in the platoon do not include him among their number. The number, by the way, for No 9 Platoon alone comprises two L/Cpls promoted to be Sergts and 4 privates to L/Cpls, so the toll of NCOs seems to have been heavy. I am waiting to hear more definite news, which I hope will be better. One of the fellows I speak of was a solicitor from Yorkshire[48]. We had many tastes in common, but also many in contrast; which is just as

it should be. We "spoke with naked hearts together"[49] and sometimes cut in half our last cigarette. The other was a little fellow – a most delightful companion, full of humour and good spirits. We three were together during all the bad times at the end and since they were both much cleverer and more useful individuals than I, I don't think the selection a good one.'

Mountfort was correct about his friend Ernest Pickering; he died of his wounds on 17 July and is buried in Abbeville.

From the surviving records a further twenty men have been identified who were wounded in July 1916, eighteen of them on the 15th. Between them they give a cross section of the sort of men who volunteered in August 1914. On 11 July Stk439 Private George Hurst from Derbyshire who had been working as a wharf superintendent on the Thames, received gunshot wounds to his head, face and chest. He was sent from the dressing station to hospital, probably at Rouen, and on 5 August arrived at King George's Hospital in London. He remained here until the middle of January and was discharged from the army with a pension in February 1917.

On 13 July Stk677 James Farrar, auctioneer's clerk born in Poplar, later resident in Putney, was wounded and had bones broken. He was invalided out of the army in March 1917.

Stk84 Private Charles Fisher, aged 32 and married with one daughter with his home in Chingford, Essex, received a gunshot wound in the knee which led to his reclassification to Class P in April 1917.

Stk60 Private Harold Costin a 32-year-old civil servant living in East Grinstead received gunshot wounds and was discharged to the reserve in May 1917.

Nineteen-year-old Stk227 Sidney Seager, was wounded in the leg and sent to the Queen Mary's Military Hospital in Whalley, Lancashire, although his family came from Camberwell in London. He was discharged from the army in July 1917.

Edward Trowbridge, a stockbroker's clerk, was wounded in the chest and discharged with a pension in April 1916. He returned home to his family in Battersea.

The 24-year-old Oliver Apted, wounded in the thigh, was, before his army service, an accountant in a rubber company in the City. He lived with his parents, brother and three sisters in Reigate. After being wounded he was sent to the 1st Western Hospital in Fazakerley, Liverpool from where he was discharged in March 1917.

Harold Betteley, Stk333, a former shipping insurance clerk, received wounds to his legs and on regaining fitness was drafted to the 23RF. With them he was wounded on four further separate occasions, in November 1916, again in early April 1917 when he was wounded in the wrist and on his return in the same month he was wounded again. His final injury was received on 1 July 1917 when he was shot in the neck and throat. After a period in Netley Hospital, Southampton, he was discharged as his injuries made swallowing and eating difficult.

Stk432, Private Francis Higginson of Wimbledon, a draper's wholesale junior salesman, was discharged in March 1917 having received gunshot wounds which earned him a spell in hospital from where he was sent for a month on the roll of 6RF.

Percy McNeill, an old boy of Owen's School in Islington, had joined the battalion in August 1914 with the number Stk469. A stockbrokers clerk, with his father and one of his three brothers in the same occupation, he received gunshot wounds on 15 July and after a spell in hospital was placed initially in Class P, but was finally discharged from the army on 20 July 1917.

More seriously wounded Private John Millar, Stk472, had his left arm amputated and was also wounded in the neck. He had been a shipping clerk and like most of the others injured at Pozières, been in the battalion since August 1914. He was discharged with a pension in December 1916.

Godfrey Melhuish was born in Anerley, south-east London, in 1891, his mother died when he was young and he and his brother were sent to a school in Folkestone before they were 10. In 1911 his father was shown on the census as a fruit importer living in some luxury in Harrow. When Godfrey signed his attestation form on 29 August 1914 he described his occupation as that of clerk.

The same age as Godfrey, and also born in Anerley, Cecil Porter, Stk797, a clerk to an export company, suffered from gunshot wounds to both knees on 15 July. Four days later after being at No 3 Stationary Hospital in Rouen, he was put onto the Hospital Ship, *St Denis* and then taken by train to the military hospital in Leeds. His discharge to category biii, allowing him to do sedentary work only because of his wounds, was agreed by a medical board in March 1917.

Harry Osborne, employed as a commercial traveller by the family firm of Osborne and Philips of Wood Lane, London, joined 10thRF on 29 August 1914. He was promoted to lance corporal (unpaid) in July 1915 just before the battalion left for France. On 15 July 1916 he received gunshot wounds to his arms and back and on 22 July was sent to the Northern Hospital in Leeds. His father was notified on 29 July that Harry was in the 2nd Northern Hospital in Beckett's Park, Leeds, improving slowly, but on 1 August he received a letter from the RF Records at Hounslow informing him that his son was missing in action. Osborne senior wrote to the Records Office respectfully pointing out their error and correcting their record of events. Harry was discharged home to 81 Elgin Road, Seven Kings, Essex on 9 January 1917, with a six month pension of 12 shillings and 6 pence per week.

Stk1296 Private Stanley Coxall from south-east London, originally trained and worked as a shorthand typist, not an unusual occupation for a man at the time. He then became an inspector of artesian wells, which supplied water to London, and was doing this job when he joined the battalion at Colchester in January 1915. His pension record notes that he suffered a number of gunshot wounds to his back and spine and also had a broken lower jaw, as well as flesh wounds and contusions.

On 31 July Coxall was described as being dangerously ill in 3rd London Hospital, Wandsworth. He recovered and attended a medical board in late October 1916. In his statement for his pension and work application he said that to continue as an inspector of artesian wells he had to have both arms fully working; however, he could take up employment as a shorthand typist as he had sufficient movement and strength to do this work.

A number of the recruits to 10RF came from overseas and, with others from the UK, were drafted into 10RF to replace those who left through illness, unfitness or promotion. Stk1349 James Fairweather, a tea planter arrived from Colombo on board the SS *Orsova* on 27 April 1915, signed up in Kingston-on-Thames on 5 May and was in France by 13

October. He had spent time some time in 31RF which was the training battalion linked to 10RF. He was not unaware of army life as he had served in the Ceylon Artillery Volunteers until 1911.

William Jones Morgan, Stk1448, at the age of 19 signed his attestation papers on 5 June 1915 at Kingston-on-Thames, one month after James Fairweather. He was allocated to 10RF and crossed with the battalion to France just eight weeks later. He was wounded in the head and shoulders during the Pozières attack. A farmer from Shrewsbury, he was discharged from the army in March 1917. Private Arthur Webster, Stk1553, volunteered to join the army in St Paul's Churchyard, London, a street near the cathedral, in the middle of August 1915. After three months training in 31st Battalion he joined the 10RF on 19 November as one of a draft of forty men. A valet, he had married Lily Patston on 12 October 1915 and their daughter, Stella Mary, was born on 14 December while her father was in France. He was wounded in the right forearm on 15 July and sent to the 3rd Canadian Hospital at Boulogne, from where he was sent to the military orthopaedic hospital in Shepherds Bush, London and later discharged from the army.

As the casualties recovered in hospital the battalion resumed training at Bresle, incorporating lessons learned in the attack on Pozières. The War Dairy records that on 25 July:

> 'Battalion practised the attack in the morning. In view of recent experiences troops now being trained to advance close up to the barrage when attacking. In the afternoon the battalion, together with the remainder of 111 Brigade, was inspected by the Corps Commander (Lieutenant General Sir W.P. Pulteney KCB, DSO) who expressed his appreciation of the smart appearance and good turn out of the battalion. He also expressed the opinion that the work done by the battalion in the ~~unsuccessful~~ attack on Pozières on 15th contributed materially to the eventual capture of that place by the Australians and Territorials.'

The word unsuccessful is crossed out in the diary. New drafts arrived the following day; two second lieutenants came from 39th Infantry Base Depot. They arrived with 198 other ranks, 99 of them being Territorials of 4th Battalion, City of London Regiment; the diarist commented that 'many are recruits of three or four months service'.

Still with 37th Division the battalion continued intensive training with special emphasis on the tasks of Lewis gunners, bombers and signallers. On 29 July the battalion, minus the specialists who continued training, marched to Ribemont in hot and fine weather to bathe in the River Ancre. The following day, 30th, the whole battalion moved along an emergency road from Hennencourt to Albert where they took over billets and prepared to relieve what the diary described in error as 7th South Lancs, it was actually 7th (Loyal) North Lancs, in 19th Division. The error was corrected in the diary on the following day when they moved to take up position between 23rd and 51st divisions in support of 101st Division in the front line. August 1 saw the men of the battalion working to deepen and strengthen the trenches between Mametz Wood and Contalmaison. They created 'T' headlands in front of the main line of trenches and put wire in front of these. Although the German lines were about 2,500 yards in front, there remained the fear of a concentrated counter-attack. The battalion HQ occupied a former German dugout on the edge of Mametz Wood. The dugout was 22 feet deep and the passage was 5 feet 9 inches in height with small bays cut into the sides. The whole edifice was 80 yards long, and had three entrances. The Germans regularly shelled the wood, killing five men during the two weeks the battalion was in this position, although other battalions in the division suffered more severely.

On 3 August the battalion moved forward to relieve 16 Royal Scots when they advanced to attack the German lines. The attack was unsuccessful as the two companies of Royal Scots, accompanied by two of the 11 Suffolks reached Intermediate Trench just north of Bazentin-le-Petit to launch a frontal assault but, like attempts earlier in the week, this was soon beaten back; thirty four men were killed from the four companies. The 10RF Diary notes that while the Suffolks occupied the trench they were not supported by the Royal Scots so had to withdraw. While 10RF were to the east of Bazentin-le-Petit they were engaged in deepening and strengthening the trenches, and there were injuries including, on 3 August, to Second Lieutenant Harold Tupper, aged 24, an articled accountant from Harrietsham in Kent where his family ran the Roebuck Public House. Originally serving in 20th London Regiment he arrived in France in March 1915 and was commissioned in January 1916. He was sent to hospital in England where, after receiving a Silver War Badge on 8 July 1918, he died on 22 July. On 4 August Second Lieutenant Tatton-Tatton and three ORs were wounded. Percy Tatton-Tatton, aged 32, born in Torquay was, in 1911, a schoolmaster living with his wife in Conway, Caernarvonshire. He survived the war retiring with the rank of captain in 10RF.

On 5 August the battalion suffered one OR killed and four wounded. The diary noted that the HQ being used, in a chalk pit, was, so far, the only German dugout found with just one entrance, possibly grudging acknowledgement of the general quality of the German defences. Seven ORs were wounded on 6 August after the battalion had moved into trenches in High Wood, relieving the 13KRRC. Work continued with D Company, under Lieutenant Penfold[50], extending and improving a trench running south-west from High Wood. They linked together shell holes and deepened the trench for about 80 yards to locate a Lewis gun at the end; during the course of the work Lieutenant Penfold was wounded. C Company under 35-year-old Lieutenant St John[51] pushed a sap forward about 80 yards from Sutherland Trench. Losses continued on 7 August when three ORs were killed, one officer and nine OR wounded and one OR was listed as missing.

During the time in High Wood two men were wounded severely enough to warrant them being discharged from the Army. On 11 August Stk47 Lance Corporal Percy Carpenter, a 22-year-old warehouseman born in Westminster was wounded by a shell. He was severely injured on his left side and received more superficial injuries to his right arm. After treatment in France he was put onto the Hospital Ship *St Patrick* and transferred to the Highfeets Hall Hospital near Southampton. Posted to 6RF on 17 November his final medical report on 31 January described his wounds and condition. It said that he was still suffering from breathlessness, his flat feet which had been strained in France were causing pain and he was generally debilitated. Lance Corporal William Haslam of C Company, a 21-year-old stockbroker's clerk, received wounds to his leg which resulted in the limb being amputated. He was in a number of hospitals in England, completing his treatment at Queen Mary's in Roehampton. He was discharged with a pension and an artificial limb at the end of June 1917, returning to his father's house in Leigh-on-Sea, Essex.

The proximity of the enemy did not mean that the battalion knew the layout of the German defences or how the lines were configured. The dense woodland had prevented aerial reconnaissance providing pictures of the trenches. The nature of the troops facing the battalion was also a mystery which needed a solution. A reconnaissance carried out on 7 August by Corporal Albert Duligall warranted an extensive entry in the Battalion Diary, and the incident was included in the citation for the award of his DCM which was published in *The London Gazette* on 26 September. Starting from the north-west corner of High Wood he crawled 400 yards along a line running parallel to the road between High Wood and Bazentin–le-Petit, he then turned to the north-west and continued. He discovered German sentries at intervals of 50 yards, and ascertained that they came from the 163rd Regiment. He next shot a German officer, and continued his journey along the western edge of High Wood, shooting a German sentry about 60 yards away. He returned safely to the battalion line. On the same day Captain Dallas Waters confirmed that the German trench ran diagonally through High Wood, about 80 yards from the British lines. The personalisation of features was continued with the extension of St John Sap to join with Penfold Sap, both named after the officers responsible for their development, completing a new front line about 300 yards nearer to the German line.

Preparations by the Royal Engineers to mine under the German trenches in High Wood were set in train on 8 August, when 10RF was relieved by their sister battalion, 13RF. The Germans had realised that any reinforcement had to use a limited number of routes and had shelled these fairly regularly. Four men were wounded in the reserve trenches in Mametz Wood, so the decision was taken to move two companies towards the southern edge of the wood. During the time in rest the battalion was engaged in salvaging equipment, burning rubbish and generally tidying the area. Under regular shellfire they had two OR wounded on 10th, six OR wounded on 11th and one more on 12th.

On 11 August in Manchester Captain Ronald Campbell died of the wounds he had received at Pozières three weeks earlier. His family buried him in the family mausoleum in the little graveyard of Keils Old Church on the Isle of Jura. Described by Maxwell as 'a Scottish Laird', Campbell was a barrister who had degrees from Cambridge University. The youngest son of Colin Campbell, the head of Clan Campbell, he had been in the battalion since its formation, and in the photograph of officers taken in Andover looks older than his twenty-six years.

On the 14th a relief by 1 Loyals meant the 10RF could move further back into Bottom Wood where they were surrounded by heavy gun batteries operated by British, Australian and French Artillery Units. A new draft of men arrived and when the battalion trained on 16 August these men were drilled together by the RSM. Baths provided a welcome relief on the 15th and 16th, the previous two weeks having been hot and without rain.

Captain Ronald Campbell, joined the battalion in Colchester. World War One Photos

Letters from Mountfort in hospital in London moved quickly from containing information about his colleagues in 10RF. He wrote of the Zeppelin raids on London and the opportunities to see friends and pay visits to the theatre and music hall. He remained in Mile End Hospital where, although his wound was fairly superficial, it was slow to heal and he became the longest serving patient from 10RF in the hospital.

The battalion moved from the Somme on 18 August, travelling by train from Fréchencourt Station to a place spelled in the diary as Ariancs [actually Airaines] south of Abbeville. They marched from here to Allery a village further to the west. Here the battalion found the lack of open latrines and rubbish sites a welcome relief from the conditions near the front line. A night in this peaceful spot was followed by a march to Longpré-les-Corps-Saints, about 6 miles away, where they took a train to Bailleul, a journey which took from 5pm to 2:30am the following morning. Back on the Belgian border, west of Armentières where they had first experienced the war in July 1915, they next moved, on the 20th, into a billet in a former flour mill in Estaires. Sited in safety behind the area being shelled, this town of 6,500 people was a revelation with open shops and civilians moving freely. The diarist noted with some relief that this was the first time for thirteen months that the battalion was in an area free from shelling. The relief was short-lived as the battalion was told they had one day's further respite before returning to the trenches on the 22nd. From here Wilkinson wrote home a short letter, with the address 'in a quiet spot under the pit heads'. After describing the bad weather and the distance covered in the previous days he goes on to describe his guard duty on the previous evening:

> 'My guard last night under the stars was quite enjoyable and the circumstances led to one of those heart to hearts with my companion which the darkness and quiet of the night make possible. Of course our thoughts were of home. His of his wife and little ones, mine of mother and home. It is very interesting trying to understand the nature of others, their points of view and their circumstances. A chap of my own age tells me how he misses his 'old woman' and longs to see his two youngsters, how when twenty-one he scraped together £1 a week at basket making and paper selling to tide over the expensive period at the birth of his son and heir.
>
> 'And then there is the City man who paid a guinea a week for thirteen months to an ear specialist and then told the specialist that 'he thought he had better see a doctor' which he did and obtained relief from pain by simple application of Vaseline.'

A change in orders on the 21st cancelled the move to the front and ordered the battalion to rejoin the 37th Division. Taking the train from La Gorgue to Calonne-sur-la-Lys near Saint-Pol, they took over billets at Camblain-Châtelain, with the Divisional HQ at Bruay-la-Buissière, about 2 miles away. The battalion continued drilling and training until 30 August when they marched in rain and wind to take over huts from the Honourable Artillery Company in the Bois du Bouvigny, south of Bully-les-Mines.

The first days of September were spent in training, specialists in their groups and the other men in companies. On the morning of the 4th Major General Count Gleichen, the divisional commander, inspected the battalion and complimented the men on their smart turn out. He also said how pleased he was to have the battalion back in the 37th Division. His pleasure was short lived as on the following day the battalion marched to Bully-Grenay and became attached to the 190th Infantry Brigade of the 63rd (Naval) Division. They took up position in reserve in the Calonne Sector and officers rapidly reconnoitred the routes to the front in case support was required.

On 6 September two companies, A and C, were sent to Fosse 10 and their place was taken in the 10RF by two companies from 10th Battalion, Royal Dublin Fusiliers. This amalgamated battalion set off the following day to relieve 13RF in the trenches in the Colonne sector. The distance to the German lines was between 100 and 180 yards and the battalion HQ was in a damaged house about 400 yards from the front line. The battalion had launched some trench mortars and sent bombers across to visit the German lines. However come nightfall the German machine gunners retaliated and strafed the area around battalion HQ and some of the trenches, but caused no casualties or damage. It was worse on the 8th when the Germans shelled the battalion lines and HQ for most of the day, killing five and wounding two men with one shell.

Trench warfare took on the rhythm the battalion had become familiar with earlier in the year. Raids, trench mortars and bombers kept the men busy. Artillery bombardments, described in the diary as 'feeble' did require regular repairs to the trenches and support lines. The battalion cleared up a mystery left by their predecessors who had reported a sniper operating from a railway truck. The 10RF identified the source of flashes as ricochets of their own bullets hitting the iron on the side of the truck.

Machine guns and Lewis guns were used to fire on trenches and to break up working parties in the German lines. Patrols were sent out but did not find any evidence of German patrols in the area. On the 11th the battalion was relieved by the 4th Battalion, Bedford Regiment and marched to billets in Verdrel. The A and C companies marched back from Fosse 10 and the Royal Dublin Fusiliers left. The reformed battalion found Verdrel to be sheltered from observation by the Germans by a belt of trees, but the accommodation and water supplies were poor. To overcome the latter problem the Engineers had constructed a concrete reservoir on the edge of the village with a capacity of 500,000 gallons.

Roland Mountfort remained in hospital until the middle of September. He then moved to join 6RF, one of the reserve battalions at Dover. His wound proved slow to heal and his A3 classification was continued so he was transferred to the 32nd Training Reserve at Longhill Camp near Dover. The men in this detail were very different from the fit, enthusiastic volunteers in Colchester eighteen months before. He remained in Dover until February when he joined a draft for 25th Battalion (Frontiersmen) RF in East Africa.

On 12 September the battalion lost its strongest advocate and figurehead. Colonel The Hon Robert White, who had recruited and led the battalion from its formation, was promoted and left to take up command of 184th Infantry Brigade. His place was taken on a temporary basis by Major Rice of the Scottish Horse who had been attached to 13RB.

By the middle of September the personnel of the battalion was very different from those who had arrived in France thirteen months earlier. Most of the original officers were gone, having been killed, wounded or promoted. The NCOs had suffered similarly, as evidenced by Mountfort's letter describing the promotions following Pozières.

However, the spirit of the battalion was not lost. Some drafts came from the Public Schools Battalion, transferred in May and took the opportunity to blend into the 10th and adopt its pride and practices. White had retained some of the officers, like Maxwell, the transport officer, and Dallas Waters, who became adjutant. Some senior NCOs, like Company Sergeant Major 'Polly' Perkins of C Company, Sergeant John Coast of the same company and Sergeant James Haddow of 11 Platoon, were original recruits who had progressed through the ranks to hold these key positions. The spirit remained.

Chapter 12

Battle of The Ancre:
September to December 1916

For the rest of the week the battalion trained at Verdrel. On 17 September 1916 they marched back to Bully-Grenay, reoccupied the billets that they had used there earlier in the month and were reunited with the rest of 111 Brigade which now took over from 190 Brigade in the area. After another two days training in wet weather they took the place of 13KRRC in the trenches near Calonne. The handover went smoothly despite the German shrapnel which accompanied the last men taking up their positions.

The HQ of the battalion was in the ruined village of Calonne, with the men billeted there living in the cellars of the houses. There was a steady, though not intense, firing of artillery and trench mortars onto the lines occupied by 10RF and the British artillery responded. The lines and wire were in poor condition and the battalion set to work to improve the situation. They suffered from frequent mortar attacks, which were trying but inflicted little damage. Suspicions that the Germans were reinforcing their positions were strengthened as the men in the front trenches could clearly hear heavy transport moving behind the German lines. The Royal Engineers exploded a camouflet on the 23rd, to destroy German mining attempts. The underground explosion created a large cavern below the surface, collapsing any shafts and tunnels in the vicinity.

Work continued to improve trenches, communication trenches and wire. An attempt to site a trench mortar was disrupted by the Germans firing a number of shells into the area, but without causing casualties. On the 26th the 13KRRC relieved the battalion in the trenches and the men moved back into support taking over the Calonne defences, which had been built by the Pioneers of the 6th Battalion, The Welsh Regiment the previous June and were described in the diary as being 'very strong and somewhat complicated'. The battalion was not rested during the days in the defences. They had to provide 200 men for the RE working and tunnelling parties, both day and night; the others were engaged in guard duties around the defences.

During the time spent in the trenches six other ranks, were wounded, most described in the diary as 'slightly'. The diary also names Sergeant A.H. Waterhouse as being wounded on the 22nd. Arthur Waterhouse, Stk568, had enlisted with his two brothers, Gerald and Stanley who were Stk566 and 567 respectively. The brothers came from Hull where their father was a seed-oil merchant. Arthur, the eldest at 33 when he signed on, was in the family business as a broker, Stanley, aged 30 was a clerk in a timber merchants and the youngest, Gerald aged 25, was an engineer. Both Stanley and Gerald transferred from 10RF to take commissions in the East Yorkshire Regiment, Gerald in November 1916 and Stanley in January 1917; Gerald later transferred to the Royal Engineers. All three brothers survived the war.

Wilkinson's letters reduced in both length and frequency for a while after his spell in hospital following Pozières. He broke his silence on 29 September to tell his father that it was some time since he had received a letter 'from Miss Seal'. There had been a few cryptic references to a correspondence with a young lady, but this is the first time he mentioned her real name. It is possible that she was a teacher who lived in Wembley.

Relieving 13KRRC in the trenches the battalion began its next tour of duty on 1 October. They had little activity, apart from a raid on the 4th, for which an officer and sixteen men had been training during the previous week under the command of the colonel in Bully-Grenay. Second Lieutenant Ground, who had joined the battalion with the number Stk101 and 21-year-old Sergeant Hunt, a draper's assistant from Plymouth, led the two parties who spent about two minutes in the German trenches, which they discovered to be unoccupied. They returned under a strong barrage fire. The Germans did not retaliate to the incursion.

The relief of the battalion by 13th KRRC was delayed by twenty-four hours because divisional fronts were being altered. They were eventually able to march back to Bully-Grenay on 9 October and spent the next day cleaning up after eighteen days in the trenches. In addition to cleaning equipment all the men had a bath and were allocated clean clothing. On 11 October Wilkinson wrote home with some news about the previous weeks, but with little detail. He did ask his father to do him a favour:

> 'Willie Roe has written me a long letter urging me to put in for a commission and I have decided to try and get it through. Will you please write to the War Office for "Application Form for admission to a cadet unit" (Form No MT. 393) and obtain the necessary signatures and then send it on to me to sign and put through. I don't know whose signatures are required but I am sending you a few addresses which may come in handy.'

Training was carried out each morning for the rest of the week. A draft of 115 ORs arrived on the 14th described as 'quality good, only one old soldier i.e. who had been to France before'. They spent the next day training and drilling with Captain Dallas Waters, the Adjutant.

On 17 October the battalion began another move, this time on foot. On the first day they marched a distance of 9 miles to Maisnil-lès-Ruitz, with no men falling out. The following day they continued to Ostreville, a distance of 13 miles, it was a dull cold day, described as being 'fine for marching'. A day to rest on the 19th, with the planned parade cancelled because of bad weather, was followed on the 20th by a further march of 11 miles to Rebreuviette. The next day's march was made a little easier as lorries took the men's packs, but the roads were in poor condition, in some places being no more than field tracks, although shown on the maps as second class roads. This necessitated putting extra horses to draw the wagons over the rougher than expected ground. The battalion covered 13 tiring miles arriving in the evening at Beauval, where forty men from each company were rewarded with a hot bath and all were relieved to find they had good billets. Moving further the next day they marched 8 miles to Puchevillers where they were put into a hutted camp in a 'dirty orchard'. They had marched a total of 54 miles in five stages with no man falling out and all men and horses arriving in good health. The battalion was now back in the vicinity of the Somme about 15 miles west of Albert.

Training was curtailed; B Company was sent out road cleaning and the others undertook short route marches. On 24 October three lost officers eventually caught up with the battalion. Captain St John, a stockbroker, and Second Lieutenant Herridge had been on leave, Second Lieutenant Stone was returning from a course and all had some difficulty in finding where the fast moving battalion was located. Still more rain made the camp even more muddy and training was restricted until the 28th when the rain eased enough to allow the battalion to practise attacking in lines, following an artillery creeping barrage. On the following day officers and NCOs practised attacking an objective some distance away using column of route and artillery formations.

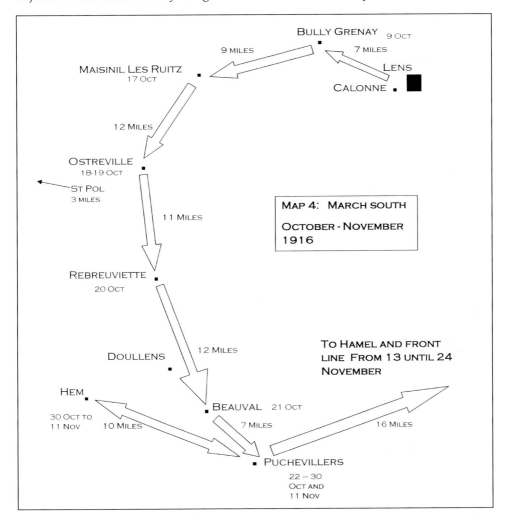

The battalion moved west, away from the fighting, and after covering about 7 miles reached the main Beauval to Talmas road where they were informed that their destination was to be a further 5 miles on at the village of Hem, with the overflow of the battalion to take up billets in Hardinval, just across the river. The weather was atrocious with torrential rain; the battalion stopped for dinner and arrived in Hem by 7pm. The next nine days were spent in light training in the morning, weather permitting, and sport in the afternoon. There were matches between the battalion and 10 Loyals, two football matches were drawn, the 10RF won at rugby. The officers of 10RF lost at rugby to the officers of 13RF and internally C Company beat D Company at rugby. On 7 November there was a visit from Brigadier General The Hon R. White, who took the opportunity to see his old battalion as his HQ was close by at Occoches. On the 10th the battalion trained in the morning, observed by Major General Williams who had taken command of 37th Brigade. A rugby match against Brigade HQ, scheduled for the afternoon was cancelled as the brigade had to prepare to move on the following morning. George Wilkinson wrote home on the 12th to catch up on the events of the previous two weeks. He had received a parcel just before the move away from Bully-Grenay and had been stuck with the volume of goodies that he somehow had to pack away. He described:

'of course every corner of my pack and haversack had been crammed and there still remained two tins of delight to be carried. I found a secret corner on the gun wagon and waited the order to move off with the feeling of triumph which so often rewards the resourceful. Our departure was delayed by an hour or two. The CO had an idea. He paraded the whole (MG) Company by the limbers and carefully went through all the weapons and found much that should not be there. He promised 28 days number one [field punishment] to any future offenders and then left us. My own tins were not found but I removed them while there was peace and they found a resting place in my jacket pockets.'

The brigade marched back to Puchevillers, arriving in the dark because of delays caused by having to wait for the passing of convoys of transport on the roads. In the mid afternoon of the 12th they moved again, reaching Varennes at 8pm. A departure at 3:30pm on 13 November was the start of a very long day of marching and finding positions. The first task for the battalion was to find the village of Englebelmer, which they reached after nightfall.

The Battle of the Ancre which began on 13 November was intended to advance the British lines northward beyond Beaumont Hamel towards Serre, Beaucourt and Grandcourt. Beaumont Hamel was captured on the 13th and an attack was made on the Redan Ridge to the left of Beaumont Hamel, but this ran into difficulties caused by the wire defences of the Quadrilateral, and the quantity of mud through which the troops had to advance. Further west the attack on Serre by 3rd Division also faltered because of the mud.

On 14 November 10RF entered the battle and advanced with the support of a tank towards a German redoubt which had been bypassed in the advance made on the previous day by the Royal Naval Division. The battalion captured 270 Germans and released 60 English prisoners without a shot being fired. They also took three machine

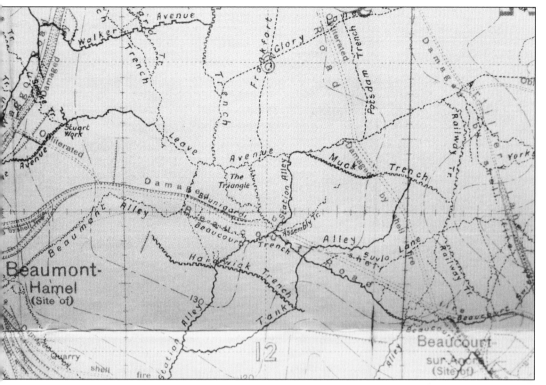

Trench map of the area between Beaumont Hamel and Beaucort fought over by 10RF in November 1916. GH Smith & Son

guns and spent much of the day collecting wounded of both sides from the area. At the same time other battalions in the 111 Brigade, 13RF and 13KRRC were advancing towards Beaucourt and their final objective of Muck Trench about 600 yards beyond the village. Orders for 15 November required the battalion to take over a portion of the new front line. A reconnoitring party advancing north up Station Alley discovered a group of Germans still in the trench, which was supposed to be in British hands, they took nine prisoners and moved on. Taking over from 13KRRC they established themselves facing the German line by 2am on the morning of the 16th.

The battalion was ordered to attack trenches in what became known as The Triangle, the junction of Frankfurt and Munich Trenches with Leave Avenue. They attacked at dawn but were held up by rifle and machine gun fire. A party of bombers reached the junction at 3:45pm but had to withdraw. One officer, Lieutenant Stephenson, was killed and another, Second Lieutenant Thorpe, was listed as missing, believed captured. The battalion was next ordered to occupy Muck Trench (the amount of mud found in it gave it its name) and to establish four strongpoints along the length from Leave Avenue to Railway Avenue, a distance of about 600 yards. The trench was occupied and attempts to establish the strong points were foiled in daylight by strong enemy barrages. Eventually under cover of darkness Second Lieutenant Ground set up two points with machine guns on the left and Second Lieutenant Moore attempted but failed to establish two on the right. These were eventually set up by Second Lieutenant Rupert Bambridge at the cost of six casualties.

Reinforcements were sent to the left side of the trench because orders had been received to attack the Triangle again, to coincide with the main attack by 32nd Division. On the night of the 17-18th the machine gun team at the left post was knocked out by a shell. The battalion diary record is brief:

> *'The officer in charge, Second Lieutenant Grey (111 Coy MGC), and nearly all the team being killed.'*

A grenade buried on the track near The Triangle. Author

View south from near Muck Trench. Author

At 6:10am on the 18th the battalion carried out the order to attack The Triangle. All the parties, with the exception of that led by Second Lieutenant Barker achieved their objectives. Barker's party was opposed strongly and was unable to enter Leave Avenue. The right flank of 32nd Division also failed to achieve its objectives and so the 10RF parties had to withdraw. One officer, Second Lieutenant Barnes, was killed and other casualties were sustained. Another attack during that night, carried out by two strong officer patrols was supposed to have artillery support, but the ranging had not been carried out so this was ineffectual. Second Lieutenant Bambridge and Second Lieutenant Heywood led the patrols, again they had to withdraw and Bambridge was wounded. That marked the end, for the time being, of the action for 10RF in Muck Trench. During the night of 19-20 November they were relieved by 13RF and two companies of 10 Loyals and retired to Station Road, moving the next day to Englebelmer.

Not all the battalion left the area in good health. George Wilkinson had been with the Left Post machine gun party when it was shelled. He wrote to his mother on 22nd, four days after the shelling, to say:

'My dear mother, I am sure you will be glad to know that I am right away from the firing line again. Fritz has given me a few scratches so I am now having a fine time in hospital and I hope to be over the worst in a few days then I can see you.'

On the 24th a telegram addressed to George's father arrived in Hammersmith, from the OC Kitchener Hospital, Brighton. It informed him that George was a patient in the hospital and:

'The stationmaster at Hammersmith will issue one full return ticket on application.'

Wilkinson wrote to his mother on 25th from hospital in Brighton giving a little more information about what had happened.

'My dear mother, You will see that I am in dear old blighty once more. All through trying conclusion with a whizz-bang which has given me a lovely black eye not to mention one or two flesh wounds. I am quite sound and ought to be getting about soon. Ain't I lucky to be dumped here? It's an Australian Hospital and I'm nearly killed by kindness.'
'I am £4 in credit so shall be all right for money when I come out.
'I've had some thrilling experiences and a miraculous escape. I was two days lying wounded in a shell hole, but I crawled [word missing] trust me. Parnell was alright when I last saw him.'

The writing is shaky, he is not clear about what actually happened and he probably has little idea of the fate of the others in his team.

A later letter to Wilkinson from his friend Stk1311 William Walpole dated 21 January 1917 gave some details of what happened:

'I spoke to Sgt Lees at his position, then went to HQ and spoke to Ground, the Officer I had spoken to in the morning and who was in command at that point. He told me you *were being carried down to the aid post. Mr Crowther also telephoned and was told you had gone. By then it was 2 or 3 days after you had been wounded. Surely you were not out there all that time? You must have had the most terrible experiences possible.'*

A letter written by Parnell suggested that Wilkinson may have received a head wound which meant he was unconscious for some of the time he was in the shell hole.

'You didn't get a pleasant 'Blighty' did you, but knowing what I do I think you have tons to thanks Providence for that you were able to get back at all. Another sixteenth of an inch in your head I suppose and we should have all been desolate.'

Letters are fewer during this period, possibly because members of his family visited him in Brighton, but he continued to receive letters from members of 10RF with news of the actions and fate of others. By 20 November 1917 he was discharged from hospital and, having had some home leave, was on his way to Harrowby Camp, Grantham, the base depot of the Machine Gun Corps. In his letter of that date he said that on the train from King's Cross he met Hubert Smith, who was the man responsible for the noises in the dugout with the accordion near Monchy-au-Bois. Smith told him that while Wilkinson was 'resting' with a sprained ankle (after Pozières) he, Smith, went down the line on a stretcher suffering from a combination of nerves and rum ration 'more of the latter so he affirms'.

Fifty-seven officers and men were killed or died of wounds in the period from 13 November to 3 December. The list demonstrates the change in character of the battalion; less than a third of the fifty-eight men who died had the prefix Stk. The geographical spread of home towns had increased, largely through taking drafts from other battalions. The Sports Battalion, 23RF, had taken a number of recruits from the cotton towns around Manchester and the occupations of warp dyer and spinner appear in the list; the 18th Public Schools Battalion had recruits without a public or grammar school background and took many from the midlands and north. Rather than the preponderance of clerks and City office employees there appeared boot makers, farm labourers and domestic gardeners. Some city jobs remain in the lists, insurance clerks, shipping clerks, stockjobbers and brokers clerks, but there were also warehousemen, furniture polishers and storekeepers. Some unusual occupations feature – the footman to a Norfolk landowner, the violinist in the Brighton Municipal Orchestra, the son of a magnetic bone doctor – but the accents, tones and perhaps style of the battalion was now different to what it had been six months previously, and would now change again as the battalion was receiving recruits to the regiment not solely from the linked training battalion. In pockets the old Stockbroker spirit remained. C Company had a group of NCOs and men who had been with the battalion either from the start or had joined early in 1916.

Chapter 13

Into 1917:
December 1916 to March 1917

Puchevillers was the base for the battalion during the first two weeks of December. The time was spent in training, parades before the brigade and corps commanders, sheltering from the rain and snow, and receiving a draft of 156 untrained men. The introduction for these new recruits must have been unsettling for the day following their arrival the battalion received orders to make their way to another unknown destination, this time to the north.

The move began on 13 December with a march of 9 miles to Doullens. The following day's march took them to Rougefay, a distance of 16 miles, meeting the GOC 37th Division at Mézerolles en route. Next day, after a march of 10 miles they finished at Oeuf-en-Ternois, with the benefit of good billets. Eighteen miles the next day in cold but fine weather and passing through Saint-Pol took them to Sachin where they were again given good billets. Nine miles on the 17th ended at Ecquedecques. A turn to the north-east and a march of 13 miles brought them to the new area where they established battalion HQ at Quentin, about a mile and a half away from Brigade HQ at Calonne-sur-la-Lys. A break for the men while officers visited the trenches in Neuve Chapelle was followed by a short 6-mile march to Vieille Chapelle and on 21 December the battalion arrived at the new trenches in the Neuve Chapelle sector. The battalion found the new area to have good billets, and a local population well disposed to the men who were imposed on them.

A total distance of nearly 90 miles in eight days was accomplished with few if any men dropping out, thus ensuring that the battalion retained its proud position as the best marching battalion in the brigade. A direct journey from Puchevillers is about 50 miles but the need to remain in the areas to the rear of the lines necessitated the diversion west and north of the direct route.

On 21 December the battalion took over part of the line from 5th Division troops of The Devonshire Regiment and The Devon and Cornwall Light Infantry. All over Christmas there were regular artillery bombardments and mortar shelling by both sides, causing five deaths among the 10RF. Relieved by 13KRRC on 27 December the battalion took up billets in a village, called in the War Diary, Croix Barbee, but is probably La Croix Barbet, where they took the opportunity to have baths and change clothes. Training and use of the rifle range made sure that the men remained sharp, and that the new recruits were assimilated. The risk of an attack meant that one platoon was on piquet duty, sleeping with their boots on to be ready at instant notice.

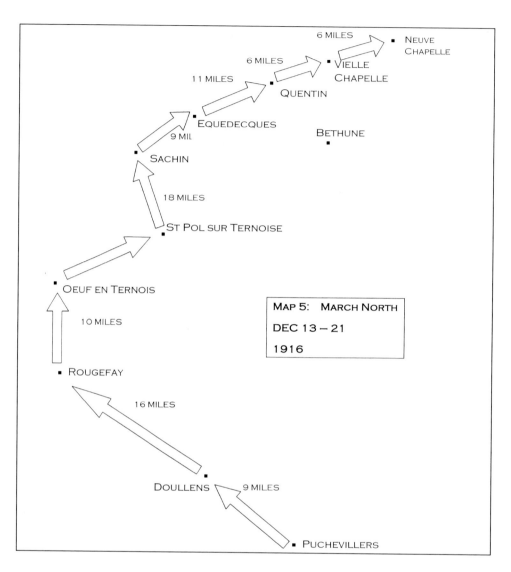

6 MILES

■ NEUVE CHAPELLE

6 MILES

■ VIELLE CHAPELLE

11 MILES

QUENTIN

■ EQUEDECQUES

BETHUNE ■

9 MIL

■ SACHIN

18 MILES

■ ST POL SUR TERNOISE

■ OEUF EN TERNOIS

10 MILES

■ ROUGEFAY

16 MILES

MAP 5:   MARCH NORTH

DEC 13 – 21

1916

DOULLENS ■   9 MILES

■ PUCHEVILLERS

On 2 January 1917 the battalion moved into reserve at Locon, where they were rejoined on the 4th by a detachment of 148 ORs who had been training in Calonne-sur-la-Lys under Captain Goldthorpe. A parade scheduled for 5th was carried out under some difficulty. The owner of the field originally selected for the purpose forced the battalion to move to another field which was waterlogged. Lieutenant General Sir Richard Haking the GOC of XI Corps praised the men as being 'the best turned out battalion I have seen in the last year'. After the parade the men enjoyed their delayed Christmas dinner and the CO read out the list of honours and awards won by the battalion. It included a Military Cross for Captain Penfold and a DCM for Acting Regimental Sergeant Major Rowbotham; five men received Mentions in Despatches.

The announcement of the confirmation by the divisional commander that the battalion had the best marching record during the return from the Ancre was well received. Two days later the sergeants had their Christmas dinner and the men had baths. After more baths the next day medal ribbons were awarded to one officer and ten ORs by the divisional commander. A group of ninety men under the command of the adjutant went to the brigade depot at Senechal Farm for training. Having lost their band earlier to the division, the battalion established its own fife and drum band which began to practise under Corporal Morris of the divisional band.

On 15 January the battalion began a week in the trenches, relieving the 8th Battalion Somerset Light Infantry. The stay was fairly quiet, with the opportunity taken to improve the wiring, there was occasional mortaring of enemy lines, which led to a response in the form of an artillery barrage on the right of the battalion lines but there were no fatalities. The Germans sent patrols towards the British lines, and the snipers claimed some successes; one German deserted into the battalion lines.

In rest at La Fosse the detachment from brigade depot returned and the men were allocated to their companies. Working parties were provided from B and D companies to work in the trenches, A Company continued with routine training and C Company undertook special training in preparation for a raid scheduled for 1 February. They remained behind to train at Senechal Farm when the rest of the battalion returned to the trenches on 26 January. To replace them in the trenches E Company was created with Lieutenant Pratt in command and Company Sergeant Major Perkins from C Company as senior NCO, taking one platoon from each of A, B and D companies. Over three nights wire was cut in preparation for the planned raid, but the Germans replaced it over night and during the early hours. Finally on 31 January the brigadier called off the raid because a new plan included a move into brigade reserve with the battalion taking up billets at Merville and La Gorgue on 1 and 2 February.

After two days the battalion was relieved and moved to Bout-Delville. The weather in early February 1917 was bitterly cold and the men had to find ways to shelter and keep warm, even in the reserve lines comforts were few. All the extra baggage was collected and taken to the brigade dump at Calonne-sur-la-Lys and from 2 February the battalion was at six hours notice to move. A group of twenty men of the 1st Artist Rifles was attached to the battalion for training. Leaving Bout-Delville, 5 miles on the first day took them to Locon, the next day they marched a further 5 miles to the south, passing through Bethune, arriving at Fouquereuil. On the third day the march took them east towards the lines of the Hulluch Sector, to the north of Lens. Here they relieved the 1st Battalion, North Staffordshire Regiment in the support trenches and sat in the thawing mud as the temperature rose and water replaced ice as the source of aggravation. On 18 February, in mud described in the diary as 'awful' the 10RF relieved the 13KRRC in the right subsector front line trenches. While the battalion was at Calonne Private Charles Wise went home on leave.

Writing after the war he recounted his experience:

'At that period it was only a ten day leave and in all my life I have never known time to pass so quickly. I can still recall quite clearly some of the things I did on my first ten day leave. Some of them were rather disappointing such as my complete inability to book

seats for 'Chu Chin Cow', 'The Bing Boys' and 'Carnival'. However I was fortunate in my efforts to get seats for the show 'Romance' with Doris Keane in the leading role. Again I was fortunate on the day I was to return to the battalion. My father came to Victoria Station with me and I had just shaken hands in a goodbye clasp when over the loudspeaker came the following announcement: "Cross Channel Boats cancelled all men scheduled to return to their units fall in an orderly queue, go to the RTO's office, get your passes stamped for an extra day, draw money for one day's rations and return here in time for the 7:30am train tomorrow."

'The following morning came all too quickly and on this occasion there was no further respite. Late that afternoon I crawled off the boat at Calais and made my miserable way to a tent that already held two dejected artillery men also on their way back. The bugle sounded "Cookhouse" and I shuffled out of the tent and down a duckboard track and lo and behold I walked into one of our battalion signallers, Alec Newton, like magic much of the lonely gloom departed. Brothers in distress we linked arms and went in to a surprisingly good tea and in the evening a 'show' by one of the professional parties. The following morning Alec and I paraded and were marched to the station and clambered onto a cattle truck. Directly opposite the door was a lady with portable harmonium and in spite of the bitter cold this gallant person entertained us with melodies in which we all joined. But oh dear! As we drew very slowly out of that Depot the strains of that very sad song 'God Send You Back To Me' floated to us on the cold air. One young soldier collapsed in tears, but no one thought any worse of him and rough sympathy was extended to the young lad. Finally with long stops at St Omer and Hazebrouck we drew into Bethune. Here we met trouble. A brassy voiced MP started on the leave party. At that time I was the type that cringed at the sound of authority; not so a party of Argyll and Sutherland Highlanders: "Go and jump into the canal you crawling lump of S—-!" The whole of the leave party seemed to erupt and the transport officer arrived and took over. He was a nice man and to our amazement sent the MP packing. Finally we were seen by the clerk who told us we would have to return the following day as it was not certain where the 111 Brigade was.

'I knew Bethune very well for we had been billeted in the town every time the Public Schools battalion came out of the trenches from November 1915 to April 1916. I took Alec to an RAMC depot and we got a stretcher and blankets each, and had a very good night's sleep. We were awakened at 6am with a hot cup of tea, washed and dressed and made our way to the Café d'Intimes and the old dame recognised me and cooked us both a good breakfast for which we paid a reasonable price and at about 8am came by way of the Rue du Vieux Beffroi, Rue d'Ecole du Jeune Fille, Rue de La Gare to the RTO's office. We learned the battalion was in the village of Philosophe so without more ado we set off. We had completed about 3km when we were overtaken by GS wagon belonging to 10RF whose driver relieved us of our packs and told us the orderly room was in Philosophe and the Transport in Mazingarbe and the battalion was in the line at Hulluch. He said he would dump our packs in the orderly room, and drove on. When we arrived at the orderly room Sergeant 'Elsie' Broad was in the office and a Captain Guy Goldthorpe told us to go to RQM Clements. This we did and he told us we could stay at the Transport Lines for our lunch and tea and go up to HQ with the ration.'

In Philosophe forty men of C Company began to train for a raid to be carried when next in the trenches. Training of the remainder of the battalion continued and there was an inspection of transport by the Divisional OC Transport. After only four days in rest the battalion returned to the trenches at Hulluch, relieving the 13KRRC. The raid was carried out as planned by C Company on the night of Thursday 1 March. The cost to the 10RF was one man wounded, Private William Whitehall, who died the following day. He was originally with the 1st Battalion, East Surrey Regiment and had been in France since October 1914. He was part of a draft from 11th East Surreys arriving in 10RF early in 1917. He had married Henrietta Underhill, in 1914, just before leaving for France and their son, William, was born just after his father died.

The battalion remained in the trenches for a further two days after the raid, being relieved on 4 March by 14th Battalion, Devon and Cornwall Light Infantry. Moving back west over rough and worn roads in cold but fine weather, with a stop in Labeuvrière, the battalion arrived in Ecquedecques, where they stayed for three days rest in reasonable billets with plenty of space as there were no other battalions in the village. On 9 March they established the HQ and two companies in Pressy and the other two companies with the transport on the other side of the river in Marest. A final march of 13 miles brought them through Saint-Pol to Buneville and the divisional training area based on Roëllecourt. The diarist proudly recorded that only two men fell out during the 35-mile march:

'and that on the first day in a snow storm, thus the Battalion's record as the best marching Battalion in 37 Div is still unchallenged.'

Training was carried out from 11 to 19 March, the emphasis being on the platoon in attack. On 20 March the diarist recorded:

'Instructions received for 2 Officers to proceed for attachment to 46 Inf Bde in Arras to reconnoitre - 3 days Capt Warner and A/Capt Shutes commanding B and D Coys respectively, selected. CO and Adj and Intell Offr and OC C Coy (Capt C R StJohn) also proceeded to Arras for a day to reconnoitre with a Bde party. Weather wet and miserable, roads skirting the city, assembly trenches and route to front line were reconnoitred assisted by CO 12th HLI at present in that sector.'

While the training and planning proceeded other events took place, notably a medal presentation which included four MMs for the battalion, and a brigade cross country race, won individually by Lance Corporal Stroud of 10RF who had just rejoined after being wounded earlier. Charlie Wise wrote that it was at 'the untidy little village of Buneville' that Stk247 Charlie Stroud returned to the battalion.

'He had been wounded in front of Berles au Bois on June 4 1916 and was evacuated to England and upon recovery was sent out with a draft to Etaples. He took part in number of foot races and one occasion ran the Scottish Champion Jock Wilson to a very close second in a three mile cross country run. However being a celebrity had its drawbacks

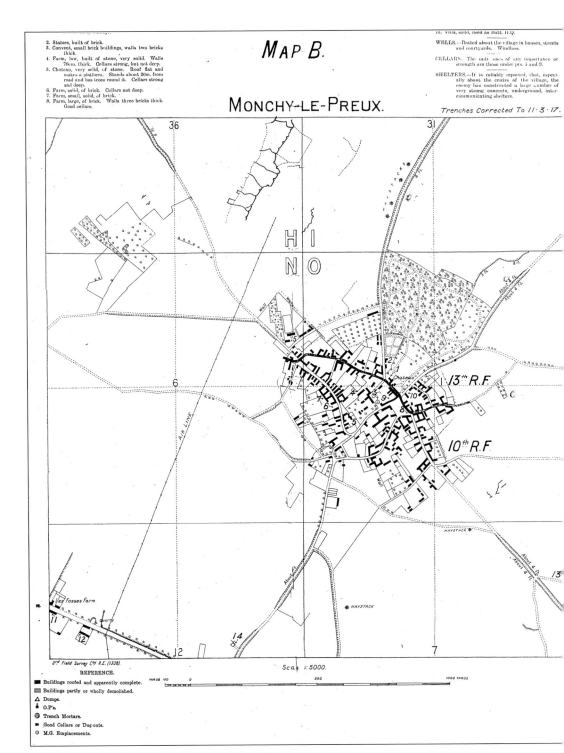

Detailed plan of Monchy-le-Preux used by 10RF in planning. Pen & Sword

for coming out of the baths one morning he ran into the RSM of the Bull Ring. Like most RSMs the greeting was in the politest language: "Here, You. Name." Charlie gave it. "You skrimshanking B———D I've been searching for you. Report to the orderly room." That same afternoon Charlie was on his way back to the battalion at Buneville. Upon arrival Charlie ran into Dallas Waters and after the usual enquiries about his health Dallas Waters asked Charlie if he played a musical instrument. Charlie replied that when he was a young boy he had played the fife in the Church Lad's Brigade. Dallas Waters told him to report to the Bandmaster and Charlie remained with the Transport Section until he was demobilised. Two days after his return Charlie entered the 37 Div three mile cross-country and came home minutes ahead of the field.'

Sergeant Stanley Whiteman wrote his memoir of the events of March 1917 after the war. A member of C Company, he began to practise attacks on a village near Buneville with the rest of the battalion.

The officers and NCOs learned that the target for their attack was the village of Monchy-le-Preux, east of Arras. Intelligence about the village had been collected in the preceding weeks and maps and pictures were distributed to the NCOs. The NCOs began their task of learning the maps and the information they contained, to the point where they could draw them from memory. This was the central sector of a major push on the German lines with the intention of breaking round and through the defensive line towards Germany. The battalion trained to perfect their execution of platoon in attack and open warfare; a significant change from the stagnant trench warfare of the previous two years.

Chapter 14

The Attack on Monchy-le-Preux: April 1917

At the end of 1916 the Allied Generals, Joffre and Haig, agreed that they would mount a co-ordinated series of attacks in the spring of 1917. The focus of the attack moved between the planning and execution stages because the situation changed over the winter. The Germans retreated to the Hindenburg Line meaning that the allied attack would be against much more strongly defended positions. The French were to move northwards from the River Aisne. The British were to attack at Arras as a diversion to keep the Germans engaged and unable to send reinforcements south. A bonus, if both plans were successfully exploited, would result from the British and French meeting up south of Cambria to encircle the Germans.

The British Third Army, which included 111 Brigade and 10RF in its 37th Division, was in the centre of the Arras attack with First and Fifth Armies on either flank. Overall the northern front was to be 15 miles long stretching from Lens to Croiselles with over 120,000 men in the storming line with a further 40,000 behind and in support. The First Army in the north was to take Vimy Ridge, the Third Army was to advance to Cambria and in the south General Gough's Fifth Army would attack the northern end of the Hindenburg line. The land over which the troops of the Third Army were to attack, was open and undulating, a series of shallow ridges, with the valley of the River Scarpe running from west to east, parallel to the direction of the attack, The planned line of advance was astride the River Scarpe with the high ground around Monchy-le-Preux as the first objective.

The first phase of the Third Army plan was to proceed through a series of lines, marking German positions, and moving towards Monchy-le-Preux. The first objective, the Black Line, was under a mile from Arras itself, and was the German front line which they had occupied since October 1914. A further 1000 yards to the east lay the second, the Blue Line, running across a feature called, Observation Ridge. There was a gap of 2500 yards to the next line, Brown, on the western flank of Orange Hill. This was the last natural obstruction before Monchy and was defended by two lines of trenches 100 yards apart. It incorporated a strong position, the Feuchy Chapel redoubt on the Arras to Cambria road. The Brown Line was the start point for the attack on Monchy itself a further 2000 yards to the east. Writing after the war Corporal Sydney Sylvester reflected that 'the attack on Monchy in the Battle of Arras was not by any means the worst of our experiences in France, but it was the first time we had broken out to open warfare from the mud and blood of trench warfare.'

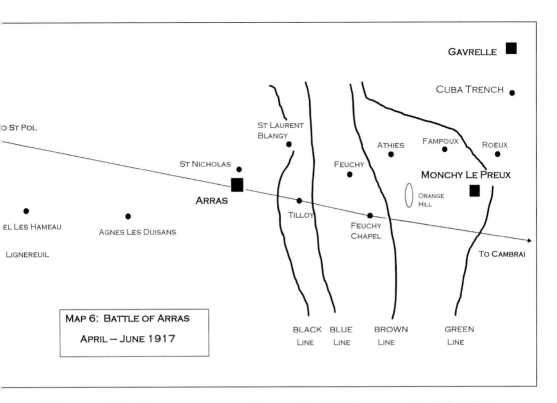

MAP 6: BATTLE OF ARRAS
APRIL – JUNE 1917

A feature of the German strategy not encountered before was that of the 'elastic defence'. A number of young German staff officers met in 1915 to consider how to maintain the maximum number of troops in fighting condition during the trench warfare that had evolved on the Western Front. They concluded that placing a minimal number of men in the front line protected the majority from artillery bombardment which by 1915 had become a standard precursor to an attack, seen at its most powerful on the Somme in 1916. The elastic defence required the men in the front line to make their presence known and so attract the usual bombardment and an attack over the top. As the attacking troops approached the front line the defenders would retreat and leave the attackers to make their way across no man's land, the wire and into the front line trenches, opposed by artillery and machine gun fire from rear positions. Once the attackers had got into the first trenches the Germans would mount a strong counter-attack on the pockets of troops which by this time could be expected to have broken formation and be under less direct control of officers and NCOs; communication with the headquarters and the supply of ammunition and equipment would be stretched. The British attack on Monchy was the first time the German General Von Lossberg was able to improvise an elastic defence in a battle.

On Wednesday 5 April in beautiful sunny spring weather, a contrast to the snow of the previous week, the battalion moved from Buneville towards the east. They halted at Izel-lès-Hameaux 9 miles nearer to Arras. Stk648 Sergeant John Coast was sent as representative of the battalion to view the tunnels in Arras. These had been constructed during the previous winter and were provided with beds, water supply and electric light and, according to Whiteman, were sufficient to hold three divisions, a total of about

60,000 men. The tunnels also incorporated a dressing station with 700 beds. The allied plan was that if the attack was held up by bad weather, men could be hidden in the caves out of sight of German aircraft. On his return Coast was in great demand by officers and men to recount what he had seen. He described the size of the shelters, the way in which men emerged for exercise after nightfall, the cramped and uncomfortable billets and the silence in the streets of Arras during the day. He said there was an amazing number of guns of all sizes in the fields around the town, tanks parked and waiting, cavalry hoping, at last, get into action and miles and miles of Army Service Corps and Engineers stores and ammunition dumps.

On Friday 6 April, Good Friday 1917, the battalion moved to Agnez-lès-Duisans a further 6 miles nearer the forthcoming battle, about 7 miles from Arras and 13 from Monchy-le-Preux, their target for the advance. Another move the following day took them closer to Arras where they were billeted in Nissen huts. If it hadn't already been clear to them it became obvious that they were nearer the action when, as Whiteman recounted:

'Kit had been taken off and hung on the floor [the huts] being made of iron no nails or hooks can be driven in to serve as pegs and everything getting snug for the night when with a sudden whiz and a roar accompanied by a rush of hot air through the hut a high velocity shell took refuge in mother earth about twelve feet from the front door. There followed a hurried exodus from the huts to a nearby roadway with high banks on each side for Hun shells, as a rule, do not travel alone but have two or three companions behind. Minutes went by, and still more, and nothing happened, only one shell had come over. After a quarter of an hour hearts lowered themselves from throats to normal positions, huts gradually became full of men again and in due course everyone having forgotten about the incident, but wondering what events the morrow would bring,"turned in" and slept the sleep of the just.'

By 10am on the morning of Easter Day, April 8, the battalion was on the move again to the east. At midday they had covered 5 miles, becoming very aware of the increased volume of the guns with every step as they moved forward. They went into a field on the side of the Saint-Pol to Arras road at Louez about a mile and a half from the centre of Arras. After they had been fed by the cooks from the travelling cookers, Colonel Rice called his officers and senior NCOs together for a briefing. Whiteman later recalled the briefing, paraphrasing what Rice had said:

'You all know, perhaps, the general attack starts tomorrow morning. The first phase of the attack will be carried out leap frog fashion. The first attacking Division on gaining its objective stays there; the next Division following behind passes through them and taking its objective stays in it. The next Division goes right through the other two in front of it and has to take possession of the Brown Line as the third German trench system is called. Then it is our Division's turn. The Brown Line is about three miles behind the present German front line. Once it has been captured we, moving slowly up behind the Division in front of us all the time, are to get into the Brown Line trenches, reorganise

platoons on account of losses, then go forward in open formation for our objective, the village of Monchy, having no one in front of us except the Germans. Artillery, both light and heavy will move forward as the attack proceeds.'

Aeroplanes carrying out observation flights reported that after passing the Brown Line there were few, if any German trenches. Any advance would be over open ground with no prepared cover. Experience from previous attacks would have led the men to hope for a good barrage to keep the Germans in their positions and also provide shell holes in which they could shelter.

Every man received fifty extra rounds of ammunition, Lewis guns were checked and inspected and rations for two days were drawn for each man. Stk594 Company Sergeant Major Reginald Perkins was sent back to the transport lines as part of the battalion reserve. His place as Company Sergeant Major of C Company was taken by Sergeant Edward Freemantle, Whiteman took over 9 Platoon, Sergeant Harold Howard was with 10 Platoon, Sergeant James Haddow with 11 Platoon and Sergeant Frank Swain with 12 Platoon. As night fell the guns began their barrage, lighting up the sky, and when the heavy guns half a mile away from 10RF joined the shooting they caused the candles to flicker and the bivouac sheets to bulge as the battalion huddled trying to sleep, knowing they would be called at 3am for breakfast.

The night sentries woke the officers and NCOs, and the men were roused to face the events of 9 April. In the pitch dark and with a cold wind blowing all ranks regretted that their greatcoats had been sent back to the transport lines the previous day. As dawn broke the sky was completely overcast with low rain clouds scudding over, a contrast to the pleasant sunshine of the previous days. At 4am the battalion moved forward and took up position behind the first line of heavy artillery. At 4:50 every gun along the front began to fire simultaneously. The Germans in the front line of trenches sent up rockets requesting that their artillery should retaliate, but the German gun positions were known and being targeted. Whiteman observed:

'With the increasing light of morning it was possible to see the German positions were one dense cloud of red, black and white smoke intermingled with dull red flashes of bursting shells.'

As the battalion took up position behind those preceding it the men passed through the lines of the guns. Whiteman described the precautions taken to avoid injury:

'Passing the line of 6, 8 and 9.2 inch howitzers with one's mouth open to reduce the possibility of concussion on the stomach leading to disastrous results and also lessen the effect on the ear drums, we advanced.'

The battalion were still in the St Catherine's suburb on the west side of Arras. It began to deluge with rain and they stopped in a wood for an hour as the troops ahead of them moved slowly forward. There was evidence that the advance was progressing when they saw about 100 German prisoners being led back. The men, who Whiteman described as having terror stricken faces, were being escorted by the Military Police and the battalion moved off the road to let them through. At 10am the battalion marched out of the wood. The artillery was packing up their guns to prepare a move forward. As the 10RF moved into Arras some wounded men were seen standing outside the dressing stations set up in cellars and shelters. By 11am 10RF again moved forward now in a file of twos, with 50 yards between platoons to reduce the size of the target if a shell happened to land nearby. This worked well as the battalion moved through Arras without halting. The leading platoon reached the entrance to the first communication trench, which led through a cemetery, and progress slowed as the men filed in. The next platoon, Number 10, was halted and two shells landed, one hitting a house, the other landed on the cobbled road just in front of the waiting men. Although he was wounded Sergeant Howard pushed forward to report to Captain St John that he had lost half of his platoon.

This incident caused the column to halt and then reverse direction for 300 yards and wait for five minutes before being ordered to turn and continue the advance. As they moved forward Whiteman fell over what he first thought was a body lying at the bottom of the trench but on investigation it turned out to be a man known to be a sufferer from shell shock. He showed the same symptoms on each occasion the battalion went into action. As they moved through the cemetery a huge blast and pall of black smoke behind them marked where a German shell had landed in one of the ammunition dumps sited around the city. Emerging from Arras they entered what at 4:50am had been the British front line; here they had a break and a smoke as they watched the shells landing on the village of Feuchy. The battalion moved up the first of the ridges ahead of them and somewhere crossed what had been the original German front line, however as Whiteman later recalled:

'There was absolutely nothing to distinguish it from the surrounding acres of brown earth. The trench would have probably been six or seven feet deep, the sides lined with wood or iron and the bottom paved with wooden duck boards. Deep dugouts there were certain to have been, supported by heavy wooden posts and a jungle of barbed wire just outside the trench and the usual litter of empty tin cans, ammunition boxes etc, but of all of this, including the Hun garrison, nothing remained, not even the outline of the trench itself.'

Just beyond the ridge they stopped in some convenient shell holes for another smoke and watched as a group of about forty Germans came past, under escort of a soldier Whiteman described as:

'A tiny Jock in his kilt, and still in his teens, who could not have had more swagger had he won the war himself as he headed the column with his rifle, bayonet fixed, slung casually over one shoulder. When about 100 yards from us he calmly handed his rifle over to the nearest German, a great big chap, and still walking in front totally unarmed, proceeded to slowly fill his pipe.'

Progress forward slowed and took the pattern of an advance of a few hundred yards and then a wait in a shell hole for an hour before moving again. The noise of battle ahead diminished as the afternoon wore on and by about 4pm the British artillery fire had reduced. As the sun was setting the battalion received an order to move into artillery formation and, led by Colonel Rice armed with his revolver and walking stick, advanced over the ridge of Orange Hill. The ridge turned out to be a plateau about 400 yards across with a gentle slope leading onward from the edge. There was even less sound and fury of battle ahead, and very little supporting shell fire. In some amazement the men of 10RF saw in front of them grass and meadow, undamaged trees and very few shell holes. There should have been men taking what could just be made out as a line of trenches along the far side of a road with trees on each side about three quarters of a mile ahead.

Those trenches were the Brown Line from where the battalion was to launch its attack, having passed through the division charged with taking the trenches. There was no sign of battle, few shell holes and even an occasional hare running through the grass. In the distance, about two miles ahead, the village of Monchy-le-Preux could be seen surmounting the hill with red-roofed cottages appearing through the green foliage of surrounding trees. As night fell so the temperature dropped rapidly and large dark snow clouds began to build, seemingly from all directions. Moving on, with the comfort of being able to see other battalions on either side, but lacking the support of an artillery barrage, 10RF continued to move towards the Brown Line trenches. Confidence began to grow that things might be all right and Stk772 Corporal William Morton called out to the men around him that this was the first walk over he had experienced. Almost as soon as he had spoken there were shots and the sound of machine gun fire accompanied by the whistling of bullets overhead and cutting through the grass at their feet.

Changing into extended order they continued to approach the Brown Line and it became obvious that the fire was coming from the trench, so the Germans still held it. The division which had been scheduled to capture the trench was nowhere to be seen and 10RF had to live with the consequences. The battalion took cover in the ditch on the trench side of the road and assessed the situation. Private Zealley was among those held up and spotted a German sniper hidden in a farm cart. He was causing many casualties and Zealley moved to get clear shot with his Lewis gun. As he moved the sniper saw him

View from the Brown Line looking back to Arras. Author

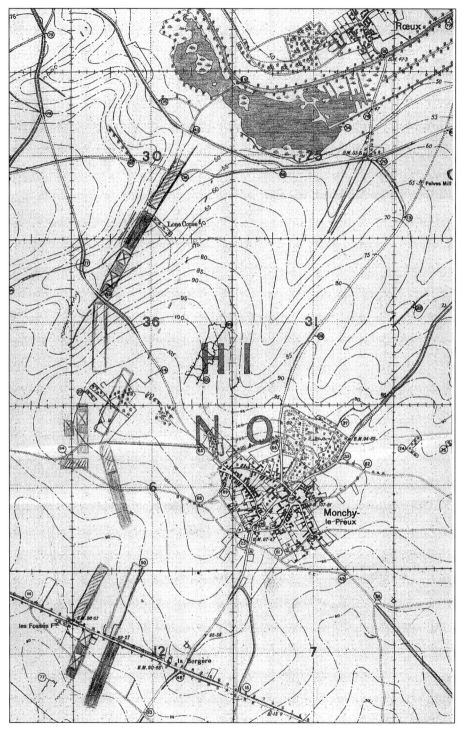

Formations approaching Monchy-le-Preux. 10RF was in the centre below the wood.

and fired, putting a bullet into Zealley's groin. Falling into a shell hole and incapacitated, he managed to crawl across the frozen ground and eventually arrived at a First Aid Post where the bullet was found in his boot, having caught in his long underwear after passing through his leg.

For those still in the ditch the sound of an approaching tank gave hope that they might have a way through forced for them to follow; however this was short lived as the tank broke down and stopped. This incident marked the end of action as the battalion was ordered to re-cross the road and dig trenches on the side away from the German trench. It was too cold to sleep and men wandered about moving to keep warm. Whiteman, Corporal Grendon and a few others spent the night burying their comrades who had fallen during the afternoon. Whiteman later recalled: 'It may not have been cheerful work but it was humane and kept one warm'.

Snow showers had fallen all night and as 10 April dawned the men had a hurried breakfast of bully beef while they awaited orders. A runner arrived with an order to fall back up the slope. Outlined against the fresh snow the battalion felt they made a tempting target, but as they moved away from Monchy they wondered if the enemy had withdrawn during the night as there was not a single shot from the German trench. On reaching the crest of the ridge they formed into four company columns and marched to a railway cutting near Feuchy, a journey of about an hour. The railway sleepers chopped up with an entrenching tool made good firewood and groups of men could be seen huddled around fires in the cutting brewing tea using water from a nearby well. After three hours, at noon, the battalion was formed up and marched back in the direction of the Germans. The snow continued to fall in squally showers, one minute unable to see, the next clear and bright. They arrived at a well-fortified trench on top of a small rise. An officer, Second Lieutenant Charles Mollinson, told the men near him that this was the Brown Line and the reason they had withdrawn to the railway cutting was to let the division responsible for capturing the trench do its job. The 10RF was starting its part in the taking of Monchy-le-Preux twenty-four hours late but as they advanced the men could see their objective about a mile and a half ahead. Whiteman wrote later:

'The whole countryside was covered in two to three inches of snow. In front in the direction of Monchy was a small rise with nothing to be seen beyond other than dull, heavy looking snow clouds. On reaching the crest of the slope looking to the right and slightly behind was the section of the Brown Line opposite where we had a go on the previous evening. About a mile away on the right was the Arras to Cambria road. Immediately in front in a fold in the ground was a brigade of cavalry, Royal Horse Guards, 10th Hussars and Essex Yeomanry. On the other side of the cavalry, with its hill top just showing, was Monchy.

We advanced through the cavalry; they were awfully excited and keen with the prospect of seeing action for the first time for many of them. I remember some of them saying "give us covering fire boys when we pass through you at Monchy".'

Advancing across the snow covered fields towards the cone of the hill on which Monchy sat, the troops saw the untouched hedges, living trees and houses with complete roofs

Near the start line for 10RF final attack on Monchy-le-Preux. The sunken road is marked by the line of trees right of centre in the photograph. Author

The red roofs of Monchy-le-Preux. Author

The slope from Orange Hill, the first time the battalion had advanced across fields and grass. Author

and walls, a sight never seen further south near the Somme. They had moved nearer to the Arras - Cambria road and could see lines of men approaching Monchy in line with them from the other side of the road, black against the snow. A few German shells and machine guns opened fire as the advancing lines breasted the slope and became visible to the defenders in Monchy. The firing was sporadic and from a distance which presented few dangers. As at Pozières the battalion was not getting the promised artillery support, and the training to advance close behind the barrage seemed a waste of effort.

About a quarter of a mile from the village the machine gun fire from the sunken road, which linked the village with the Arras – Cambrai road, became more intense and progress forward became a series of rushes from shell hole to shell hole, surrounded by the smoke and suffocating gases from high explosives. More and more men fell killed or wounded and about 300 yards from the bottom of Monchy hill both the 10RF, and the 13RF which was advancing on the left, were brought to a halt by machine gun fire. Whiteman found himself sharing a shell hole with Corporal Grendon, Sergeant Coast and two privates. Things got worse at about 4pm when a light field gun appeared at the top of the street leading from the village and began to fire down onto the battalion. The battalion Lewis gunners combined and after about half an hour the gun moved back into cover of the houses.

To the right of 10RF a group of men from the Yorks and Lancs Regiment broke out in groups of four and ran towards the village. After a few yards those who survived, eight out of the original twenty-four, took cover in the nearest shell hole. Bending almost double, Sergeant Coast tried to move to another shell hole but had covered barely 10 yards before he was hit in the head and fell dead. At about 5pm the snow began to fall and soon became a blizzard obscuring the village and reducing visibility to a few feet at best. Writing later Whiteman recalled:

'Each and every man simultaneously became possessed with one idea viz that this was the chance he was waiting for to get across the 300 yards intervening space and right into the Germans with bomb and bayonet before they had time to realise what was happening. Corporal Grendon, me and the others from the shell hole dashed forward with the rest and must have covered 150 yards when the screening blizzard thinned out as suddenly as it had commenced revealing the whole battalion to a man running forward. Immediately the Germans opened fire with all the machine guns from the sunken road. Our poor chaps fell like ninepins and all round figures were stretched out dead and wounded in the snow.'

Whiteman managed to find a small shell hole and curled up to keep his head below the level of the ground. Second Lieutenant Mollinson was in a hole on his right and Captain St John accompanied by Sergeant Freemantle in another a short distance behind him. Whiteman saw that the Germans had dug a short trench at the foot of the hill, but they had to run up the slope behind to a small barn to get ammunition. By letting the snow fall on the back of his helmet and then turning it round so the white front merged with the snow he was able to snipe at the men moving up the hill. He could only manage to take a couple of shots at a time as the snow on the front of the helmet melted making it stand out so he had to sink down and turn it round. Corporal Henry Grendon had been wounded in the shoulder during the rush forward and as he made his way to the rear to find the Aid Post he was wounded a second time in the same shoulder; he eventually made it back to a hospital in England.

Once it was dark Whiteman got out of his hole and looked to see who else had survived. He found about sixteen unwounded men from various companies. Second Lieutenant Mollinson had disappeared and there were no other officers or senior NCOs further forward. Accompanied by Corporal Sylvester and the group of men he made his way back to find the rest of the battalion. As they made their way in the dark a shout was heard from a man needing a stretcher. At first thinking it was Grendon's voice Whiteman sent the rest of the group on with Sylvester and set off to find the source of the voice. He discovered not Grendon but Lance Corporal John Turner, one of the men drafted from 3rd Royal Sussex earlier in the year. He had been shot through the body and had both legs smashed but as Whiteman wrote 'despite this fairly cheerful'. While with Turner, Whiteman heard the sound of another man moving across the snow towards them. He waited and issued a challenge which was replied to by Captain Frank Shutes who had taken over C Company in addition to his own D Company as Captain St John had been badly wounded.

Whiteman and Shutes began to carry Turner back and after a few yards came across the body of Corporal Morton, who a few hours earlier had been proclaiming a walk over. Taking Morton's groundsheet they lay Turner on it and began to part carry, part drag him along. Four hundred yards further on they came across another group of men from A, D and C Companies who were with Company Sergeant Major Sharp searching for the battalion. They spread out in extended line to search for wounded as they headed back. They found the battalion's machine gun officer, Lieutenant Twyman, lying in a shell hole being tended by two stretcher bearers, but he died shortly after. Word came along the line that Sergeant Smith, the Pioneer sergeant who usually stayed with HQ, had been found. From Smith, who had been left behind to guard a battalion dump of equipment when HQ had moved forward, they learned that Colonel Rice had had his arm blown off, and was being taken back to Arras; the adjutant, Captain Guy Goldthorpe, had taken command of the battalion.

As they talked a shell landed about 40 yards away, swiftly followed by a second which exploded about 10 yards away. The group of fifteen men who had been spread out, had come together to find out what they had to do next and in a few moments would have been on the move again. As it was eleven of the men were hit and fell across each other, dead and dying, leaving only Sergeant Smith, Whitehead, Sylvester and Captain Shutes unwounded.

A further 200 yards towards Arras the four survivors found a sentry sitting in a shell hole. He was able to direct them in the direction of a deep German dug out which had been taken over by the battalion HQ. Captain Shutes went into the dugout, re-emerging a few minutes later with Captain Goldthorpe, and the group set off back towards Monchy. They were joined by another group of men from all the four companies who, as Whiteman recalled:

'did not seem to know much about what was to happen or what had happened, only that they had been taken back from just in front of Monchy soon after darkness had set in on the previous evening and had been waiting in dugouts since then and that now they were out in the snow again bound for they knew not where and were too fed up and fatigued to care.'

On arriving at a small wood about 300 yards from the foot of the hill the men were halted, a distance of about 50 yards was paced out from the edge of the wood and the men were told to dig themselves a trench and get some sleep. They had a group of 13 Rifle Brigade to their right who had already got their trench down about four feet. Later, at about 3:30am, an officer from 10RF, Second Lieutenant Passenger, arrived with a group of Royal Engineers who began to dig. The trench was declared to be deep enough by 4:30am and as the men spread their groundsheets on the floor to have a sleep an order arrived for Captain Shutes to tell him to take his men 'over the bags in half an hour for another attack on Monchy'.

A dim dawn twilight began to show, and with it a group of 10RF who had been withdrawn overnight as far back as the Brown Line and were now being sent forward to join the remnants of the battalion. They were carrying supplies of bully beef, biscuits and a jar of rum. They shared out the bully and biscuits but Sergeant Mellings buried the rum jar, vowing to return to find it later. The men collected their equipment together and, as Whiteman recalled later, at 5am:

'Without any fuss or excitement we climbed out of the trench which had apparently been dug to no purpose. There was none of the romance associated with 'going over the top' in novels – no stirring strains of marshal music, no colours flying in the breeze.'

There was no artillery support, and Whiteman described the mood of the men:

'No one seemed to care what happened that morning, everyone was mentally and physically finished as we advanced mechanically in a long line towards a hedge which stretched away to the right from the little wood in front. There seemed to be a surprising number of troops advancing with us on both left and right.'

It was Wednesday 11 April. The bodies still lay where they had fallen during the advance in the snowstorm the previous afternoon. The Germans had put more machine guns in the sunken road and they began to take a toll on the attackers who ran for cover and quickly filled the few shell holes available. Captain Shutes who had command of two companies, was wounded in the thigh and had to withdraw, leaving control in the hands of junior officers. Machine gun fire from a small cottage on the left was causing causalities and Stk818 Corporal Frank Scales, who was Lewis gunner of C Company, trained his gun on the cottage. An officer ordered him not to open fire as it was believed that it was occupied by British troops, but Scales ignored this and fired, shattering windows and breaking the woodwork. Firing from that quarter ceased immediately. On entering the cottage later men of 10RF found the bodies of dead German machine gunners, they had been firing from one window and Scales shot them through another one.

There was still no artillery support, but two tanks appeared just ahead of the advancing troops, one heading for the sunken road, the other for the village. The Germans saw one advancing tank and began running up and down the sunken road. All of a sudden the firing from the road and the village stopped. The attackers emerged from their shell holes and other places of concealment and began to run towards the village. Others joined them and Whiteman became aware of masses of men in all the surrounding fields heading for Monchy. They swarmed up the single road, passing the still-moving tank which was making its way into the village. The capture of the village had, in the original plan, been assigned to 10 and 13RF but there appeared to be representatives of almost every regiment in the British army as Whiteman recalled.

'Along the street and up the hill the crowd surged; it was a similar crowd that one sees issuing from the gates after a football match. All bayonets had been fixed before getting out of the trench but I don't think anyone had occasion to use them.'

The village was still standing, the houses virtually intact and some had a feel of the Marie Celeste with coffee still boiling on the stove and the table laid ready for a meal. The Fusiliers took about 150 prisoners and received the tearful thanks of two old Frenchwomen, once they realised that the newcomers were 'Les Soldats Anglais'. The

The Mairie and school later destroyed by shelling.

The new Mairie in Monchy-le-Preux. Author

original scheme, carefully rehearsed at Buneville now required the 10RF to continue through the village for about 300 yards and then to dig in in preparation for the expected counter-attack. The plan had envisaged this happening on Monday afternoon but it was now Wednesday afternoon as the remnants of the battalions made their way to their designated places.

Emerging from the centre of the village the troops were standing on the crest of a ridge which descended steeply into a wide valley, soon christened the valley of death, which rose to a ridge on the other side, about half a mile away. They could see the garrison from Monchy retreating across the fields and a large group of British set off in hot pursuit, stopping occasionally to fire a couple of rounds at the fleeing Germans. The pursuers went through a small wood where they took some prisoners, but they were suddenly opposed by machine gun fire which killed and wounded quite a few of the party. Whiteman was the only 10RF man in a group of King's Own Scottish Borderers who were sharing a shell hole. In front they could see men frantically digging holes and putting earth banks in front to provide them with some shelter.

Corporal Sydney Sylvester had been with Whiteman as they sheltered in the gates of the chateau. Moving forward with his two Lewis guns Sylvester lost track of Whiteman and, using the cover of the right hand wall of the cemetery, he found a building which he described as a stable. He had a good field of fire into the valley where he could see a trench about 300 or 400 yards in front. He set up one gun on either side of the stable and waited. A German field gun was shielded by the wood behind the trench and Sylvester did not want to risk exposing his position until he had to either defend against a German counter-attack, or support a British advance; he could see a few men in khaki digging in on the right a few hundred yards behind his position. The other feature of interest to Sylvester was the raised road about half a mile away on the right. This was the Cambrai to Arras road and was being used by German troops and transport moving towards Monchy.

One of the supporting tanks could be seen burning in the sunken road; the other emerged from a wood and with a wave from one of the crew, set off towards the ridge ahead with bullets ricocheting off its hull. On reaching the slope rather than advancing to drive out the Germans, as the watching troops hoped, the tank turned back to the village and as it climbed back burst into a sheet of flame having been hit by a German whizz-bang. Two men rolled out of one of the side hatches, their clothes on fire, rolling in the snow in an attempt to extinguish the flames.

Sylvester recalled seeing a figure in khaki crawling up the slope in front of his position. They brought him in and found he was an officer who said that his tank had been right round the village. After giving him first aid and checking his papers, Sylvester sent Private Reginald Hesketh back with him into the village to report their position.

The allied artillery dropped a few shells between the village and the men in the forward positions, but it was not a supporting barrage. A few of the men in the holes in front had been killed and others wounded; a few began to crawl back but as they went so they were hit again.

A plane, showing the black lines of a contact aircraft appeared and began to fly slowly along the British line sounding its klaxon for those on the ground to identify themselves, and thus the British positions. Fuller and Whiteman began to prepare the flare in the bottom of their shell hole, but at the last minute they looked up and saw the Maltese Crosses of a German plane, rather than the Royal Flying Corps roundel. They abandoned the process of lighting the flare.

The men in the holes in front of Whiteman were now all either dead or wounded, the Germans began shelling Monchy and some moved forward and round the flanks. All the British began to move back and Whiteman and Second Lieutenant Fuller ran separately up the slope of the valley of death having agreed to meet in the cemetery which was at the village end of the sunken road. Thinking it was quieter in the direction of Arras they decided to look back across the sunken road to see if they could find more 10RF men. They were just crossing the road when a piece of shrapnel from a shell which had landed near the Arras – Cambrai road about 200 yards away, hit Second Lieutenant Fuller in the chest and he fell dead.

Whiteman joined a group of Scottish soldiers in the sunken road looking over the valley of death towards the Germans. Discovering Sergeant Frank Swain and about half a dozen privates from 10RF Whiteman took up a position in front of the road as the Germans were now shelling the road and village with some intensity. The 10RF men could see the Germans in front, as well as the impact of the shelling on the village which, having survived so far was now being systematically destroyed. The shells flew over their heads and landed in the sunken road wounding and killing those sheltering behind the banking. Men of the Machine Gun Corps moved into the sunken road, and set up a barrage fire, aiming high to drop bullets onto the German guns across the valley.

German troops were forming up opposite, being driven into position by an officer on a horse and wielding a whip or stick. They advanced towards Monchy and before disappearing into a fold in the ground they came under fire from the machine guns in the lane and a Lewis gun further forward, which Whiteman learned later, was operated by Corporal Sylvester of 10RF at his stable building. The MGC men continued their fire despite the volume of shells landing among them. Whiteman caught sight of the cavalrymen they had passed earlier in the day approaching the village from the direction of Arras. He thought that the mounted troops would pass quickly through the village to avoid the shelling, advance down the slope and into the Germans in the valley. The horses entered the village, but did not reappear. Despite the shelling they had stopped and because the Germans had succeeded in reducing the volume of machine gun fire from the MGC in the sunken road more artillery guns transferred fire onto the village. Immediately horses, most riderless and many wounded, emerged from the village fleeing in all directions. Whiteman and others left the shelter of the sunken road and managed to catch some of the horses which they used to carry wounded men back towards Arras. When Whiteman and his group returned there was no one left standing in the sunken road. All the MGC men had been killed or wounded and the guns were lying shattered along and across the road beneath the banking.

As he explored the area behind the road Whiteman came across Sergeant Freemantle bending over a shell hole and talking to Lance Corporal Turner who had been left behind the night before with both legs shattered but who was still alive and fairly cheerful. They managed to get Turner to a nearby dressing station but he died later, leaving a widow, Lilian who he had married in 1914. Whiteman and Freemantle turned back towards Monchy. The cavalry regiments had lost over 500 horses but the riders had managed to take cover in cellars and dugouts and were involved in the preparation of the defences ready for the expected German counter-attack.

At the edge of the cemetery Sylvester's party were joined on the left by a number of dismounted cavalrymen who were experiencing their first action. They quickly set up their Hotchkiss gun and began blazing away at the enemy; although Sylvester had tried to explain to their officer why he had been holding fire. Sylvester's left hand gun opened fire on the German field gun, hitting some of the crew. The right hand gun opened up on the enemy troops advancing along the main road, scattering them to the sides of the road and delaying their progress. Eventually the left hand Lewis gun position was hit and when Sylvester regained consciousness he was lying with both legs out of action and a useless left arm. Lance Corporal Graham carried him on his back into the stable. As he was borne along Sylvester was hit again by sniper fire. Some men of the West Kents joined him in the stable putting on equipment and cleaning their gun. As they stood in the door of the stable a shell landed and with a blinding flash, yellow smoke and fumes, Sylvester was covered in debris which included bits of flesh and blood. Night fell and the German shell fire became more desultory.

About midnight the British troops saw a column of figures coming from the direction of the German trenches. They were in lines four abreast, not a formation normally used for a surprise attack. The defenders, including Whiteman, were ordered to hold fire until ordered to shoot. As the tension mounted and the figures moved closer to a distance of 50 yards a challenge was issued from the defenders' line. 'The King's' came the reply; the King's Royal Rifle Corps from 7th Division, part of the designated relief. It transpired that they had marched out from Arras, missed the turn to Monchy and overshot into no man's land. Realising their mistake they had turned and approached the village from the German side. They were fortunate to escape without any casualties.

A simple command to 'return to Arras' encouraged the defenders to retrace the 5-mile route. The navigation was difficult over the snow covered fields and when they got to the roads they found them packed with traffic going towards the front line. Eventually Whitehead, Freemantle, Swain, Haddow and a few others stumbled into Arras at about 3am on Thursday 12 April. The battalion moved back to Izel-lès-Hameau where the list of those confirmed missing got longer. When companies paraded on Sunday the 15th Whiteman recalled 'there were more gaps than there were men'.

The battalion War Diary covering the same period gives a prosaic impression of a more ordered series of events. For 11 April, the Wednesday two days after the start of the attack, when Whiteman began his day advancing mechanically on the hedge separating him from Monchy, the diarist recorded:

> '3am orders received to attack and take Monchy-le-Preux. After a stubborn resistance the village was entered and occupied, the enemy placing upon it a very heavy barrage. By 3pm all were entrenched about the western edge of the village except for a small advanced post on the eastern side of the village. Enemy shelling very intense and the Cavalry who entered the village about 11am suffered severe casualties. At 11pm the battalion was relieved by The Queen's (12th Division).'

The battalion HQ moved to Feuchy Chapel arriving at 2am on 12th where they spent what was described as a terrible night in snow and very low temperatures. Buses arrived at 5am on the 13th to take them to the huts at Agnez-lès-Duisans from where they marched to Izel-lès-Hameau on the following day. Sylvester, still in his stable at Monchy, was eventually discovered by men of 1st Essex who carried him down to their Aid Post. With a septic thigh that had swollen horribly he was given what he described as a big injection and was rushed to the advanced hospital in Arras where he was operated on. On April 20 he was put on a hospital ship to England.

On 19 April the battalion moved again towards the Germans, first to billets at Agnez-lès-Duisans then east again to St Nicholas, a suburb of Arras and, via Athies, to what had been the German trenches between Roeux and Gavrelle, north of Monchy. Whiteman looked across to Monchy and commented on how transformed it looked from being the village with red-roofed houses surrounded by trees to the ruins with shells still falling 'as though wanting to blot it from sight'. They entered the front line on Saturday 21 April, just over a week after they had left Monchy.

During the period from 9 to 22 April ninety-three men and two officers were listed as killed in action or died of wounds. The diary records 12 officers and 240 other ranks as being killed, wounded or missing between the 9th and 11th; about half the strength of the battalion was lost. Among the dead was Wilkinson's great friend Arthur Parnell, who

BRADLEY, SPENCER MAXWELL, L.-Corpl., No. 914, Lewis Gun Section, 10th (Service) Battn. The Royal Fusiliers (City of London Regt.), elder *s.* of Spencer Redfern Bradley, of Daraeq Lodge, Streetly, near Birmingham, by his wife, Annie Maud, dau. of William Vale ; *b.* Penns, co. Warwick, 23 Sept. 1891 ; educ. Warwick Grammar School, and on H.M.S. Conway ; was an Engineer ; enlisted in Aug. 1914 ; served with the Expeditionary Force in France from July, 1915, and died in the Base Hospital, Dames, Camiers, 20 April, 1917, from wounds received in action at Monchy-le-Preux on the 11th. Buried in Etaples Cemetery. The Commanding Officer of his Company wrote : " Your son was a great friend of mine ; we were in the ranks together for nearly two years, and he was one of the best fellows I have ever met. He was very popular in the battalion, and died as he lived, absolutely loyal." He was a keen sportsman, playing cricket for the Warwickshire Gentlemen and the Leamington Club, and was a member of the Warwickshire Beagles; *unm.*

Spencer M. Bradley.

Max Bradley who had been with Sylvester during the advance was wounded as he made his way back. World War Photos

died of his wounds while in hospital in Etaples. Also buried at Etaples is Corporal Max Bradley, the machine gunner who won the bombing competition at Mézerolles.

Recovering from his wounds in England, Wilkinson received two letters in early May. The first, dated 4 May, from Corporal William Walpole, writing from Broadfield Farm in Hertfordshire so not subject to censorship, was able to give some details.

> *'I have bad news for you. Poor old Trahearn was shot in the neck by a machine gun when we were going up into the village of Monchy-le-Preux and afterwards I had a letter from Mr Trahearn to say he had died at a clearing station. It was jolly hard luck for he was able to walk to the dressing station in spite of the wounds. Abdul Hamid was wounded, not seriously I think. Joe Winsberg was sent back to be a machine gun instructor in Blighty so I am the last surviving 10th Fusilier of the old MG section left untouched. It was good to get news of Otten. He left us after Pozières and we heard nothing, Hember saw him at Grantham.'*

The second, dated the 5 May, came from Sidney Wing, who was born in 1890, and in the 1911 census was recorded as living in St Pancras with his parents and working in his family's catering business. In 1912 he married Elizabeth Wakelin; they had three children: Charles born in 1913, Florence in 1914 and Mabel in 1915. Drafted into 10RF from 14th Royal Sussex late in 1916 he survived the war and died in 1948. In the beginning of his letter he mentioned that Parnell and Max Bradley had both been killed, he continued:

'As you may guess a large number of the old boys are now officers but give me a cook's job before any officer's place, it certainly suits me best as I have got my little family at home. I now possess three dear little children my youngest being eighteen months. I hope someday to see them all again. We have had some narrow scrapes of late but as you know "a miss is as good as a mile".'

Another letter he received in May was from Douglas Otten who had been mentioned in Walpoles' letter. He had been transferred to 151 MGC in 50th Division. In his letter of 14 May he was searching for news:

'Just a few lines to let you know I am alive and well and hoping that you are the same. You see they have got me out here again but still we live in hope of a Blighty.
    Have you heard from Parnell? I wrote to him about a couple of months ago but up to the time of writing have received no reply.
    Well take care of yourself but don't come out here again.'

Otten wrote again on 5 July:

'I was awfully sorry to hear about the boys being killed especially poor old Parnell and Webber but I suppose it is all for the best.'

Chapter 15

Battle of Gavrelle and Beyond: April to October 1917

The battalion re-entered the Battle of the Scarpe, which was part of the continuation of the Battle of Arras, on 22 April 1917. They held a front of about 250 yards, with the 13RF and 13KRRC on their left. They were ready to move forward, the plan requiring each company to provide four waves of advance with 50 yards between each. Initially the advance went to plan. The first line followed close behind the artillery barrage as they had rehearsed in training. After reaching the German's second line things began to go wrong. The 63rd Brigade situated to the right of 10RF had moved too far left and the battalion on the immediate left of 10RF was slow in coming forward leaving them open to enfilade machine gun fire. They waited until the confusion was sorted out and resumed the advance along a road. A patrol was sent to find out if the Germans still occupied Cuba Trench and they returned to report it empty. By this time according to the report in the diary the battalion had been reduced to three officers and about fifty other ranks in fighting condition as they moved to occupy the trench at 9:30am; soon after they were joined by men from 13RF and 13KRRC.

While waiting for the arrival of 63rd Brigade the battalion sent out a patrol towards the crossroads which lay just under half a mile ahead. Over fifty prisoners had been taken; the battalion had moved over a mile forward and was secure in Cuba Trench which was now consolidated as part of the new British front line. The Germans had clearly not given up without a fight as the battalion had lost most of its officers and men killed or wounded; the German barrage, which had been intense, was now directed onto Cuba Trench.

For the next three days, from 24 to 27 April, the battalion worked to consolidate Cuba Trench by deepening it and placing sandbags on the edge of the parapet. Patrols were sent out but returned to report continued German presence just ahead, with accurate snipers. The Germans attempted to reinforce their line along the road ahead of Cuba Trench. Men were seen to be running forward towards the road, and a number were seen to fall to the rifle, machine and Lewis gun fire from 10RF. German artillery continued to batter the line of Cuba Trench, and occasionally moved over the trench to shell the road 200 yards behind which was being used to bring up supplies. Each night patrols were sent out to prevent a German assault and try to cause damage to the enemy.

Early on the morning of 28th the battalion extended its frontage along Cuba Trench to the north. They were to support the 13RF and 13KRRC who were to attack the Brown Line sited along the road half a mile ahead. At 4:25am an artillery barrage opened the

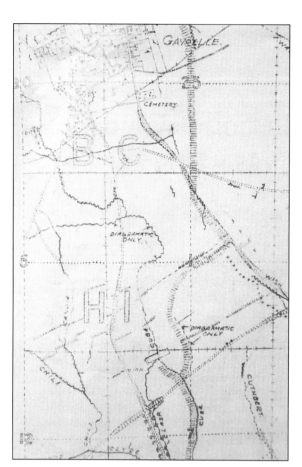

Gavrelle. Cuba Trench is in square I.

Cuba and Cuthbert Trenches.

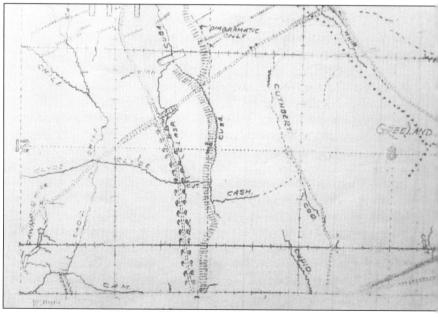

advance and the Germans responded immediately by shelling the trench and the road. After establishing battalion HQ in Cuba Trench a patrol was sent to the right to get in touch with 63rd Brigade. Contact was made with 13RB on the left, but this battalion had lost touch with 13RF.

German troops were seen moving towards the crossroads and a larger group emerged from the south side of Railway Copse, about a mile and three-quarters ahead; presumably these were reinforcements heading for the crossroads and trenches along the road. They were dispersed by intense machine gun and artillery barrages. The patrol sent out at 2:30pm to find 63rd Brigade returned to report that Cuthbert Trench, about 300 yards in front of Cuba Trench and held by the Germans, had been extended and was now joined to the post at the crossroads. Afternoon moved towards evening and the German artillery fired more intensely onto Cuba Trench. During the night some Royal Engineers with support from eighty men of 10RF dug a trench and strongpoint in front of Cuba Trench to disrupt any German counter-attack.

The 29th was a relatively quiet day and in the evening the battalion, after a week of fighting, was relieved by 9 Scottish Rifles. The relief was accompanied by a German barrage from artillery and machine gun fire. A march of about 3 miles took the men back to the transport lines at St Nicholas, arriving at 2am. The journey of 13 miles took three hours because the roads were congested with traffic and troops moving to and from the battle east of Arras.

During the week of the Battle of Gavrelle the battalion diary recorded that four officers were killed, and six wounded. A total of 256 other ranks were lost, 42 killed, 192 wounded and 22 missing. The 'Ditchers' lost another twenty of their number, and the prefix Stk was becoming increasingly less common in the battalion.

Among those reported dead was Pioneer Sergeant Arthur Smith who, earlier in the month, had been guarding the battalion dump at Monchy. Another killed was the son of the vicar of Ifield, Lance Corporal Alan Gibson. His friend Stk76 Private William Drughorn, whose father was the owner of Ifield Hall, had been killed at Pozières. Drughorn's father, Sir John Drughorn, had been accused of trading with the enemy and was tried in January 1915. He exported iron ore from Sweden to Holland, both neutral countries, but the final destination was said to be Germany. He was found guilty but fined only one shilling. William Drughorn reportedly changed his name during the trial.

Second Lieutenant Cowie was killed on 23 April; his brother, Lionel Cowie, also served in The Royal Fusiliers, fighting with 2RF in the same battle and his death was reported on 24 April. Both are remembered on the Arras Memorial. One of the wounded was Lance Corporal Edward Branch; he had been wounded before but returned and this time his wound, to his back, was more serious. He spent four months in hospital before returning to the Regimental Depot in August from where he was discharged from the Army in October 1917.

From the end of April until the middle of June the battalion was in rest, training, reserve and providing support to engineers and tunnellers. During the period from 1 to 18 May 1917 the battalion was at Izel-lès-Hameau. New drafts of men and, on the 12th, eight officers, arrived and were integrated into the battalion. Major Smith, who had been temporary CO was promoted to Lieutenant Colonel and given command of the battalion;

the third holder of the position in just over a month. Severe losses among the Lewis gunners, signallers and stretcher bearers needed urgent replacement and the early days of training were spent identifying and beginning to train the new specialists. After two days to tidy up and reorganise, the battalion took part in a tactical exercise at Lignereuil about 8 miles away. On the 11th men undertook musketry training, and a half day's exercise on 12th was followed that night with a march by compass bearing from south of Ambrines to Givenchy. Much of this was similar to the basic training exercises carried out by the original members of the battalion when in Colchester and Andover, the new arrivals were often much less well trained and basic skills had to be developed in France.

After church parade on 13 May the Brigadier General presented a Military Medal ribbon to Stk1138 Corporal Benjamin Townsend. He and others had won this award during the action at Monchy; Stk657 Corporal Stephen Dean and Stk1129 Corporal Sydney Sylvester, who had been wounded, were given their medals in hospital. The specialists rejoined their sections for the brigade exercise at Lignereuil on 15th where they practised following an artillery barrage, represented by advancing drummers. The training on 17th was cancelled because of rain and thunder. At an inspection of the battalion the corps commander congratulated them on the standard of dress and smartness of the men which he said, 'was in keeping with the traditions of the battalion'.

A 9-mile march in fine weather on Friday 18 May brought the battalion to very good billets at Berneville. Here they spent the night and next day marched to the Schramm Barracks in Arras. Late the following evening they left Arras and marched to the old German lines at Tilloy-lès-Mofflaines. Shrapnel shells hit the camp in the early morning and late evening of Wednesday 23rd but no men were injured and bayonet practice continued under the specialist NCOs from brigade. Company training followed baths for the men on 24th and the diary listed the officers mentioned in despatches in *The London Gazette* of 15 May; Lieutenant Colonel Rice, Major J.D. Waters, Captain F.W. Shutes, Second Lieutenant T.L. Ground DSO, Quartermaster and Hon Lieutenant J.D. Rickard.

Following company training on the 25th the first platoon set off at 8:30pm to begin the relief of 8 East Lancs in the reserve line. The battalion HQ was established in old stone quarries at La Marlière near Wancourt, on the south side of the Arras to Cambrai road, about a mile from the cross roads with the road to Monchy. Here they were near some artillery batteries, which attracted occasional shelling from the German lines. They were employed in supporting a New Zealand Tunnelling Company by providing three shifts of one NCO and twenty-four men to support the digging of tunnels for the placing of explosives under the German lines. A further party of one NCO and ten men provided carriers for the tunnelers and 2 officers with 100 other ranks provided support for the Royal Engineers and the commanders of front line battalions. One working party of 7 officers and 250 men were shelled in a communication trench as they moved in groups with 100 yards space between each group; there were seven casualties, two of whom died.

For the next four days, from 28 to 31 May the battalion provided large working parties to salvage the paraphernalia left behind following the advance in April. On the night of the 30th a party of one officer and 100 men was sent to support the line while a group from the battalion in that line went out on a raid. The raid was cancelled that night, but took place on the next one, when the 10RF men took their place in the front line, and the remainder of the battalion stood to in the support trench.

On the night of 1 June the battalion was relieved and marched back into Arras, the last company reporting in at 4:15am. As usual when returning from a spell in or near the front line the first day was spent in tidying clothing and equipment. The next day part of the battalion used the range at Liencourt for musketry practice while the others undertook specialist training. A cricket match in the afternoon between 10RF and 13RB, with additional entertainment provided by the divisional band, resulted in a win for 10RF. Organisation of the battalion for training began in earnest on 5 June with a number of specialist classes being formed for junior NCOs, musketry instructors, bombers, rifle grenadiers, signallers and snipers. Once these administrative aspects had been arranged the battalion moved by bus to Sains-lès-Pernes and then continued on foot to Fiefs, where they spent the night, before marching the last 6 miles to the peaceful Beaumetz-lès-Aire situated on a plateau just over a mile wide with steep sided valleys on both sides. Here they found the billets to be rather cramped as 13RF was also in the village, but by moving two companies down to the village of Cuhem they relieved the pressure.

The battalion spent the next two weeks in training in what the Battalion Diary described as idyllic, if sometimes rather too warm, weather. The battalion had not been given any specific tasks to prepare for in anticipation of their return to the trenches. In consequence more basic skills, bayonet practice, musketry, attack and outpost duties formed the basis of the training. The usual activities of digging trenches and wiring featured heavily in the programme and two night operations were carried out during the fortnight. This emphasis on getting the basics right was necessary to get the men who had arrived in recent drafts familiar with the battalion, and particularly their platoon and company. On a lighter note a cricket match between the battalion and the brigade staff took place on the 17th, the Brigadier and the CO both taking part; 10RF were the victors. Involvement in 112 Infantry Brigade sports day was limited, but the battalion did take third place in the only event for which they entered, the obstacle race. Administration and paper work had increased as the war progressed and the battalion received authorisation to appoint an assistant adjutant, Second Lieutenant R.S. Baker was appointed to the position.

On Saturday 23 June the men put on their packs and haversacks and, fully laden, left Beaumetz-lès-Aire at 6:25am to moved eastward to Isbergues, a distance of 14 miles; they were all in their billets by midday. On Sunday morning at 4am the battalion began the 16 mile march from Isbergues arriving at their next billets in L'Egernest, 3 miles north-east of Hazebrouck at 11am. The marches over three days had proved too much for some of the new men drafted into the battalion. Over 300 men, nearly half the battalion, had arrived in the previous six weeks. Not all were sufficiently fit to complete the march and the divisional commander ordered all men who had dropped out to parade for inspection. A number of them were sent back to the base depot for further training and reassignment; others were moved to the Divisional Employment Company where they would provide support for engineers and service corps. The rush to get men to the front, the poorer health of many of the new recruits, many of them conscripts, and the limited basic training to develop fitness resulted in many arriving at front line battalions in a poor state of readiness. This contrasted with the ten months training for the original members of the battalion and proved the wisdom of the process, despite the frustration it caused among the 1914 cohort wanting to get to the action.

On Wednesday 27 June the battalion moved across the land in the Ypres Salient recently captured from the Germans and took position in the support trenches with the battalion HQ in Lumm Farm south of Wytschaete. On the following day they moved forward and took over from 15 Royal Irish Rifles in the front line. B Company, in the front line with C Company, were shelled during the night of 29th with nine casualties, four being killed outright. More men from B Company were killed on 1 July when their section of the trench was shelled again. Two of those killed, Midwinter and Biggs, had been transferred from the Army Service Corps, two others, Davey and Ambrose, had previously served in the 3rd Battalion, Norfolk Regiment and Thompson had been in the Middlesex Regiment.

Work continued to improve the trench and salvage equipment and also to send patrols towards the German lines. Until the night of 4-5 July no contact had been made but on that night two enemy patrols were located on the north side of the Blauwepoortbeek, a stream running across the ground in front of the 10RF trenches. One patrol was engaged but retaliated with bombs and machine guns. The 10RF patrol returned to their trench, collected two Lewis guns and went back to break up the German working party. A patrol of twenty men led by an officer was sent out the following night to identify which regiment of German troops was facing them. Although it cost nine men wounded and three missing no information was obtained. Eventually on the 8th 13RF arrived to take over the trenches and 10RF made their way back to the reserve trenches around Lumm Farm where they spent the next few days tidying, carrying out salvage work in the immediate area and sending large working parties forward to work on the front line and communication trenches. On Tuesday 10 July the battalion was relieved in the support

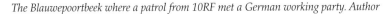

The Blauwepoortbeek where a patrol from 10RF met a German working party. Author

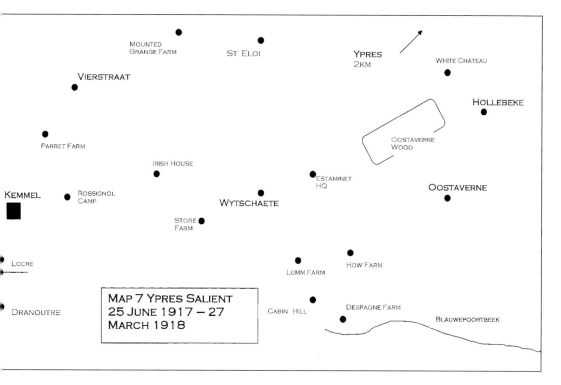

MOUNTED
GRANGE FARM
ST ELOI
YPRES
2KM
WHITE CHATEAU
VIERSTRAAT
HOLLEBEKE
OOSTAVERNE
WOOD
PARRET FARM
IRISH HOUSE
ESTAMINET
HQ
OOSTAVERNE
KEMMEL
ROSSIGNOL
CAMP
WYTSCHAETE
STORE
FARM
LOCRE
HOW FARM
LUMM FARM
MAP 7 YPRES SALIENT
25 JUNE 1917 − 27
MARCH 1918
CABIN HILL
DESPAGNE FARM
BLAUWEPOORTBEEK
DRANOUTRE

trenches by 8 Somerset Light Infantry and the men marched back six miles from the lines to rest at Dranoutre.

Monday 16th was devoted to baths, obtaining clean underclothing and fumigating uniforms. The billets were sprayed with creosol solution, which gave temporary relief from the lice. For the next ten days the battalion was engaged in training in assaults, providing working parties for the Royal Engineers to prepare practice trenches for the assault exercises; and musketry practice was carried out at Bailleul. The brigade commander's inspection planned for the afternoon of the 25 July was cancelled owing to inclement weather, but instead the battalion received orders to prepare to move to the front line on the 26th. An opportunity was taken to have more baths on 25th before the battalion moved up to take over the line from 10 Yorks and Lancs just across the Blauwepoortbeek from their last position in the trenches.

Work was started to deepen and strengthen the line of shell holes and patrols were sent out to ascertain the position and level of activity of the enemy. German shells passed over the trenches to land around Despagne Farm, about three-quarters of a mile behind the trench, but rather close to where B Company was situated in the reserve line and just in front of battalion HQ sited on Cabin Hill. Second Lieutenant Messenger led a successful patrol to gain intelligence about the enemy during the night of 28 July. He later received a letter from the divisional commander congratulating him on the quality of information he sent back.

On the following day the battalion moved back about a mile and a half to bivouac in

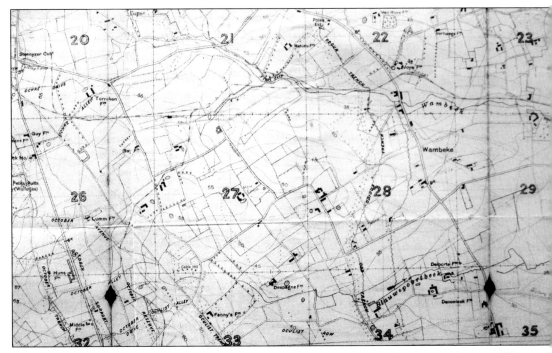

Trench map around Lumm Farm, in square 26 and to Wambeke road where the front line trenches were. GH Smith & Son

West of Wytschaete showing Store Farm, square 29, and Irish House, square 23 where the battalion rested. GH Smith & Son

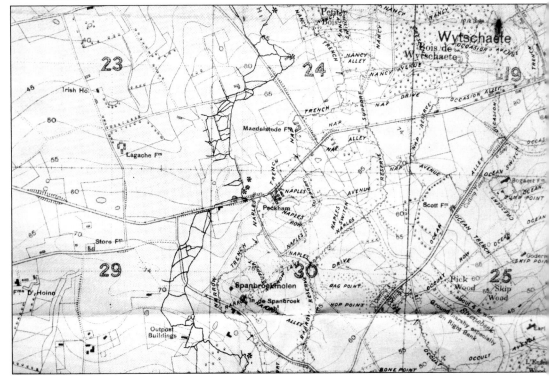

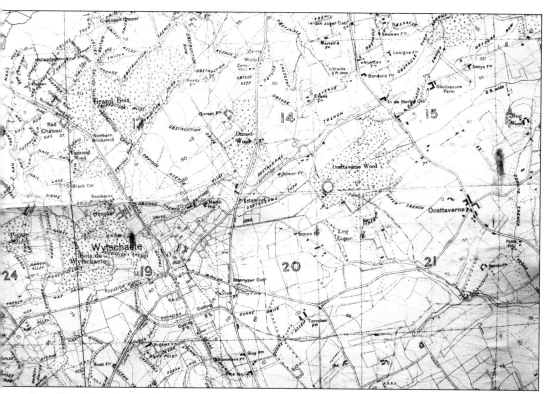

East of Wytschaete showing Oosttaverne Wood and the estaminet used as battalion HQ. GH Smith & Son

a field by a raised road between Wytschaete and Kemmel. Rest was short as early in the afternoon they received orders to move forward again that night to near Lumm Farm, where HQ was located. Later in the same afternoon two companies moved forward to provide support to two battalions near How Farm; A Company moved up in support of 8 Somerset Light Infantry and D Company with 10 Yorks and Lancs. The battalion continued to lose men, the Diary records that one man was killed in action and two others wounded with another missing; Second Lieutenant Messenger was wounded on 31 July.

During the night 10 Yorks and Lancs moved forward a short distance to establish a new trench on the east side of the road from Oosttaverne to Warneton and 10RF moved to support them in trenches on the west side of the road and slightly further back. The positions were strengthened, mainly by laying wire in front over night. Patrols were sent out to ascertain the strength and position of the enemy and two enemy snipers were shot by snipers from 10RF. On the 3 August A Company moved into the front line to relieve C Company which settled itself into the reserve trench. The following afternoon this trench was heavily shelled for about four hours, three men were killed.

On the 6th, after a quiet day during which the weather improved a little, the battalion was relieved by the 48th Australian Battalion and moved back to shelters near Store Farm, about a mile and a half west of Wytschaete. The next day the baths at Kemmel were made available to the battalion and the men spent twenty-four hours tidying and cleaning themselves and their equipment. From this date until the last week in August, a period of twenty-one days, the battalion trained in the area of the billets, had inspections by

German Bunker near Nr Oculist Row, Wytschaete. Author

Open ground crossed by D Company in their raid on German bunkers in September 1917. Author

senior officers and their gas equipment and respirators were checked by the divisional gas officer. Sniping was practised under specialist instructors and on 16 August there were changes in the command of the battalion.

The CO, Lieutenant Colonel R.A. Smith MC, who took command when Lieutenant Colonel Rice was wounded in April at Monchy, left and was replaced by Lieutenant Colonel Cyril R. Carter, a regular officer with the King's Own (Royal Lancaster) Regiment, who had most recently been acting second-in-command of 10 Loyal (North Lancashire) Regiment. Major Dallas Waters, who had served with 10RF from its foundation, returned to take up the second-in-command position having spent a short time with 13RF.

The battalion had established the tradition of celebrating the anniversary of its foundation, 29 August. In 1917 the celebration was held a few days early, on the 25th, because a return to the trenches was imminent. Prizes were awarded by the Divisional Commander to those winning races and competitions. During the evening the divisional concert party 'The Barn Owls' provided entertainment in the hut maintained by the Church Army. During the afternoon the battalion received the expected orders to move into the support trenches to the north next evening.

On 26 August the battalion relieved the 8 Lincolns in the support area due west of Wytschaete. On the following evening they moved through Wytschaete to relieve the 10 Loyals and take a position in the front line with their HQ near Oosttaverne Wood, about a mile north of their previous front line area. The three days in the front line were quiet with patrols sent out each night. A German MG post was located by a patrol from D Company and A Company's patrol saw German soldiers marching away from the lines. The battalion was relieved by 13KRRC and set up HQ near the estaminet by the crossroads mid way between Wytschaete village and Oosttaverne Wood. A raid was planned for the night of 31 August, to be carried out by men of D Company intended to destroy a number of German blockhouses in the vicinity. On the night of the 29 August patrols were sent out and much enemy movement was observed in the area on the ridge lying north of the Wambeek.

Early on the morning of 1 September a party of three officers and seventy-nine ORs from D Company, under the command of Captain Frentzel were ready to carry out raids on German dugouts and strongpoints. They set out at 2:30am in five parties led by Second Lieutenants Garman and Usher, and Sergeants Carter, Hilton and Macklin. The raid was carried out in bright moonlight, but the insurgents managed to bomb four dugouts inflicting a number of casualties. Second Lieutenant Usher and one other man were wounded and another five men were initially posted as missing. The battalion received a congratulatory message saying:

'The Divisional Commander is very pleased with the enterprise shown by 10RF in preparing and carrying out the raid this morning. He regrets that the raiding party were not able to reap the full benefit of the operation owing to the time allotted being too short.'

That night the battalion was relieved by 19 King's (Liverpool Regiment) and on 3 September marched back to Kemmel. The next day men had baths at Locre and the equipment was cleaned and companies reorganised. After training on the 4 September the remaining 'Ditchers' held their annual dinner. The whole battalion spent the next two days in digging a cable trench near St Eloi, and during the night of the 6th moved to an area three miles north-east of Wytschaete, centred on the village of Hollebeke. Over the next four days in the front line most of the time was spent in salvaging equipment and tidying up; each company sent out patrols but failed to find any sign of the enemy in the immediate vicinity. On the 10th at about midnight the diarist recorded that about 100 'Mustard' [gas] shells landed between the posts and the support company causing some casualties among B Company, who were in the support trenches. That night the 20 Kings Liverpool relieved 10RF, who made their way back to Irish House just over a mile to the west of Wytschaete. The brigade commander arrived at the battalion in the afternoon to present Military Medal ribbons to Sergeant Carter, Corporal Packham, Lance Corporal Graham and Privates Meadowcroft and Robertson who had taken part in the raid on 1 September.

On the morning of 14 September the battalion moved north to an area behind the original British front line under orders from 19th Division, and took up a position in Bois Carre; next evening they moved half a mile to the east to take up a position in another wood, the Bois Confluet. For the next two days carrying parties were sent to support the 19th Division, and the battalion was informed of the award of a MC to Second Lieutenant

Bois-Carre and Saint-Eloi. GH Smith & Son

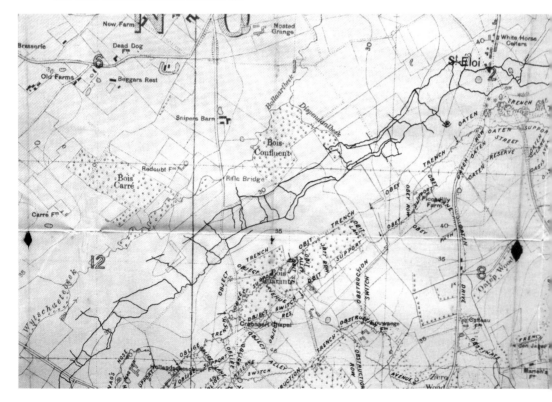

Usher and a DCM to 24566 Corporal Arthur Fellowes for their parts in the raid on the 1st. Fellowes' citation, published in *The London Gazette* of 25th January 1918, read:

'For conspicuous gallantry and devotion to duty during a raid on the enemy's trenches. He took command of a party when his officer had been hit, led them forward under heavy fire and bombed four dug-outs. After the raid, he immediately volunteered to go and look for some men who were missing, and continued the search, though continually fired on, until daylight. On the following night he again led another search party, approaching to within ten yards of the enemy's position. He set a splendid example of initiative and courage.'

The battalion provided guards for the prisoner of war cage at Bailleul and at another cage nearer to the Bois Confluet. This reduction in numbers led the battalion to reform into a combined company to support an attack by IX and X Corps on the night of 20 September. Until 27 September the composite company continued training, but also had to provide working parties at a place written in the War Diary as Zevecoten, but which is marked on modern maps as Zevekote. On 28th the reduced 10RF relieved the 13 Royal Sussex in the front line. There was limited communication between the companies in the front line and HQ. No telephone lines had been laid and movement by runners was almost impossible because of German snipers and machine guns so pigeons were employed to pass important messages. The companies in the line sent out patrols each night to ascertain the position and strength of the enemy opposing them. The bright moonlight made patrolling difficult and the patrols faced active snipers and machine gunners who caused casualties and deaths on most nights. Just after dawn on the morning of the 30th the Germans attacked the position held by 13RF, on the left of 10RF. The attack was repulsed but German grenades caused casualties in some of the 10RF outposts.

Another attack on 1 October was also repulsed, but the enemy barrages remained at an intense level. Any shelling by British guns was responded to by a return barrage from the Germans targeted on the support trench line. Throughout the day on the 4 October detachments were sent to support battalions in the front line. At one point only forty men were left to support the whole sector, but at about 5pm two companies of 8 East Lancs arrived to reinforce the battalion. Equipment and ammunition boxes were buried by shells bursting, as were a number of men, but rapid action to dig them out limited the number of casualties. The battalion was relieved from its position in the support trench by 11 Royal Warwicks and on the 8 October, after being relieved by 13KRRC the battalion was moved first to Croix Rouge, then the Hooge Street Tunnels and then Bois Camp.

Training at Kemmel and baths at Locre occupied the battalion for the next three days and they then returned to Hooge Street Tunnels in Reserve. The next ten days was spent in training at Boeschepe near Mont Vidaigne. On the 22nd a detachment of 100 men under Captain Wickham left to make roads near Ypres in support of 13KRRC; the rest of the battalion left Dranoutre on 26 October to go into scattered billets in the Strazeele – Merris area near Hazebrouck. While there the Corps Commander awarded Military Medals to Stk1857 Lance Corporal O. St Arnaud Duke of B Company and 48692 Private George May of C Company, the citations for both are recorded in the War Diary as being for 'Courage

Oriel St Arnaud Duke, back centre, with his family in Barbados, 1919. David O'Carroll

and devotion to duty 27 September to October 6 October 1917, East of Ypres'. Another MM was presented to 20363 Private William Miller of C Company, attached to 111th Infantry Brigade HQ, for 'great personal courage, cheerfulness and devotion to duty East of Ypres 27 September to 4 October 1917'. Private Thomas Seale, 3079, of D Company, attached to 111 Brigade Trench Mortar Battery, received his MM for 'conspicuously gallant conduct on 4 October 1917', he was part of one of the detachments sent into the front line on that day to support another battalion.

Oriel St Arnaud Duke was one of the original volunteers in the battalion. Born on the island of Montserrat, West Indies, in 1898, his father was a doctor who was born and qualified in Ireland and had begun to practise in the West Indies in 1875. Oriel arrived in Liverpool from Montreal in July 1907 on the SS *Ottowa* accompanied by his mother and two sisters. He returned home and joined the local regiment, but on the outbreak of war he travelled to England and, at the age of 18 years and six weeks, enlisted in 10RF.

Twenty-nine men were killed in the period between April and October 1917; often an individual day saw one or two men killed, by sniper or random shells. The average age of the men killed was nineteen, the first time this figure had fallen below twenty, and only five, or 17 per cent had the prefix Stk, or had been renumbered following being wounded; the proportion of 'Ditchers' in the battalion was continuing to fall. Another 'ditcher' who had left was Stk925 Sergeant Ernest Carter MM who entered Pirbright Camp in November 1917 to train for a commission.

Chapter 16

Winter 1917 – Spring 1918: November 1917 to March 1918

The beginning of November 1917 found the battalion in billets at Rouge Croix, near Kemmel. They trained and were inspected by the brigade commander and held church parades. There was also a Yukon Pack competition, which A Company won and so progressed to the divisional competition. Here they were beaten by 13RB, who went forward to represent the division in the brigade competition. The Yukon Pack is constructed by wrapping equipment and spare clothing in a groundsheet and tying the pack with rope, mounting this on straps and carrying on the back. The style of warfare had changed from that of being stuck in a trench to a more mobile one of moving forward, establishing positions and then moving again. For troops on the move the Yukon pack was more effective in keeping man and equipment together than having to transport large packs on wagons. The combination of the change in warfare methods with the damage to roads as shells landed to clear and cover the advance meant that as the army moved forward it was impossible to find transport to move personal equipment, the need for ammunition and bombs being the priority.

The battalion marched out of Rouge Croix at 8am on the morning of 8 November and established themselves in Rossignol Camp, about three miles to the east. Here they continued training but also provided working parties for tree cutting and improving water supplies. On the 17th buses took the battalion 6 miles, through Wytschaete back to the sector near Hollebeke. Headquarters was once again established in the grounds of White Chateau with C Company in the front line just outside Hollebeke, B Company in close support, in Oak Reserve Trench, D Company at White Chateau in support and A Company in reserve further north. On the morning of 18 November men of C Company captured two Germans of the 3rd Bavarian Regiment near Hollebeke. On the following evening two more Germans approached a post in the front line but escaped. A larger party of about ten Germans approached posts in the front line on the morning of the 20th but were dispersed by gunfire from the trench.

The Germans brought up reserves and the British Third Army lacked sufficient backup to establish a secure foothold. In the mud near Ypres the companies of 10RF moved round on 21 November, D Company relieving C Company, which moved back to reserve. After being shelled on the 22nd C Company moved on the following day to Oak Support Trench and, augmented by twenty-five men from B Company, exchanged places with A Company. An approach to the front line by a party of Germans on the 24th was again

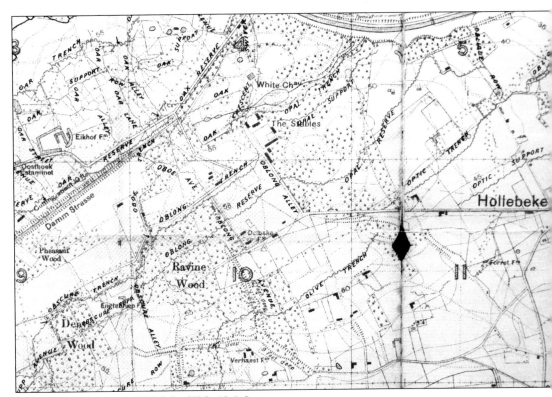

White Chateau and Hollebeke. GH Smith & Son

rebuffed, this time leaving one of their number, again a member of 3rd Bavarian Regiment, lying dead. On 25 November the battalion was relieved by the 8th Battalion, Lincolnshire Regiment and moved through St Eloi to Moated Grange Farm. On Wednesday 5 December the battalion moved 2 miles to the south-west, marching through Vierstraat to Parrett Farm where they took up billets in the huts erected in the fields around the farm buildings. The remaining week in 'rest' was spent in providing working parties for the Royal Engineers and in training. A visit to the baths at Siege Farm and a battalion church parade provided some relaxation but in the ongoing cold and wet weather the mud began to thicken and spread.

A return to the same sector of line north of Hollebeke on Thursday 13 December was complicated by the relatively small number of men now with the battalion. Shortages caused by the attrition and battles of 1916 and 1917 were really beginning to impact on battalions in the front line. Men were being transferred from the support arms, particularly the Army Service Corps. Beyond a fairly basic level, their training had not been focused on infantry tactics and fitness. The move of these and other men who had been rushed through training after minimal screening when they were conscripted, into the tougher conditions of front line battalions had already resulted in some dropping out of marches and being returned to depot, or less physically demanding tasks. Now the battalion was increasingly dependent on the less fit and skilled men to provide their core. They did not, in the main, lack keenness and enthusiasm, but in an increasingly mobile war both they, and the new officers coming from the officer training units, lacked the expertise to exploit situations as they emerged. The number of regular officers who had been fully trained before the war had been radically reduced by the fighting in the first three years. Rapid promotion from relatively junior ranks meant that a lieutenant in 1914 might be a lieutenant colonel in 1917. While some of these grew rapidly and matured quickly into the role of leading a battalion others found the task daunting and weaknesses showed. It sometimes took a while until the senior commanders realised the seriousness of a situation and took action to remedy it.

In his letters written after the war Charles Wise, battalion runner, who spoke warmly of Colonel Rice, Captain Goldthorpe and others he met in the course of his duties, was outspoken in his criticism of the major from the King's Own (Royal Lancaster) Regiment, appointed to take over in October 1917, and who remained in charge until the following January:

> 'Then again we had a period in the Salient when we were commanded by a truly white livered person named Carter, a Regular from the Kings Regiment. He was drunk on nearly every occasion he ventured out of his pill box.'

In a later letter he expanded further:

> 'He joined us at Kemmel and when you took him out at night to visit Companies his one refrain was 'Hurry, Hurry'. Once inside his pillbox he never came out and his batman had the filthy task of emptying huge tins of urine and excrescence. He was the laughing stock of the battalion.'

Cyril Carter was 28-years-old and had begun the war as a Lieutenant. Without knowing the man's history and experience it is difficult to do other than take at face value the testimony of those there at the time. It is possible that shell shock had taken its toll on this man, or perhaps he was not strong enough to combat the sights he had seen. Whatever the reason the condition of the man leading the battalion must have increased the pressure on other officers and NCOs to keep the men carrying out the tasks allotted to them, and the old pride in the battalion must have suffered.

Back in the sector with their HQ in the grounds of White Chateau, because of the reduced numbers, the battalion reorganised into three companies, identified by numbers rather than letters. The company commanders were listed in the diary as being Lieutenant H.H. Green, replaced by Captain Rupert C. Bambridge on 16 December; Captain Reginald C. Penfold and Captain Ralph S. Wickham. Every two days the companies rotated through the front line, Oak Support Trench and the reserve trenches near White Chateau.

A gas attack on Tuesday 18 December killed two men, Private Rennie Hammond, aged 19, a boot maker from Northampton, and Private Robert Havercroft, aged 35, a draper's assistant from Goole in Yorkshire, who left behind a wife and children. The gas also wounded Lieutenant Docking and former railway clerk Second Lieutenant Eayres, together with three ORs. Lieutenant Green was wounded on 20 December while patrolling the front line trenches, he survived. The battalion continued to rotate through the positions and completed their wiring on 21 December when they were relieved by 8 Somerset Light Infantry and moved to the north. They continued to work over Christmas, carrying out wiring and support but voluntary church services were held on Christmas Day. Baths at the Brasserie, just outside Vierstraat, provided a bit of warmth in what was proving to be cold and misty weather. Working parties, although serving in forward areas, were unharmed and the battalion ended 1917 back at the huts of Parrett Camp where they held their Christmas dinner on 1 January 1918.

During 1917 the battalion lost 252 men and 5 officers killed, but many more through wounds. Although some recovered and returned to 10RF more were in receipt of a pension or were transferred to other battalions from the infantry base depots. Other men were lost from the ranks to officer training units where for six months they learned how to be what were called 'temporary gentlemen' before returning to action. The proportion of those who bore the proud prefix Stk before their number declined rapidly. In the battle of Pozières in 1916 about 91 per cent of the men killed were original members of the battalion; at Monchy in April 1917 only 27 per cent of the dead had the prefix Stk and by the last big battle of 1917 the proportion had fallen to 17 per cent.

Christmas festivities over, the battalion returned to its normal routine of cleaning up and spent a day wiring in front of the support trenches. Still with three companies, now reverted to the former A, B, C, nomenclature, the rotation began again with little action apart from shelling on Sunday 6 January in which one man was killed, Private Ralph Nind a 35-year-old married man from Northampton, who had been employed as a clicker, cutting out the leather pattern, in the shoe industry.

A successful raid was mounted on the German posts on the 10th when Lieutenant Harlow and ten men from D Company went out at 2:50am to identify the regiment of the soldiers facing them. They attacked a post south of Hollebeke and killed or captured the entire garrison. Two prisoners, men of the 93rd Infantry Regiment were brought back with their machine gun. A total of one Military Cross, two DCMs, one bar to a Military Medal, two Military Medals, and five Green Cards showed the effectiveness and success of the raid. The same evening the battalion was relieved by the 48th Australian Battalion and they marched west to Tournai Camp. The next morning they marched to Dickebusch, nearer to Ypres, where they got into railway cattle trucks and travelled to Ebblinghem, midway between Saint-Omer and Hazebrouck from where they marched south towards the canal and took up billets at Wardrecques.

Now 25 miles away from Kemmel, the battalion took the opportunity to clean up, change worn out boots and clothing and reorganise the companies. Training and drill filled much of the following days as new men were integrated into their squads, platoons and companies. The inevitable inspection, this time by the divisional commander, took place on Monday 21 January. Training was resumed and on the 25th the army commander presented medal ribbons to Captain Rupert Bambridge who received a bar to his Military Cross. Sergeant Arthur Fellowes was awarded a bar to his DCM, the citation in *The London Gazette* of 26 January 1918, which refers to an incident when in the Ypres Salient in October, read:

'For conspicuous gallantry and devotion to duty. During a hostile attack on our trenches he was of the greatest assistance to his company commander whilst his company was proceeding through an intense barrage to reinforce the front line. Later, he took command of two posts, repulsing repeated attacks during a period of eight hours, and holding the enemy at bay until our counterattack developed. Thanks to his magnificent example of coolness, determination and efficiency the situation, which might have become extremely critical, was retrieved.'

He was also awarded a Military Medal for his part in the raid on 9 – 10 January. Corporal St Arnaud Duke, Stk1857 who had been awarded the Military Medal in October 1917 was presented with his bar to the MM. Lance Corporal Charles G. Robertson, 58769, Lance Corporal E. Meadowcroft, 228082 and Private George May, 48692 were all presented with the Military Medals they had won in the D Company raid at the beginning of September. Corporal Walter H. Packham, 32570, was awarded a bar to his MM on 29 January 'for conspicuous gallantry and great courage during the raid by D Company east of Hollebeke on the night of 9 - 10 January'. For his part in the same raid Private Edward W. Butters, 22200, was awarded the Military Medal.

The month of January 1918 ended with further days of training, a route march to Saint-Omer and field firing. Training continued on Friday 1 February and the following day the battalion was successful in winning five first prizes in the brigade sports. Church parade was held on the 3rd, the members of the Roman Catholic faith were permitted to attend a voluntary service in the village church. Prepared in body and spirit the battalion boarded a train on Monday 4 February and arrived at Dickebusch to relieve the 11 Warwick Regiment in MicMac Camp. At this camp a number of new officers arrived and were allocated to the companies. Captain Archibald G. Tanner and Lieutenant Willie B. Home-Gall, whose father was a well-known author, joined D Company, Acting Captain A.F. Watson MC went to A Company and Second Lieutenants Horace C.B. Sandall and H.E. Abbott strengthened C Company, under the command of Captain Thomas Huntington. The Battalion Diary did not record the departure of Lieutenant Colonel Carter but *The London Gazette* of 28 January announced that 'Temp Major J.D. Waters was to command a Battalion and be Temp Lieutenant Colonel'. During the course of the war he had risen from the rank of second lieutenant to that of lieutenant colonel of the battalion. Further training and reinforcements of officers were accompanied by the presentation of further awards, Company Sergeant Major George Gregory was awarded the Belgian Croix de Guerre. For their parts in the Hollebeke Raid Second Lieutenant Harlow received a bar to his Military Cross and Stk1692 Lance Sergeant R.W. Field and 9715 Corporal Sydney Powell were awarded the DCM. The citations in *The London Gazette* of 28 March 1918 described the events, which give a little more detail on the raid by D Company in January:

'Sergeant Field: For conspicuous gallantry and devotion to duty. When in command of a section of a raiding party on an enemy machine gun post, he, on reaching the post came under fire of a machine gun. He threw a bomb which put the gun out of action and while the rest of his section dealt with the garrison he took the machine gun and its ammunition

and carried it back to our lines. The completeness of the attack in which the enemy garrison was either killed or captured was in great measure due to his leadership.

'Corporal Powell: For conspicuous gallantry and devotion to duty. When in command of the scouts leading a raiding party on an enemy machine-gun post, he led the party most skillfully by the best route, although a machine gun opened fire on them at close range from the flank. During the struggle he and another NCO overpowered one of the enemy and brought him in as a prisoner. His conduct contributed largely to the success of the operation, throughout which he showed great courage and resource.'

The continuing shortage of officers is shown by diary entries for 8 February when three temporary second lieutenants joined the battalion from the Honourable Artillery Company. A few days later another entry records the arrival of three more temporary second lieutenants this time from the 12th Battalion Royal Fusiliers.

Providing working parties in the front line, having bath parades and continuing to receive replacements took the next two weeks in February. This group included Temporary Second Lieutenant Frederick Docking, born in Croydon, an apprentice seed and fruit grower living in Essex who had first arrived in France serving with the Australian Imperial Force in October 1914. He served with the 12th AIF before being commissioned; he served as an officer with both 10RF and 14RF. Of the others, four had also been serving soldiers, two, Temporary Second Lieutenant John Andrews and Temporary Second Lieutenant Albert Root, both aged 20 and both commissioned in November 1917, had served with the 8 City of Londons, where Andrews had won a Military Medal. Former Corporals Ernest Yarker and John Lovett, also commissioned in November 1917, had previously served in 19 London and Royal Engineers respectively.

The period of providing working parties and reorganising ended on Thursday 21 February when the battalion moved up and took over part of the front line from the 6 Bedfordshires and 13RF. They were east of Ypres with the headquarters at Glencorse Wood in an area which had seen heavy fighting in the previous August. On the night of 25 - 26 February a German soldier of the 84th Regiment made his way across no man's land to surrender. On the following night the battalion suffered the loss of 21-year-old Temporary Second Lieutenant Eric Ward. He was wounded by shell fire and died of his wounds the following evening. On the night of 27 February three companies moved into Manuwatu Camp, leaving C Company in the Hooge Tunnels under the command of 13RB.

From then until 4 March the battalion remained in support, providing working parties and each day the company in support in Hooge Tunnels was relieved. All the companies moved up and replaced 13KRRC in support when the latter moved forward into the front line on Tuesday 5 March. On the 8th and 9th the Germans shelled the Joppa and Jericho trenches occupied by 13KRRC causing a large number of casualties. The battle continued, with the Germans getting into the British line at one point. The commanding officer of 10RF, Lieutenant Colonel Dallas Waters, took command of the brigade sector and ordered up B Company to provide additional support. Communication became confused as telephone lines were cut and messages depended on runners getting through. Captain Tanner, who had been in charge of D Company for four weeks was wounded and made his way back to HQ to report the situation. German soldiers occupied part of the British front line trench system and had set up machine guns. The whole of A Company was tasked with carrying bombs forward, managing to get thirty-six boxes up to the men in the front line. B Company led by Captain Bambridge was ordered forward to support.

The situation was becoming desperate, further supplies of bombs were needed and the only men available to move them were the HQ detail of the battalion, supported by the HQ detail of 13KRRC. Two junior officers, Second Lieutenants Dester and Scott were detailed to lead the party. These officers had been commissioned from the ranks of 24 Royal Fusiliers in March 1917. Dester was 39-years-old, a native of Derby who had worked as a clerk before the war, his father was a railway engine driver. The battalion mounted three attacks during the night of 8 - 9 March. The first, by B Company, was not successful, because there was only a limited supply of bombs in their part of the line. A frontal assault on a machine gun post by a group from B Company under Second Lieutenant Burch provided a cover for another group, under a 21-year-old Scot, Second Lieutenant Edington who had served in the ranks of the Lothian and Border Regiment, to get to the rear of the post, but although they inflicted casualties they could not hold the position and Edington was severely wounded in this operation.

At about 10:40pm B Company had managed to establish a block in the trench and set up a Lewis gun where they were joined by men from A Company who had a supply of bombs. Captain Bambridge organised and led a second attack involving both A and B Companies. Three parties, each comprising about thirty men were to advance towards the front line using three access trenches. Two red Very lights were fired at 12:15am and the advance began. Second Lieutenant Sandall led his party along Post Line and although strongly opposed, they managed to hold their position despite the number of bombs coming over from the Germans in the trench ahead, one of which killed Sandall. Second Lieutenant Burch, who had been commissioned from the ranks of the Coldstream Guards, managed to progress along Smart Support Trench to the junction with Smart Trench and, with support from the other party from A Company, established a stronghold, at which they received the bombs being carried up by the headquarters party.

The third attack was carried out at dawn. A line of men was set up to relay bombs to the men at the front of the attack. The attack started from Post Line and Smart Support simultaneously and, assisted by the regular supply of bombs, moved forward. Snipers also provided support keeping the enemy engaged as the bombers moved. Some of the Germans began to run towards the chateau, where C Company had its HQ, a large number of the attackers were killed by machine gun and rifle fire. By 6:45am the enemy had been cleared from the trenches. Positions were rapidly consolidated and posts re-established where they had been before the attack. The battalion lost two officers and eleven other ranks, killed and five officers and forty-seven other ranks had been wounded, three men were unaccounted for.

The battalion had also won its first and only Victoria Cross. Lance Corporal Charles Graham Robertson was 38-years-old when he won the award. D Company was involved in the action during the afternoon of 8 March when they had been sent forward to support the King's Royal Rifle Corps and then were pushed back during the early evening. Lance Corporal Robertson's citation in *The London Gazette* on 9 April 1918 describes his part in the action:

> '*He repelled a strong attack by the enemy, realised that he was being cut off and sent for reinforcements, while remaining at his post with only one man, firing his Lewis Gun and killing large numbers of the enemy. No reinforcements arrived, so he withdrew, and was then forced to withdraw again to a defended post where he got on top of the parapet with a comrade, mounted his gun and continued firing. His comrade was almost immediately killed and he was severely wounded, but managed to crawl back with his gun, having exhausted his ammunition.*'

Charles Robertson was born in High Bentham, Yorkshire, on 4 July 1879, the son of Ellen Graham, who was described on the birth certificate as a domestic servant. The name of his father is unknown and at the time of the birth Ellen was staying with her sister and brother-in-law, Thomas Boothman, who registered the birth. Charles' name was registered as Charles Prince Graham and when he was included in the 1881 Penrith census his name was shown as Charles P. Robertson, aged 1. He was brought up by his mother's other sister and her husband, James and Catherine Robertson at 137 Graham Street, Penrith, Cumberland, but they later moved to Dorking where Robertson lived for the rest of his life.

Charles Robertson served in the South African (Boer) War as a member of the 34th Company (Middlesex) Imperial Yeomanry. He was later employed as a booking ticket clerk by the London and North Eastern Railway Company. He re-enlisted at the outbreak of the First World War and joined 10RF in France in November 1915. He was allocated the number Stk1591 but at some stage was wounded, taken off the roll and when he returned was given the number 58769. He won the Military Medal for his

Lance Corporal Charles Robertson, who was awarded the Military Medal in January 1918 and the Victoria Cross in March 1918.
World War One Photos

part in the D Company raid on 1 September 1917 near Wytschaete. After time in hospital at Ipswich, he was discharged from the army in December 1918, with the VC, MM and Silver War Badge to add to his South African and other medals.

The battalion reformed putting two companies in the front line, one in reserve at the chateau and another at Jargon Tunnels in the southern sector of the battalion area. On 10 March the two companies in the front line were relieved and the battalion took up its position in brigade support. On 14 March men from C Company operated dummy figures placed out in no man's land to distract from a real raid by 112 Brigade. Between 17 and 20 March the men were engaged in carrying out salvage work under direction from the Royal Engineers and they had baths at Vijverhoek. Following a lecture, attended by all officers and senior NCOs on 'The Finance of the War', Major General Williams, the

Divisional Commander, addressed the battalion to congratulate them on their part in the action of 8 and 9 March. Further praise was heaped in the battalion the following day when the Corps Commander, Lieutenant General Sir A. Godley, came to present Military Medal ribbons to six men for their part in the events earlier in the month. In his speech he congratulated the officers and men on their work. He expressed pride in having such a battalion under his command and said he was confident that wherever the battalion was that part of the line would be safe.

Writing to Sydney Sylvester after the War Charles Wise reflected on the time the battalion spent in the Ypres Salient:

> 'In June 1917 we were sent to a pleasant spot called Beaumetz Les Aires. This was a truly good 'mike' [skive, cushy number] for we had one morning parade and then we were free. We did not realise that such freedom would have to be paid for and awoke to reality on 25 June 1917 when the Ypres Salient claimed us for its own. Our merit as a First Class Battalion was well beyond the shadow of a doubt when such a wonderful soldier as Field Marshal Earl Plumer kept the battalion in the Ypres Salient for nine solid months and I feel that insufficient honour was done to our Companies in the line. Conditions were indescribable and I tell you that the mud at Beaumont Hamel was comparable with the Ypres Salient mud, and we had it with us the whole time from June 24 1917 to March 27 1918 it will give you some idea of what it was like.'

Six men with the prefix Stk were killed during the nine months in the Salient. Of a total death toll of 104 this continued to whittle away at the few original members still with the battalion.

Chapter 17

The German Spring Offensive: March to August 1918

On 21 March the Germans launched their Spring Offensive. The signing of the Treaty of Brest-Litovsk between Germany and Russia, which ended the fighting in the east, had released large numbers of troops for Germany to transfer to the western front. The Allies had known that the Germans were preparing to make an attempt to win the war before the arrival of the American troops preparing to cross to Europe, which would have brought overwhelming numbers to bear on the shrinking German army. The German attack was focused at Arras, Lys and Aisne, ground that had been taken from them the previous year and in some cases was not yet fully defended or with a secure trench system. The tidying and digging and wiring of the previous weeks, including the work involving 10RF and other units in the area, were not enough to prevent the German artillery from clearing ground to allow the fast moving infantry to follow up with light weapons. They covered ground quickly and ignored the need for transport and heavier equipment to consolidate positions; this task was left to the units following.

The German tactic was to drive a wedge between the British and French Armies between Arras and the River Oise and then they presumed that the British would retreat to the coast and the French towards Paris, both attempting to defend their key points. The British Fifth Army was facing the German advance. Comprised mainly of conscripted battalions with little training and less experience, it fought valiantly to stem the advance and the commanders took steps to move more experienced units into positions to face the Germans if they broke through. The tactics employed by the Germans, using fast moving, lightly armed and well trained soldiers, were totally different from those experienced earlier in the war, and the training of the men facing them had not prepared them to face these tactics.

The 10RF as part of 111 Brigade, in 37th Division of Third Army was in Forrester Camp, about two miles south-west of Ypres on the road to Kemmel. When the main German artillery barrage began the camp was within range of the heavy guns. On the afternoon of 21st a shell landed on one of the Nissen huts occupied by A Company, killing fourteen and wounding eleven others; in consequence the battalion was moved that evening to the west towards Dickebusch taking accommodation in Malplaquet Camp. A third of those killed had not been long with the battalion having joined as a draft from the 99th Training Battalion; many of them were aged 19.

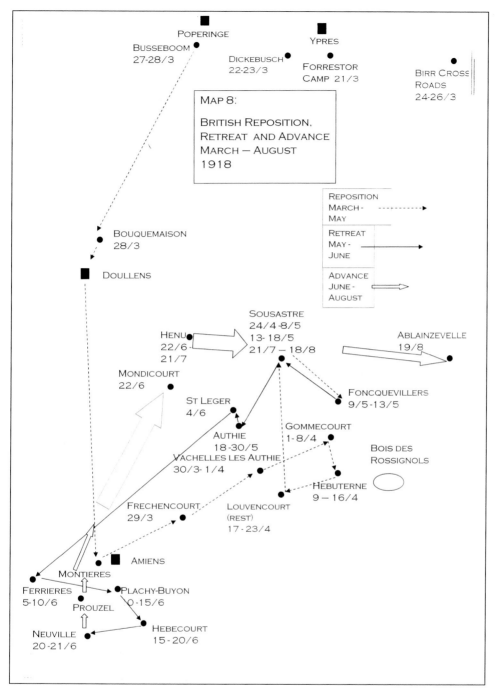

MAP 8:

BRITISH REPOSITION, RETREAT AND ADVANCE MARCH — AUGUST 1918

REPOSITION MARCH - MAY	·········▶
RETREAT MAY - JUNE	⟶
ADVANCE JUNE - AUGUST	⇨

POPERINGE

YPRES

BUSSEBOOM
27-28/3

DICKEBUSCH
22-23/3

FORRESTOR
CAMP 21/3

BIRR CROSS
ROADS
24-26/3

BOUQUEMAISON
28/3

DOULLENS

SOUSASTRE
24/4-8/5
13-18/5
21/7 – 18/8

HENU
22/6 -
21/7

ABLAINZEVELLE
19/8

MONDICOURT
22/6

ST LEGER
4/6

FONCQUEVILLERS
9/5-13/5

AUTHIE
18-30/5

GOMMECOURT
1-8/4

BOIS DES
ROSSIGNOLS

VACHELLES LES AUTHIE
30/3- 1/4

HEBUTERNE
9 – 16/4

FRECHENCOURT
29/3

LOUVENCOURT
(REST)
17 - 23/4

AMIENS

MONTIERES

FERRIERES
5-10/6

PLACHY-BUYON
10 -15/6

PROUZEL

HEBECOURT
15 - 20/6

NEUVILLE
20 -21/6

After the funerals the battalion moved towards the fighting. They travelled by train from Dickebusch to Birr Cross Roads, just east of Ypres on the Menin Road. New orders meant they had to move quickly south to form a buffer of experienced units. Another train took them to a point near Poperinghe and they marched from there to Red Horse

Shoe Shop Camp, near the village of Busseboom. The next day A, B and C companies marched to Hopoutre, a station newly created on the outskirts of Poperinghe. They were put on a train to Bouquemaison, about 4 miles north of Doullens, arriving there at about 3:45 the following morning. Having to move far enough west to avoid possible German shell fire, the trains and marching swung the battalion west and then south, with their final destination being on the Somme. A move on the following day, Friday 29 March, involved a march to Doullens and a train journey south to a place written in the battalion War Diary as Mentieres, near Amiens. A 9-mile march to the north-east, through the city of Amiens took the battalion to billets at Frechencourt, written as Freshincourt in the Battalion Diary; a day's total journey of 16 miles marched and 23 miles by train. The march on Saturday 30 March was of about 12 miles and brought the battalion to Vauchelles-lès-Authie, about 8 miles south-east of Doullens, the town where they caught the train on the previous morning. On April 1 the battalion moved towards their final destination, this time into the brigade support line near Gommecourt.

During the move more awards were confirmed by telegram and letter. A telegram arrived on Sunday 31 March informing the 10RF of awards made in recognition of the events of 8 - 9 March. Lieutenant Colonel Dallas Waters and Captain Bambridge were awarded the DSO; Captain Penfold received a bar to his MC and Captain Tanner and Second Lieutenant Edington were awarded Military Crosses. Sergeant Fellowes received a bar to his DCM and DCMs were awarded to Sergeant Poole, Corporal Spencer and Lance Corporal Holt. The citations give detail of the events, indicating the desperate situation and determination of the battalion:

'Sergeant Poole, London Gazette 26 June 1918: For conspicuous gallantry and devotion to duty. When the enemy had attacked and gained a footing in the front line he took part in three counter-attacks. He was of the greatest assistance in leading bombing parties, and when his officer was wounded he took command and continued to lead his men forward. He drove the enemy back out of the trenches and completely restored the position. He showed splendid leadership and determination.

'Corporal Spencer, London Gazette 25 June 1918: (New Eltham) For conspicuous gallantry and devotion to duty during an enemy attack. He was in command of a Lewis-gun post on the left of the position which bore the brunt of the enemy's initial attack, and the subsequent bombing attacks. He repulsed four determined attacks, which lasted for eight hours, and when all his men were put out of action, he continued to fire his gun alone until reinforcements arrived. He set a magnificent example of courage and determination.

'Lance Corporal Holt London Gazette 25 June 1918 (Manor Place SE London): For conspicuous gallantry and devotion to duty during an enemy attack. He led his section forward in daylight through a heavy barrage to reinforce the front line. He repulsed several determined thrusts by the enemy, and kept his Lewis gun in action until all the team had become casualties and all his ammunition was exhausted. He showed great courage and determination.'

The fighting the battalion was about to become involved with was taking place to the east, involving the 13RF, and north-east and the Germans were moving towards the support positions. Battalion officers reconnoitred for positions in the old German trenches. Because the direction of attack was now from east and north-east what had been the German front line became one of the reserve lines. The next front line was established in the old German third line, where D Company and part of B Company formed part of the main line of resistance. Headquarters occupied the second German line, transport and quartermasters were at Coigneaux.

The Germans had taken Rossignol Wood, on the side of the road between Gommecourt and Puisieux and on 4 April 63 Brigade mounted an attack. Although they moved forward they failed to achieve their objective and that night the Germans mounted an attack on the position to the left of 10RF, held by 42nd Division. A Company were the nearest 10RF troops to this and they had to change formation to allow The King's Royal Rifle Corps to take up position in the trenches in front of them. Shelling continued to inflict random casualties; the transport section suffered when a party returning to Coigneaux, having delivered the rations to those further forward, was shelled, killing Sergeant (acting CSM) Arthur Lindsell and wounding a driver; Sergeant James Newman managed to extricate the party from what had become a difficult situation.

From their position in support the battalion provided 8 officers and 170 men to carry rations forward to 63 Brigade. Early in the morning of 6 April the transport lines at

Hébuterne Church, the whole village was described as being in ruins when 10RF returned in 1918. Sharp Collection IWM

235

Coigneaux were heavily shelled, but there were no casualties. In the afternoon the battalion received orders to relieve part of 63 Brigade and after a speedy reconnaissance the battalion moved up at 7:30pm; working in atrocious conditions of mud and waterlogged trenches the relief took until 5am. The following evening a party under Second Lieutenant Riley attempted to establish a post nearer the German positions but almost as soon as they began to move up the sap they came into contact with the enemy. One man, 66807 Private Ronald Jackson, aged 20, a native of Liverpool and formerly a member of 3rd Battalion, Liverpool Regiment, was killed.

On Monday 8 April B, C and D Companies were relieved by 13 KRRC, A Company remained where it was in support. The following day an order was received that the battalion was to extend its line to take over the Hébuterne sector with the battalion HQ sited in the middle of Hébuterne village, which had been shelled early in the war. This relief worked better than that of a few days previously and, having set off at 5:15pm, the troops were in position by 10pm. That night the battalion was put in a state of extreme vigilance as an attack was expected imminently. The 10th was fairly quiet with occasional shelling on forward areas and the HQ moved to the edge of an orchard surrounding Hébuterne nearer the front line. A German bombing raid on the Australian troops adjacent to 10RF on 11 April was followed by severe shelling on Hébuterne village. At 6pm HQ received intelligence that the next German attack was expected on the part of the line occupied by the battalion. Maintaining its high state of vigilance the battalion 'stood to' between 4 and 8am on the morning of 13th but there was no attack.

After a day and night of intermittent shelling onto the support area, on 14 April the battalion received notice that it was to be relieved on the night of 16 – 17 April. The 5th Battalion, Manchester Regiment carried out the relief and 10RF moved back to a bivouac site about 3 miles to the west where they spent the night before marching to billets in Louvencourt where they spent the next week in resting, training and a rifle competition, won by a team from D Company which beat the HQ snipers. The sergeants from A Company won the senior NCOs' competition and the officers from HQ beat the other officers' teams.

An entry in the War Diary for 21 April sounds similar to those earlier in the battalion's history when confidence and self-belief was high. It reports that the number of admissions to hospital for the battalion was much lower than any other in the division. It notes:

'*The Commanding Officer congratulated the battalion on this very good record which reflects the greatest credit on all concerned specially on those who overcame their ailments and stuck it under very bad weather conditions, the Medical Officer and all who with him helped to maintain the health of the battalion.*'

Captain Roy Benjamin, an Old Etonian who had been commissioned in 12RF, was put in charge of a working party to improve the defence of the Red Line. He led a party made up of two officers and forty other ranks from each company. They began to work on 22 April, the same day that there was a Lewis gun competition on the ranges. It was won by a team from A Company, although one of the D Company teams had the best average.

On the 23rd an officer and two other ranks from each company travelled by bus to Souastre to spend the night with the companies they would replace the next day, and to be prepared to act as guides for the transfer. The advance party was joined the following day by the remainder of the battalion which bussed to Souastre and marched from there via Bienvillers and Monchy-au-Bois, both places occupied by the battalion in 1916, and then on to Quesnoy Farm, on the road between Monchy and Bucquoy.

On the first day in position, Thursday 25 April, the Germans shelled the trenches occupied by B Company, causing two casualties. That night the transport again came under shell fire when bringing up rations, but escaped without any casualties. For the next two days the battalion remained in the trenches, at the receiving end of intermittent shell and small arms fire. They moved from support into the front line on 28th when they took over from 13RB; they remained until 5 May, seeing little action apart from occasional shelling. On the evening of the 5th the 13KRRC took over the front line and 10RF moved back into brigade support. The next action occurred on Wednesday 8 May when the battalion moved forward to support 13KRRC when it carried out a raid on the enemy trenches at Bucquoy.

On Thursday 9 May the battalion moved back into familiar territory, at least to those who had survived from 1916, when they took up position in and around Foncquevillers. After a quiet first day the peace was shattered on the 11th when an estimated 10,000 shells, a mixture of high explosive and gas, landed in the village. Among the casualties were the commanding officer, the second-in-command, the adjutant, the medical officer and 18 officers, together with 300 men who all made their way down to the casualty station. Captain Tanner went from the battalion reserve, to take command, accompanied by Lieutenant Baker, the assistant adjutant.

Charles Wise recalled later what he had seen on that day. His letter demonstrates the level of destruction, but how the injuries led to rapid promotion for those remaining and the taking of responsibilities which, in the normal course of events, would take years:

'In the disaster of May 1918 at Foncquevillers my guardian angel was well to the fore. About 11:30pm Colonel Waters sent for me to take a message to Brigade whose headquarters were situated at Souastre, Brigadier Francis was commanding the 111 Brigade at the time. The deportment (sic) of 10RF was as follows: A Company in Snipers Square, B and D Companies were in the village and C Company and HQ were in a place called Beer Trench. Early in the morning of 11 May while I was still at Brigade HQ the Germans opened a colossal gas shell barrage. It was later reported that 10,000 shells landed on Foncquevillers and the result can be well imagined. One curious factor remains, Snipers Square escaped and the majority of A Company escaped also. At about 4am I was told by the Brigade Major to go out to the Transport Lines, report to Captain Tanner and our assistant Adjutant Lieutenant Baker and guide them and all available troops back to Foncquevillers. The scene on our arrival there beggars description. Men were lying blinded and in their own vomit all along the Hebuterne to Puiseux road. Long lines of men were being guided along, each man with his hand on the shoulder of the man in front. Red Cross ambulances were collecting men lying in the road, loading these cases into the ambulances and taking them away.*

'Captain (later Major and later still Lieutenant Colonel) Tanner took over command of the battalion and on 13 May the remnants of 10RF came back to the Transport Lines. We moved from there on 18 May to the village of Authie and there was a strong rumour that the 10RF was to be broken up. However, the Divisional General was having none of that and drafts made up the battalion to 'Full Strength'. Much of the old spirit was gone but once again I was fortunate. I first received two stripes and was put in charge of the Runners Section.'

In total 32 men died between the day of the attack and 1st June but the loss of more than 260 wounded resulted in another radical change to the structure and nature of the battalion. The injured were taken to clearing stations and field hospitals near Doullens and then moved quickly to hospital in Rouen, with some going to Le Tréport. One of the wounded who survived was Stk1411 Ernest Towler who had returned from an injury received in November 1916. He had rejoined 10RF on 28 May 1917, just less than one year before the gas caused bronchitis and conjunctivitis. He was discharged from the army in January 1919, still unable to talk above a whisper because of paralysed vocal chords. There were even fewer to carry the traditions of the 10RF and the speed of the German advance, resulting in losses in all the battalions facing them, meant that new recruits were rushed to France from training battalions or transferred from non-combatant regiments.

The battalion remained in position for two days until 13 May when they were relieved by 13KRRC and moved back to Souastre. Awards were announced to men from B Company for gallantry during the fighting in early April. Stk480 Sergeant Richard Newman and 8621 Private George Howson received the Military Medal for gallantry and devotion to duty on 5 April and 22383 Corporal Harry Ellery with Stk1684 Private Arthur Hayman were awarded theirs for their parts in the fighting near Gommecourt on 7 and 8 April. Training continued over the following days, and a draft of 128 men arrived on 17 May and on the 18th the battalion moved to Authie, taking up billets in tents and huts. Ten newly appointed temporary lieutenants and second lieutenants arrived; an NCO, Stk497 Sergeant Leslie Poole DCM MM was given a commission in the field and appointed to D Company.

The battalion worked frantically to get back into a fighting condition. Training, drill and practising on the range when wearing small respirators occupied the next few days, and four more officers and forty-four men arrived on 23 May. Following an inspection of billets by the brigade commander all junior officers and NCOs attended a lecture from the divisional gas officer. An officer's tactical exercise was attended by General Sir Julian Byng, Commander of Third Army. In the last week of May specialist training occupied most of the time, interspersed with tactical exercises but there was time for a football match against 13RB in the first round of the divisional competition; the 13RB were the victors. Training and baths continued after the battalion relieved the 8 Lincolns in the Reserve Purple Line on 31 May.

The 10RF remained in reserve until 3 June when they exchanged positions with the 1st Battalion of the 3rd New Zealand Regiment and moved into billets in St Leger. On Wednesday 5 June buses arrived and the battalion moved from a position on the St Leger to Authie road and travelled to point along the Molliens - Vidame - Amiens road, marched through Amiens and at about 9am on the morning of 6 June, arrived in Ferrières, about 6 miles west of Amiens. Three days when they were part of GHQ reserve supporting the French Army gave time for more training around the village. Another move at midday on the 15th to Plachy-Buyon, a short bus journey ending at about 3pm, followed by five further days of training and then a night march starting at 9pm, took the battalion to Hébécourt. Relief by the 1st Battalion of the 74th French Regiment on 20 June preceded a march to Neuville and marked the end of the battalion's time in reserve to 31st French Corps and, with the rest of the division they were transferred to IV Corps, part of Third Army. An overnight train journey on 21st took the battalion from Prouzel via Mondicourt to billets at Henu, about 5 miles west of Foncquevillers.

On 24 June, just over six weeks after the gas attack at Foncquevillers, the battalion took up a position in the front line near Bucquoy. While the battalion were working on the trenches, Second Lieutenants Potts and Milway from B Company, and Lieutenant Dudley from D Company each led a daily foray into no man's land to locate the position of the enemy or to attack and attempt to capture prisoners; most failed to find any enemy. The battalion was relieved on 2 July by 1 Essex and went into divisional reserve. Although the battalion diary does not record any casualties during the spell back in the trenches six men are recorded in Soldiers Died in the Great War as having been killed in action during this period.

While in reserve in Stout Trench each company was allocated a day at the baths and on 7 July the battalion moved into brigade reserve in the hamlet of Essarts, west of Bucquoy. Days were spent in providing working parties to support the Royal Engineers, most days saw little enemy action but there was some intermittent and light shelling on the 10th and 11th. Four thousand shells, mainly gas but with some high explosive were fired onto the enemy trenches about 5 miles in front of the line occupied by 10RF on the 19th and 20th. The 10RF must have felt that this was some recompense for the Foncquevillers attack they had suffered eight weeks previously. Relieved by 13RF on the 20th, the battalion moved to rest in Valley Camp at Souastre. The usual rest activities of cleaning, training and providing working parties were complemented by sessions on the ranges for C and D companies and specialists engaged in training. Rain made the ground difficult to traverse, and when they relieved the 8 Somersets in the front line they found that the trench sides and walls were badly affected by the rain. Patrols led by junior officers came across more evidence of enemy activity than in the previous period in the front line.

Relieved on 1 August, the battalion went into brigade reserve and began a week of providing working parties for the Royal Engineers, before moving back to divisional reserve in Souastre on Friday the 9th. Meanwhile further south the Germans were being pushed back from the ground they had captured in the previous months. The date of 8 August is regarded as the one on which the German Spring Offensive ended and, after a period of strengthening, the Allies began their advance back across France towards the Hindenburg Line.

Chapter 18

The Hundred Days: August to November 1918

For the first two weeks after the Germans had been pushed back from Amiens life in the Ablainzevelle sector remained the same. The battalion spent periods in the front line, sending out patrols to check the position of the enemy and periods at Souastre for training and preparing for the next phase of the war. On 19 August the battalion moved into position to support an attack on Ablainzevelle.

The 10RF was in the centre of the attack with 13RB on the left and 13KRRC on the right. An artillery barrage was timed to prepare the ground for the attack and eight tanks were allocated to support the advance, their role to move forward as the artillery barrage lifted and the troops began their advance. The use of tanks became more organised as the number available to work with the infantry increased. The tanks remained 50 yards behind the artillery and machine gun barrage, with the infantry a further 50 yards behind. The rate of advance was set at 25 yards per minute with the guns lifting together to allow the advance to follow closely behind. The orders instructed the tanks to take out the German machine gun and other fixed posts, and to breach gaps in the village to allow troops to enter. Once the companies had reached their objectives the tanks were then to manoeuvre to protect the positions in front of the captured lines to prevent an immediate counter-attack. The battalion also had air support, with communication by flashing discs and flares from the troops in the vanguard of the advance when the plane sounded its klaxon. If the plane's observer spotted any German troops mounting a counter-attack they would drop a red-brown smoke flare on the position.

By 3:55am on the morning of Tuesday 20 August the battalion had taken up their positions in the advance trenches ready to attack having used the mist which had formed overnight to provide cover. The artillery and machine gun barrage opened fire at 4:55am and the leading companies began to move around either side of the village of Ablainzevelle. B and D companies worked their way round the south side of the village and moved onto the ridge to the east, reaching their objective by 5:30am when D Company began to consolidate their position. C Company was scheduled to mop up the village, but were delayed by a machine gun post which had been too close to the start line to be dealt with by the artillery. Action by the troops on the ground quickly dealt with the post, capturing the crew and gun.

Prisoners, about fifty-six in total, were taken as were six machine guns and two trench mortars. While the battalion consolidated its positions the 63rd (Royal Naval) Division moved through at 5:45am to attack its objectives around Logeast Wood. The 10RF lost

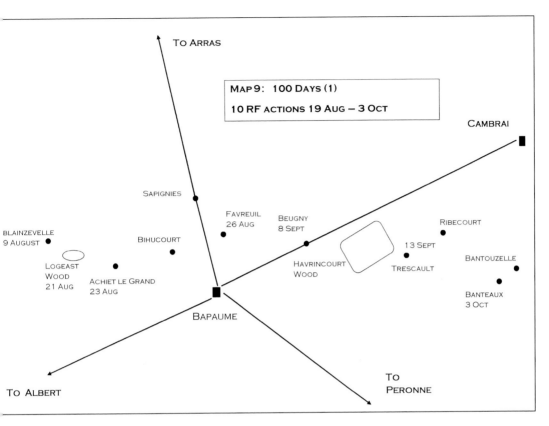

To Arras

MAP 9: 100 DAYS (1)

10 RF ACTIONS 19 AUG – 3 OCT

CAMBRAI

SAPIGNIES

FAVREUIL
26 AUG

BEUGNY
8 SEPT

RIBECOURT

BLAINZEVELLE
9 AUGUST

BIHUCOURT

13 SEPT

BANTOUZELLE

LOGEAST
WOOD
21 AUG

ACHIET LE GRAND
23 AUG

HAVRINCOURT
WOOD

TRESCAULT

BANTEAUX
3 OCT

BAPAUME

TO ALBERT

TO
PERONNE

one officer and seven other ranks killed during the advance, the War Diary does not record the number wounded.

By the next day the British had cleared Logeast Wood and 10RF were bivouacked on its south side. On Friday 23 August 111 Brigade was ordered to attack the village of Achiet-le-Grand. 10RF was to be support battalion and took up a position on the north-east corner of Logeast Wood. The attack was launched at 11am with an artillery barrage which the advancing troops followed closely and covered the mile to the village within an hour. The artillery put a bombardment down onto the village and at 1:30pm 10RF passed through the other two battalions at which point they discovered that the German garrison was fairly strong and putting up some resistance. After fighting their way into the village the opposition was overcome and one platoon of nineteen men of 10RF led by Second Lieutenant W.F. Smith captured 118 of the enemy. Although the battalion had occupied the village and advanced to the east it was realized that the battalion clearing the ground to the south had been held up by machine gun fire, leaving the right flank of 10RF exposed. They held their position, despite a heavy bombardment of mainly gas shells during the night. On the evening of the 24th they were relieved by 112 Brigade and moved back to the railway cutting just outside the village. The battalion lost three men killed in covering nearly two miles, clearing the village and capturing prisoners and guns. This was in marked contrast to the much greater losses suffered while holding trenches and in previous attacks where little ground had been made and held.

On the following evening at 6:30pm the battalion moved forward to take up its position, again as battalion in reserve, for the attack on the village of Favreuil. They had to cover nearly 4 miles from the railway cutting at Achiet-le-Grand and as they were crossing the road between Sapignies and Bapaume they came under heavy shellfire. The battalion made its way forward towards Favreuil and discovered the 13KRRC pinned down by machine gun fire ahead of them. The 10RF diverted to the south and moved below the ridge to the south-west side of the village, from where they advanced up a valley on the flank of the defenders. An assault on the flank of the trench to the west of the village caused the defenders to surrender, giving the 10RF sixty prisoners and twelve machine guns. However, the Germans were dug in strongly to the north-east of the village, using orchards as cover.

After nightfall Second Lieutenant Cecil Woodcock led a platoon along the north side of the village, when they were fired on. They rushed the machine guns which opposed them and captured one gun and its crew. Another platoon, working its way up the centre of the village, was also fired on from the orchard after it had made contact with 13RB. However, the probing forward from a number of directions had a positive effect as the Germans, realising themselves to be virtually surrounded, withdrew under cover of darkness. A platoon of 10RF, led by Second Lieutenant Arthur Usher closed a gap in the line 400 yards to the east of Favreuil and by 3am the village had been secured. At 6:30am on the morning of 27th the battalion was relieved and moved back.

The War Dairy recorded that in the five days of action 1,366 prisoners, 75 machine guns and 1 field gun had been captured. During this period the battalion had moved forward a distance of some 7 miles at the cost of thirty-two men and one officer killed, the majority lost on the last day of the advance when they were caught in the barrage crossing the road near Sapignies.

The next four days were spent in company training, a battalion tactical exercise and a church service after which, on Sunday 8, they moved further forward to Beugny. Now in a position on the straight road between Bapaume and Cambrai, the battalion had a day to clean up and wash their clothes before the next move on 10 September a further 6 miles to the east took them to the edge of Havrincourt Wood. Here they took up the role of reserve to the brigade and carried equipment and materials for 13KRRC.

On Friday 13 September the battalion moved to a position in the front line, with one company on either side of the Trescault to Ribecourt Road. Following a barrage at 5:30am the 10RF companies moved forward. The advance was successful with the troops moving into the valley and capturing, between the two companies, five machine guns and twenty-two prisoners. Lieutenant Messenger, in charge of the advance on the north side of the road, reported that because of casualties, he was requesting another platoon to be sent forward to strengthen the posts which had been established. Sending out patrols to try to make contact with 184 Brigade to the left, the company found only enemy troops, meaning that their position was dangerous as it was an exposed salient projecting into the enemy lines and on a forward slope. This danger materialised when the trenches came under heavy enfilade machine gun fire resulting in a number of casualties.

At midday fresh German troops, armed with light machine guns and grenades, counter-attacked. Fighting in the trenches was hand to hand, and 10RF were pushed back down the trenches. Colonel Tanner reported the position to brigade and was told to withdraw from Chapel Wood Switch. Lieutenant Dudley began to withdraw, but the enemy was moving forward rapidly and machine gun fire onto the road from Trescault made the carrying of ammunition and bombs to the troops in the trenches very difficult and hazardous. Captain Benjamin with A Company set up a defensive flank, with support from one company of 13KRRC and from this position launched a counter-attack which pushed the Germans back. At 6:20pm Second Lieutenant Smith led a determined attack pushing through two strong blocks to capture the remainder of Derby Trench, capturing one machine gun and killing some of the enemy. The Germans retook sections of Derby Trench at 7pm but Second Lieutenant Boodle led another foray which pushed them back again. C Company moved to replace the fatigued A Company, but Captain Benjamin remained in the trench to command action.

James Wooler, his death was only confirmed when a friend was released from prisoner of war camp after the war. Alan Metcalfe

Overnight the opportunity was taken to move ammunition and grenades to the front companies and Stokes mortars maintained a regular fire on the enemy in Derby Trench. An attack led by Second Lieutenant Paterson pushed the enemy back, but was stopped when a plane bombed and machine gunned the attackers causing casualties. Plans were made for another counter-attack; Colonel Tanner decided that to make any progress he would need artillery support. While waiting for a decision on the attack the battalion organised for defence. A report sent to brigade at noon resulted in the decision to remain in the position now held as the ground that had been lost was of limited value. On the night of 15th–16th the battalion was relieved by 13RF and 1 Essex and moved to the Lebucquière area about 5 miles behind the fighting line.

In the three days from 13 September the battalion lost one officer and twenty-six other ranks killed. One of those killed was 66093 Private James Wooler, a Yorkshireman; at first it was thought he was among a number of men who had been captured. It was only when his friend Private Ayling was released from POW camp at the end of the war that Wooler's family was told of his death.

Moving back from the front line to a point east of Havrincourt Wood on the 16th, the arrival at billets in Lebucquière, allowed C and D companies a no doubt welcome opportunity for baths at the nearby village of Velu. On the 18th the battalion had to move quickly to the Canal du Nord to support against a German counter-attack. The danger passed and they returned to their billets on 18 September and spent that and the next day completing the clean up and bathing details. Friday 20 September, a week after they began the fight near Trescault, a move west to Thilloy, just south of Bapaume, gave an opportunity for training, which was continued after a further move further west to Pys. The Battalion War Diary for September is signed by Colonel Tanner but although the event is not recorded with a specific date, Colonel Waters, who had been gassed in May at Foncquevillers, had returned during the month and resumed his command.

The battalion returned to the advance just west of the village of Banteux with B Company in the front on the right, and C Company on the left with A and D companies in support. Patrols were pushed forward and posts established nearer to the banks of the Canal de L'Escaut. On 1 October patrols reported that the Germans had retreated to the east bank of the canal, attempts made to cross that night were not successful as all the bridges had been destroyed. The events of 3 to 6 October were reported in an appendix to the War Diary:

'On the night of 3rd/4th October the battalion was in the Front line of the Division on the west bank of the Canal de l'Escaut….

'The enemy were in occupation of Bantouzelle and had machine gun posts guarding the bridges over the canal. The canal was a serious obstacle to further advance as all bridges had been destroyed except for one by the factory and this was under close machine gun fire; moreover the canal was reported to be unfordable.

'At about 8pm on the night of 3 October an officer patrol approached the factory bridge and as the patrol stepped on the bridge a small explosion occurred resulting in a further destruction of the bridge.

'However at 4:30am a strong attempt was made to push across the canal and establish an outpost line on the western side. The bridge having been roughly repaired to enable men to pass across in single file, two platoons of D Company under Second Lieutenant R.A. Jones and Second Lieutenant W.B. Laws succeeded in crossing the canal. They were immediately counter-attacked by a large number of the enemy on the right flank and owing to their exposed position and to the danger of their being cut off with no communication to the rear, the platoons were ordered to withdraw and a Lewis Gun placed in position on the western bank.

'Three men of D Company who had previously been missing returned at about 5:30pm having been cut off in the morning when the Platoons retired. They had stayed out all day in a shell hole on the eastern side of the canal and at dusk came back by fording the canal.

'4 October, the battalion was relieved by 13KRRC and 13RB and took up position as battalion in Brigade Reserve.

'On the morning of 5 October the 13KRRC and 13RB crossed the canal in pursuit of the enemy who had retired during the night. The 10RF moved forward and took up the positions previously occupied on the west bank of the canal. At nightfall the battalion moved across the canal, still as battalion in reserve.

'6 October. The battalion remained in its position. In the evening a warning order was received that the battalion would attack the Masnieres – Beaurevoir line on 8 October.

'7/8 October. At 10pm the battalion moved to the position of assembly for the attack on the next morning. The night was dark and stormy and as the Companies moved to *the position of assembly they came under a certain amount of hostile shelling. Captain R.N. Benjamin O.C A Coy and three men of A Coy being wounded by a shell in Cerneaux Wood. The battalion was in position by 12 midnight.*

'The orders were for the battalion to capture part of the Masnieres – Beaurevoir line within Divisional Boundaries the attack to be carried out in a S.E. direction. As the battalion had to cover a wide front 3 Companies were put in the front line and one in close support and mopping up. One Company of 13RB was temporarily attached to the battalion and was kept in reserve.

'Each company advanced on a two platoon frontage with 100 yards between each line of platoons. Each platoon advanced in section 'blobs' with scouts in front. One platoon of C Company was allocated to B Company to mop up the Beaurevoir Line on the battalion front. One platoon mopped up Bel Aise Farm as the leading companies passed through and the remaining two Platoons were left to hold the Beaurevoir Line.

'The assembly position was an ill-defined bank which had earlier in the night been marked out with a tape line. A barrage was put down at Zero hour approximately 300 yards in front of the assembly position and at Zero +4 advanced at the rate of 100 yards in four minutes. Close up to this barrage the companies advanced at Zero hour at 4:30am.

'There were two strong systems of wire running in front of the Beaurevoir Line and as this had not been sufficiently cut some difficulty was experienced in getting through it and heavy machine gun fire was opened on the leading troops from concrete machine gun posts inside the wire. Having successfully passed through the wire no more serious opposition was met with and the leading Companies quickly reached their objectives closely followed by troops of the 112 Infantry Brigade who passed through them to the Divisional second objective. The 13KRRC who were attacking on the right of the battalion did not reach the objective until about one hour afterwards having encountered severe opposition. Until the arrival of this battalion Mezieres farm and Little Houses were held by the right (B) company 10RF.

'About 200 casualties were suffered by the battalion all either at the assembly position, which the enemy continually shelled during the night, or in getting through the wire.

'The barrage was uniformly good throughout but was not successful in destroying several machine gun posts in the wire in front of Bell Aise farm. These were eventually overcome, the German gunners being either killed or captured. A considerable number (uncounted) of prisoners were taken in and around Bel Aise farm.'

The advance was continued until 9 October when the division halted and then on 10th they were relieved and on Friday 11th October moved back to Ligny, near Bapaume where they had a period of rest and were inspected by the divisional commander who congratulated them on their work in capturing Bel Aise Farm. Work on the ranges, in company exercises and baths filled the period until the 21st when they were put on transport and travelled to Bethencourt, about 10 miles north-east from their last position in the front line. The advance had circled south of Cambrai and was heading north-east. The constant harrying and chasing of the German forces was intended to lead to their exhaustion and end the war.

The plan was for a 5th Division attack on 23 October to take the village of Beaurain,

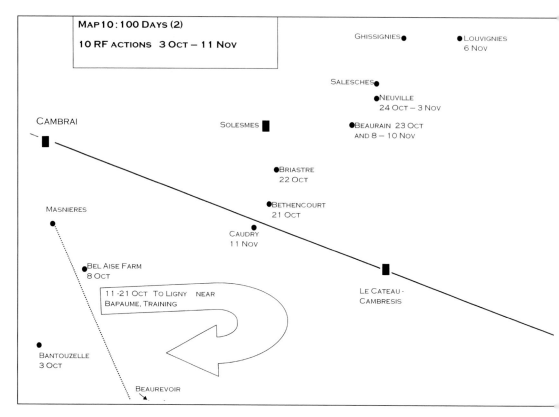

Map 10: 100 Days (2)

10 RF actions 3 Oct – 11 Nov

GHISSIGNIES●   ●LOUVIGNIES
                        6 Nov

SALESCHES●

●NEUVILLE
24 Oct – 3 Nov

CAMBRAI   SOLESMES ■   ●BEAURAIN 23 Oct
                                 AND 8 – 10 Nov

●BRIASTRE
22 Oct

●BETHENCOURT
21 Oct

MASNIERES
●
                CAUDRY
                11 Nov

●BEL AISE FARM
8 Oct

11 -21 Oct To Ligny   NEAR   LE CATEAU -
Bapaume, Training   CAMBRESIS

●
BANTOUZELLE
3 Oct

BEAUREVOIR

about 3 miles beyond the River Selle. After achieving this they were to push posts forward to establish a line to Ghissignies, another mile and a half to the north-east. The Battalion Diary report of the action uses, for the first time, the 24hour clock:

> 'On 22 October the battalion moved forward and occupied cellars in Briastre. The village was shelled intermittently throughout the afternoon and night but no casualties were incurred. At 0600 hours on the morning of 23rd the battalion was in position north of the railway with the 1stBn Essex Regt on the immediate left.
>
> 'At 1000 hours 13KRRC and 13RB moved forward to the attack of the Green Line, information having been received that Beaurain had fallen. At 1430 information was received that the 13KRRC had reached their objective and patrols had been sent forward to ascertain if the village of Neuville and the railway embankment was clear of the enemy as far as the River St George.
>
> 'About 1500 hours the Brigade Commander held a conference in Beaurain which was attended by the Commanding Officers of 13KRRC, 1 Essex, 10RF and the Artillery group commander when it was decided to resume the advance at 1715 with an artillery barrage. The first objective was a point along the road and another point immediately to the NE of the River St George. The barrage would dwell for ten minutes across the river.
>
> 'As a result of the information received from patrols of 13KRRC that the ground was

clear of the enemy as far as the river the above orders were subsequently altered and the battalion was to move forward as far as the river and the advance to start from the far side at 1730 hours. There was very little time for this information to reach the leading companies who were already moving to the original assembly position; the orders were communicated to the leading Company Commanders but not in sufficient time to enable them to reach the river in time to start close up to the barrage. On reaching the road the leading Companies came under machine gun fire at very close range from the railway.

'An Officer and some men of the 1st Battalion, Lincoln Regiment, 21 Div, were found who said that they were the leading troops of 21 Div and that they were held up by heavy machine gun fire from the railway and on their right flank. It soon became apparent that the railway was strongly held by the enemy with machine guns.

'A company and the left platoon of C Company reached the river but the right platoon of C Company was unable to advance owing to strong opposition from the railway. It was realised that no further advance could be resumed on the right without an artillery barrage along the railway. D Company 13KRRC were to advance and mop up the eastern side of the railway establish a post at the corner of the hedge and form a defensive flank on the line of the railway facing east. C Company 10RF were to advance along the west side of the railway. A company to be positioned along the road; B Company in close support and to hold the road running east and west ; D Company in reserve in the sunken road.'

No adequate barrage fire was opened and C Company 10RF and D Company 13KRRC were again unable to advance as very heavy machine gun fire was opened on them at

Mairie at Beaurain. Author

close range from the railway although, as the War Diary report described, 'a bold and gallant attempt was made and heavy casualties incurred'. Owing to the failure of the artillery barrage it was decided not to press the attack on the railway.

It now became an urgent matter to establish a line on the Green Dotted Line or as near thereto as possible to enable the 112 Infantry Brigade who were to resume the advance at 0400 (on the 24th) from the Green Dotted Line under barrage to take up a position to the rear of the Line. A and B companies were therefore ordered to get forward on the left, C Company forming a defensive right flank to their advance. This was successfully accomplished. A and B companies, having established themselves on the Green Dotted Line, sent back guides to lead up the 1st Battalion Hertfordshire Regiment (112 Infantry Brigade) by a covered approach and by 0345 this battalion was in position in the rear of the Green Dotted Line.

At 0430 hours as the barrage covering the advance of 21 Div reached a point about 200 yards east of the railway, another attack on the enemy posts on the railway was made by C Company with Lewis gun fire, rifle grenades, and Stokes mortars. When the 1 Herts had passed through the Brown Line 10RF formed a defensive flank along the railway down to the river.

In this position the battalion was relieved at about 1600 on the 24th by 8 Somersets and proceeded to billets in Neuville for the night.

Two men from 10RF were killed during this attack but 13KRRC who were alongside them at the railway line lost sixteen. The taking up of billets in Neuville again showed the confidence that there would not be an immediate counter-attack from the Germans. There was also a desire to keep pressure on the enemy by remaining in close contact, and the limited number of troops available meant that units could not have long periods of rest between operations. Training was carried out, baths were set up and there was a voluntary church service.

November began with 10RF in billets in Neuville with other units of the brigade. At a state of readiness in case there was a counter-attack the brigade was defending the line north-east of Ghissignies, about 2 miles from Neuville. Two companies, A and D, were moved forward to add strength to the flank near Ghissignies. Conferences for officers were held on Saturday 2 November, the first at divisional level the second for all officers in the battalion. The topic was the forthcoming attack to gain ground to the north east of Ghissignies. The orders for the attack which was scheduled to begin on the night of Sunday 3 November, required 10RF to retain its role as support battalion until the Blue Line, about 500m east of Louvignies when it would pass through 13KRRC and continue the advance to reach the Dotted Blue Line a further few hundred metres east. From this point the 112 Brigade were to take over and make their way through the Forest de Mormal and take up position along a line on the eastern side of the forest, the whole advance covering a distance of about 5 miles.

In Colonel Waters' report of the action he recounted that the battalion left Ghissignies on time at 0030. They stopped in Salesches for a hot meal and by 0500 were in position on the railway to the east of the village. Here they were shelled and Lieutenant Usher, commanding A Company, was killed. At 0530 the battalion advanced, with B and C companies in the lead and A and D following to give close support. D Company pushed

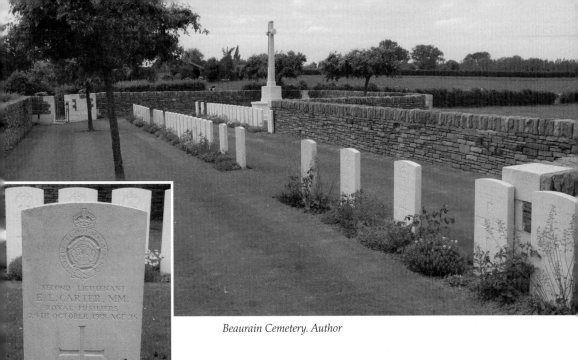

Beaurain Cemetery. Author

Second Lieutenant Ernest Carter MM, formerly Stk 925 is buried in Beaurain Cemetery. Author

through Louvignies and killed and captured a large number of the enemy. The battalion reached its objective on time and took up positions. The Germans put a barrage onto Ghissignies, which was the base for battalion HQ, and later moved to target the Blue Dotted Line, where the battalion was established, and Louvignies. This made communication between the troops in the line and HQ very difficult and even the establishment of an advanced report centre did not ease the situation so battalion HQ moved to Louvignies when the shelling died down sufficiently, to be nearer the front line. They established a position on the Blue Dotted Line at 2000, and were soon after ordered by brigade to withdraw when they marched to billets in Beaurain.

They took over 300 prisoners, three field guns, one lorry and a number of machine guns during their part of the advance. They lost one officer killed and two wounded and five other ranks killed and forty-four wounded. The march back to Beaurain, a distance of some 5 miles, was begun at about 2030 and took until 0130, described as 'a long march, men very tired'. They had again been on the move since midnight of the previous day and fought over an advance of about 3 miles.

The billets in the village of Beaurain were described as being 'very bad'; the weather was wet and the battalion rested and were reorganised during the next 48 hours. On Thursday 7 November Lieutenant Usher, whose parents lived in British Honduras, Private Cheeseborough, Private Elliott, Private Pearson and Private Verness were all buried in the cemetery at Beaurain with full military honours where they joined another 'Stockbroker', Second Lieutenant Ernest Carter who had enlisted as Stk925 and won the Military Medal during the raid on 1 September 1917. After training at Pirbright he received his commission in May 1918, and rejoined the Regiment first with 6RF at Dover

249

and then transferring to 10RFs sister battalion 13RF in France on 19 September 1918. He was killed by shellfire near Salesches on 24 October.

The battalion remained in Beaurain on the 8 and 9 November, carrying out training in companies. A church service was held on Sunday 10 November and on the morning of the 11th a move to new billets in Caudry was ordered. The War Diarist recorded:

> 'On the march near the village of Bethencourt the Divisional Intelligence Officer (Lieutenant Archbold) rode up on a motor cycle and informed the Commanding Officer that the Armistice had been signed by the Germans. This was quickly communicated to the men who responded with cheers. There were celebrations in the evening in Caudry. The battalion drummers marched into the Grande Place playing National Anthems and other patriotic songs. The sky was illuminated by Very Lights and ground flares and there was much cheering.'

It was not just in Caudry that the men who had volunteered in August 1914, and their successors, celebrated. A letter from a former 'Stockbroker' described events in Grantham.

Private George Wilkinson, Stk575, who became 25428 in the Machine Gun Corps was the author of many of the letters in this book. He had been wounded in Muck Trench near Hamel on 17 November 1916 and spent twelve months in hospital in Brighton, then London, before a posting to Harraby Camp at Grantham, the main MGC Base. He was then sent to a rehabilitation camp at Alnwick, where he was told that the injury to his arm would probably mean that he would not be sent back to France. In February 1918 a reclassification as B1, fit for Garrison Duty abroad, led to a posting back to Grantham where he was given clerking duties in the Records Section. Life was fairly tedious but he wrote home on 12 November 1918 in his typical descriptive style:

> 'OO-OO-OO-OOOT went the air raid warning yesterday about 10:45am. We left work and stood at the office doors not knowing how to act or what to do. We wanted to jump and scream, but no one started. The word passed along from mouth to mouth "It's signed", "It's signed". I sat down at my desk again. I put my hands in my pockets. I couldn't think – I went to the door again, men were standing about in groups everywhere gazing at an aeroplane circling above dropping smoke signals. Then bursting onto the parade ground came a procession of men from the MG school singing at the tops of their voices, arm in arm, making for the town, which had been out of bounds for ten days or so. Everyone laughed. The Orderly Room Sergeant was frantically trying to get his men to carry on with their work but they left him almost alone. Then came the band followed by a laughing and yelling mob pulling a handcart on which was a life size model of the Kaiser on his hands and knees. Crowds joined the mob and round the town they went for about an hour singing the national anthems of the allies. They besieged the shops for flags and ribbons and the lady from the American YMCA joined them with a huge American flag and the whole procession returned to camp waving flags and bedecked with ribbons. I watched their return – I couldn't cheer, I could hardly see – I smoked – my hands were so awkward I could hardly take the cigarettes from my case; and the church bells were ringing. A half holiday was announced. At dinner a pint of beer was waiting for us. After

dinner I went out into the town. Hundreds of flags had sprung into sight – one wondered where they had come from. The Town Crier was ringing his bell and announcing that the Mayor was meeting the Burgesses of the town at 3pm and was attending a service of Thanksgiving at 3:30pm in the Parish Church.

'I hurried on through the town, two tipsy tommies were being handed cigarettes by two officers; wounded tommies were standing on a bench opposite the Town Hall cheering various passers by and ringing a hand bell; in a side street a big woman with bare arms was assisting some children with the aid of a clothes prop to fasten some streamers across the street; a car full of officers was careering from end to end of the town its occupants whooping. I entered a shop, had some coffee and cakes but was off in a moment.

'Later I went with Halbert to the service in Church. The church was full to overflowing by 3pm. A corpulent lady sat near me with a small American flag pinned to her pocket and her hair trimmed with stars and stripes ribbon. I could see a man standing in the aisle some distance off with several small Union Jacks hanging round his shoulders.

'The congregation stood up as the Mace bearer entered followed by a big man in uniform wearing three stripes and another wearing two. Then came the Mayor and numbers of other grey-haired men followed by about fifty military big-wigs. The organ played 'Land of Hope and Glory' in soul-stirring fashion and then a service of praise followed.

'At night troops thronged through the streets singing and shouting. I managed to secure a seat at The Empire and witnessed a Revue. We sang the National Anthem at the commencement of the performance; gave three hearty cheers and then settled down soberly to enjoy the show. I finished up the evening with supper at the Club and then a quiet talk with Halbert in the office as to what the news really meant and how it would affect us.'

Chapter 19

After the Armistice:
November 1918 to March 1919

There was little effect on the rhythm of life in Caudry. On 12 November there was company training, on 13th General Sharper, the Corps Commander, made a speech congratulating the division on its efforts in the preceding weeks and distributed medal ribbons to four men who had won a bar to their Military Medal and forty-two who had been awarded the Military Medal. The awarding of medals was a potentially controversial process, requiring not only evidence of bravery, but also that the recommendation by the commanding officer should be written in what was seen to be the correct form. Writing after the war Charles Wise described to Sydney Sylvester the process as he had seen it from his rather more privileged position as a battalion HQ runner. Colonel Rice had commented to him, during a walk around the trenches, that he did not think many of his recommendations would be accepted as 'he wasn't a Whykemist', that is he hadn't attended Winchester College, the alma mater of many senior officers. In the action at Monchy Colonel Rice was wounded and the writing of citations was left to the Adjutant, Captain Goldthorpe and perhaps the new CO, Colonel Bonner. Both Goldthorpe and Bonner were killed at Gavrelle less than three weeks after Monchy. Any matters for clarification would be passed to the new CO and adjutant, neither of whom was at Monchy. An instance of perceived unfairness cited by Charles Wise is echoed more generally by other writers[52]:

> *'of later years I can believe that "kissing went by favour when the rations were given out". B**** W*******, Batman, now walks about sporting an MM and Bar and I take leave to doubt if he ever saw the inside of a front line trench.'*

There is no doubt that the awarding of medals for acts of bravery was anything but a scientific process. Acts of bravery were recognised but others were lost forever as the potential recipients, such as the unknown man who stood with Lance Corporal Robertson on the top of the trench near Hooge in March 1918, were killed in the action and only the VC, Albert Medal or a Mention in Despatches could be awarded posthumously.

On the morning of Saturday 16 the battalion gathered for a lecture from the commanding officer on a number of topics, one of which most certainly would be close to their hearts, the education and demobilisation schemes. A service of thanksgiving was held on Sunday 17 November in the Barn Owls Theatre in Caudry. The 10RF sent a representative contingent of six officers and forty other ranks; immediately this service ended the battalion held its own church parade. The battalion received a further lecture on demobilisation and education on Monday 18, this time from the divisional education officer, and there was certainly some relief that just a week after the Armistice plans were being made for the troops to return home. The demobilisation scheme had to take account of the fact that an army was still required in Germany and Italy, as well the commitments in Russia and the Empire. The scheme had provision for those with scarce industrial skills, or whose jobs had been kept open for them, to have a level of priority. Those who had volunteered early in the conflict were demobilised before those who were conscripted, and the 18-year-olds of 1918 were to be released from service last. There was a concern that with fighting ended the troops still needed for consolidation and tidying up duties would become bored and restless, the solution, to keep them busy.

Training activities continued and on Wednesday 20 November the divisional commander inspected the 111 Infantry Brigade, under the command of Lieutenant Colonel Dallas Waters, and including 10RF, commanded by Captain Knight. There was a divisional parade on Friday, inspected by Major General Williams, the next day there was a battalion parade by the CO, after which he inspected the billets. No rest on the Sunday as after the church parade the brigade commander in his turn inspected the billets. Monday 25 saw the battalion carrying out a 6-mile route march and on Tuesday 26 educational training followed the CO's parade at 0900. More educational training on Thursday and then a parade inspected by Brigadier General Francis on Friday 29 November completed the week.

On Sunday 1 December the battalion began to move north-east into the area which had been occupied by the German army. A morning march between 0845 and 1330 on the 2nd took the battalion through Beaudignies to Wargnies-le-Petit, a distance of about 12 miles. The 3rd was spent in tidying but A and B companies marched just over one mile to see the King pass by on his tour of the front; the other two companies went to see him on his return the following day. Football and education courses returned to the programme, and a route march on Friday 6 took the battalion over the border into Belgium which was, as the diarist recorded, 'for the first time since the advance'. The whole of the next week was taken up with football and education and on Friday 13 December the conditions for judging the marching competition were produced, to be used as 37th Division moved to the Gosselies area, a distance of about 50 miles. No doubt the battalion must have thought its history gave it a good chance in the competition. The standards related to the record of march discipline: the lowest percentage of men falling out on each day of the march and the lowest percentage of men admitted to Field Ambulance between 13th and 20th. These clearly set the standard high to ensure that the men were not allowed to become soft, or to lose discipline during what some were beginning to see as time filling and inactivity.

The battalion moved first to Houdain, on the outskirts of Bavay, the source of some wonder to the men as this was the first village they had seen for many months which showed hardly any damage. This was followed by a march to Louvroil and the men were none too pleased to find that they were again marching on cobbled roads, which were very hard on the feet and brought back memories of the early days of their time in northern France. A rest on the 16th was followed by a relatively short march along the valley of the River Sambre to Marpent, covering 7 miles and lasting three hours. The next day they marched to Peissant, crossing the border into Belgium, again taking about three hours to achieve the 10 miles. More wondrous sights awaited them on the following day when they marched to Anderlues; that which greeted them on entering the town led the diarist to record:

> 'After having passed across the desolate and shell pocked country since 21 August it was indeed wonderful to arrive at such a town as Anderlies (sic). The trams were running and the streets and shops being lit by electric light.'

The entry on 20 December recorded the end of the march:

> 'The battalion moved from Anderlies [sic] at 0905 hours en route for Jumet a village just north of Charleroi which was to be the battalion's final destination. Although the battalion was by no means the first to march into Charleroi the enthusiasm of the inhabitants had by no means diminished. The battalion arrived at Jumet at 1330 hours not one man having fallen out of the march since the entry into Belgium on 14th. The billets here are wonderfully good, nearly all the men being in beds. The only disadvantage being the battalion was so greatly scattered.'

The 21st was a day of inspection, of feet and rifles, and a church parade. Although there was hope since 11 November that men would be going home, it was on Sunday 22 December that the first man left for England to go through the demobilisation process and begin his final leave. The routine of education and football began again, although on Christmas Day there were voluntary church services. The Christmas festivities were postponed until Saturday 28 December when celebrations began with a football match against the Brigade Machine Gun Company, which 10RF won 5 goals to 2. The Diary records on 31 December:

> 'This being the last day of 1918 it is interesting to recount that there were 50 'Ditchers' left in the battalion.'

The figures and information available from Medal Rolls, the Commonwealth War Graves commission and the Soldiers Died in the Great War database give some indication of the fate of many of those who joined the battalion in August 1914. Men with numbers from 1 to 1453 were included in the 822 who crossed to France in July and early August 1915. Three hundred and sixteen of these men, about 39 per cent, were killed, either with the battalion or with units they were commissioned into or served with after being wounded and transferred. In the battalion as a whole between July 1915 and November 1918 a total of 670 men and 49 officers died.

The year 1919 began with the battalion giving a party for the children of the families where they were billeted. On 2 January a memorial service, attended by all the Roman

Catholics in the battalion, was held in the parish church of Gosseiles. Working parties were provided and instead of being the battalion in the line, as in the days of war, each battalion took turns to carry out the fatigues and other duties falling to the brigade. Football matches, one of which the battalion lost, were continued and parades kept discipline rigid and equipment clean and tidy. On Wednesday 8 January there was a conference of all officers, warrant officers and sergeants to decide on the form of Divisional War Memorial; a statue was later erected at Monchy-le-Preux. A representative group of officers and men attended a memorial service in the parish church in Jumet on Sunday 12, a voluntary service being held for the rest of the battalion.

More lectures on demobilisation and on post war reconstruction were given by senior officers. The need to retain a military presence in Germany to maintain control and help with reconstruction led to a search for volunteers to undertake this work. Although men were being demobilised and the proportion of conscripted men who were allocated to the army had been reducing from January 1918, the supply of conscripts could not be turned off immediately. Training had been continuing in England and new drafts were still sent out, a total of 201 men arrived over 28 and 29 January. The battalion paraded on 3 February for the Presentation of Colours to 10RF and 13RF. The Divisional Senior Chaplain, the Reverend Marshall, consecrated the silk colours and they were presented to the battalion by Lieutenant General Harper on behalf of the King. After the war the 10RF colours were placed alongside the Battalion War Memorial in St Michael's Church, Cornhill, London. They were later stolen and at present the bare staff remains just above the roll of honour.

Activities were found to keep the men busy during the time waiting for demobilisation. Second Lieutenant Shields resumed education courses using the Ecole Moyenne. Classes were held in French, book-keeping, shorthand and arithmetic and it was expected that all men not involved in brigade duties would attend. A lecture on venereal disease was given by a major from the Royal Army Medical Corps in the battalion recreation room. A divisional guard mounting competition on February 11 involved a sergeant, corporal and six men from B Company, they came joint second. Education programmes continued and lectures by senior officers were arranged for the whole battalion. Major General Montgomery lectured on 'Waterloo' on the 13th and on Saturday the 15th Brigadier General Hubbuck spoke on 'The Malay Peninsula'. On the evening of the same day 420 people attended a fancy dress ball hosted by the battalion. Prizes were given for the best costumes and the participants were helped with their outfits by the Barn Owls, the local civilian theatre and the families where they were billeted. As a result of all this effort the men's costumes were described in the Diary as being 'of a high standard'; the dancing went on until 1:30am on the morning of 16th. Hopefully it was a better dance than the one at Colchester to celebrate Christmas in 1914.

Another spell of brigade duty from the 18th to 25th kept working parties busy, two officers and fifty other ranks guarding the supply railhead at Roeux; one sergeant and six other ranks were on guard at Lodelinsart and others provided the Brigade HQ guard. The men not involved in these duties continued to attend the education courses. Although relieved from routine duties on the 25th the battalion provided a party of two officers and fifty other ranks who went to load salvaged ammunition on to trucks at

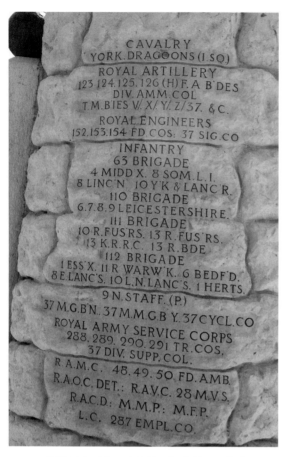

37 Division Memorial, Monchy-le-Preux. Author   *37 Division Memorial, Monchy-le-Preux. Author*

Courcelles-Motte Station. The final entry in the War Diary for February 1919 recorded that 253 men had been demobilised during the month and, because the numbers of men remaining in some battalions was so reduced, that the divisional football league had been abandoned.

The reduction the number of men proceeded apace with 10 officers and 200 other ranks marching to the station at Charleroi on Saturday 1 March to travel to the Rhine. These men had volunteered to remain in the Army and were being transferred to the 23RF. Because a number of the volunteers were on leave the actual numbers seen off by the rest of the battalion was 7 officers and 162 other ranks. The next day a draft of seventy-four men went to the IV Corps Concentration Camp at Marchienne-au-Pont for demobilisation. In response to the significant reduction in numbers the battalion reorganised into HQ and one company. On the 4th the battalion was so involved in fatigues and other duties that parades were not possible. The outbreak of influenza, which had caused thousands of deaths throughout Europe, had led to a temporary ban on men attending dances and concerts, but on 5 March this was lifted. The division was reduced to cadre strength and moved into a more concentrated area around Jumet and Lodelinsart and 10RF took over billets from 13KRRC in Lodelinsart which were viewed as being 'not very good'. The battalion transport vehicles, other than two double limbers, were taken to the barracks at Charleroi. The battalion accounts and property had to be dealt with properly and an audit board was convened on the 13th to check the canteen accounts.

A football match was mounted on the 22nd between the 10RF and Brigade HQ; Colonel Waters and five other officers turned out for the battalion. The War Diarist wryly noted 'The Brigade supplied the referee and won the game!' Another match between 111 and 112 Brigade officers was held on 24th. Again the diarist whimsically records the outcome with the phrase 'the 111 Infantry Brigade played a winning game but lost'.

The last entry in the 10RF War Diary was made on 31 March:

'By this time the battalion was only 162 in strength a great number of these were on leave, on commands etc. The battalion Transport consisted of two mules, two limber carts and a mess cart. With the exception of football matches etc life became rather dull and everybody was anxiously awaiting orders for the cadre to return to England.

J.D. Waters, Lieutenant Colonel, Commanding 10th Battalion Royal Fusiliers.'

Chapter 20

Postscript

Brigadier General Robert White ended the war commanding 184 Infantry Brigade, where he was well regarded as a leader who won the respect of his men. Aged 58 when the war ended, he returned to live at Pembroke Lodge in Richmond Park, owned by the widowed Georgina, Lady Dudley, who had supported the battalion and had worked for the Red Cross. He died in November 1936 and a memorial panel to him was erected in St Michael and All Angels Church, Himley at the same time as memorial panels were set up to commemorate the Earl and Countess of Dudley. Another panel was erected in St Michael's Church, Cornhill, London alongside the Memorial Roll to the battalion, and the Battalion Colours.

Lieutenant Colonel John Dallas Waters, aged 29 when the war ended, married Lettice Egerton Warburton, aged 36, the widow of Captain John Egerton Warburton who had been adjutant to 10RF in the early months of the war. They were married on 6 February 1919 while the battalion was in Belgium. Lettice Warburton had two daughters, Elizabeth born 1908 and Priscilla born just after her father died in 1915. Dallas Waters became Permanent Secretary to the Lord Chancellor, was Deputy Sergeant-at-Arms in the House of Lords between 1919 and 1930 and, in 1940 was appointed as Registrar to the Privy Council. He died in January 1967 having been Deputy Lieutenant of Cheshire, Master of the Cheshire Hunt and President of the Catholic Vincent de Paul Society, an organisation established to tackle poverty and disadvantage.

Major the Honourable George Keppel, was by the end of the war lieutenant colonel of the Highland Light Infantry. He had been employed by Sir Thomas Lipton but in 1927 he left London with his wife, Alice, who had been mistress to Edward VII; their great granddaughter is Camilla, Duchess of Cornwall. They bought a Villa at Bellerguado, near Florence, where they lived quietly in a marriage described as being 'of love and laughter'. Returning to England during the Second World War, when they lived at the Ritz Hotel in London, they resumed their life in Italy in 1946 where Alice died in September 1947 and George two months later.

Captain Maurice Sharp returned to Coutts Bank in 1919, having left on ten days summer leave in July 1914. After being wounded at Pozières he had been an adjutant in a training battalion in Edinburgh and Catterick, before joining the Intelligence Corps and being posted to South Russia. He married Violet Alice Wood in 1923 and went to work in the Finance Department of the Sudan Civil Service, returning in 1926 and rejoining Coutts. At the outbreak of war in 1939, having joined the Officers Emergency Reserve, he was sent to the Pay Corps, first in Canterbury, then in Gibraltar, where one of his duties was paying troops in Malta, and then Leeds. In 1945 he was demobilised and again

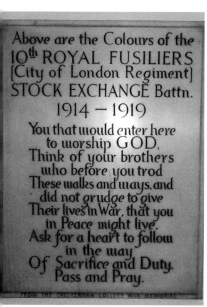

Above are the Colours of the
10th ROYAL FUSILIERS
[City of London Regiment]
STOCK EXCHANGE Battn.
1914 – 1919
You that would enter here
to worship GOD,
Think of your brothers
who before you trod
These walks and ways, and
did not grudge to give
Their lives in War, that you
in Peace might live.
Ask for a heart to follow
in the way
Of Sacrifice and Duty.
Pass and Pray.

General White's memorial, St Michael's Church, Cornhill, London. Author

10RF Memorial, St Michael's Church, Cornhill, London. Author

returned to the Coutts Trustees Department, which he finally left in 1953 to be ordained. After serving as curate at Green Street Green, Kent he became a minor Canon of Rochester Cathedral. He died in Maidstone in 1978, age 82.

The Reverend Ellis Partington later served as chaplain to the 1/5 York and Lancaster Regiment where he won a Military Cross in 1917 and a bar to the MC in 1918. After the war he returned to parish duties in London becoming Vicar of St Mary the Less, Lambeth, South London, in 1919 moving on to be priest-in-charge of St John, Southend, Lewisham in 1923, and vicar of the parish from 1928 to 1943. He was appointed a Canon of Southwark Cathedral, between 1935–36 and an Honorary Canon from 1936. He moved from Lewisham to become Vicar of All Saints, Tooting Graveney, London in 1943 the same year as he was appointed Select Preacher at Cambridge University. He died in August 1957 at Uckfield, age 72.

Lance Corporal Roland Mountfort, spent time in hospital in London after being wounded at Pozières. His wound was slow to heal and while with the 32nd Training Reserve Battalion in Dover he decided to apply for a commission. Before his papers were completed he was put onto a draft to join 25RF known as the Frontiersmen. Like 10RF many of the original recruits shared a common background, this time having worked or served in Africa and the Empire. Big game hunters, explorers, naturalists and men with experience of the Boer War found their way into the battalion which, naturally, was sent to East Africa. Poor supply lines, illness and fatigue after being forced to chase a skilful German general through thousands of square miles of bush, took its toll of men and by the end of 1917 its effectiveness was ended. Mountfort spent time in hospital with tropical diseases, but in March 1919, just before he left the army, he was commissioned. Returning to the Prudential in London he began to study for law examinations but became ill with cancer and died in May 1930, aged 40.

Lance Corporal Robertson VC returned to Dorking where he lived all his life. He married in 1939 at the age of 60; his bride was Doreen Gascoigne who was 21 years his junior. He served in the Home Guard during the Second World War and died on 10 May 1954.

A number of men who had arrived from parts of the then Empire were faced with the decision of whether to return home or remain in Britain. Oriel St Arnaud Duke had arrived with his mother from the Caribbean to England before the war to attend school. He reached the rank of sergeant in B Company and was awarded a Military Medal and a bar to the MM. He returned to Antigua in 1919 with his brother, Valentine, who had served in the Royal Navy. Oriel then joined the Leeward Islands Police, and was awarded an MBE for quelling a riot in Dominica. He rose to the rank of Commandant of Local Forces in Barbados during the Second World War. He was retired in 1948 following a dispute with the Island's Colonial Secretary and became the security officer for a department store in Barbados. He died in 1975, aged 77.

Lance Corporal Edward Branch who arrived from Trinidad in September 1915 had been discharged from the army following a wound to his back received at the Battle of Gavrelle in April 1917. On discharge he returned to his parents' home in Antigua and then went to work as a chemist on the island of Barbados. James Fairweather returned to Ceylon (Sri Lanka) in 1917 a passenger on SS Marseilles. Wounded at Pozières he had convalesced with a clergyman at Littleport, Cambridgeshire. Once he had been declared medically unfit for further service he became anxious to return to Ceylon, where he was a tea planter, largely because his army pay stopped when he was discharged, but he could not receive a pension until he arrived in Ceylon. The ticket to Ceylon cost £37, a large sum at the time. By 27 June he was putting pressure on the War Office:

'To suppress further delay I have communicated with the Secretary of State for the Colonies stating definitely my case and shall do likewise to the Secretary of State for War. No doubt I shall derive some satisfaction from this course.

'My intention is to leave at my own expense, nevertheless on my arrival in Ceylon I intend deriving satisfactory retribution from the Government there.'

A War Office letter of 2 September arrived at Littleport Vicarage to inform him that he should:

'Report yourself to the Military Staff Office at Royal Albert Docks by 2pm on September 4. Train leaves Fenchurch Street Station at 12:35pm.'

A letter from the records department of the Regiment to the War Office, dated 27 November recorded that:

'Passage to Ceylon was granted for 4 September 1917 but it appears that the man had sailed for Colombo on 14 August.'

Captain Knight went to Borneo. Captain Fane, who had joined the battalion in November

10RF Roll of Honour, St Michael's Church, Cornhill, London. Author

1915 and later joined the Tank Corps, moved to Houston, Texas. Lieutenant Docking, who had lived in Essex where he worked for a seed producer, had originally volunteered to join the 12 Battalion Australian Infantry. He served with both the 10RF and 14RF and after the war sailed for Tasmania, later working in Brisbane as an advertising executive. Second Lieutenant Edington received his medals while working for a tin mining company in Borneo.

Not all those with overseas connections returned home. Rupert Whiteman who had arrived in Europe for a holiday in June 1914 stayed in Britain after the war. He married Kathleen Totton in Croydon in 1922 and died in Colchester in 1972. Stk928 Private Alan Champion had joined in August 1914, his father from Perth in Western Australia was working for the South Australian Government in London as an immigration agent. Champion was commissioned into the Machine Gun Corps and his medals were sent to the office of the Agent General for South Australia in London.

A memorial service was held in 1922 and the old comrades arranged to meet up. Maxwell wrote to Sharp:

'My dear Sharpey, So glad you are going to the memorial ceremony, mine is a white ticket so we can stand shoulder to shoulder, or hand in hand.

Now I want you, without fail, to lunch with me before the ceremony at the Garrick Club. General White says he can come and I am asking Dallas Waters, Fred Russell-Roberts and Birley but don't know if they can come. I shall go in uniform as the card tells one to wear it.'

Members of the battalion continued to gather for memorial dinners for a number of years after the war. In 1964 a number of survivors from the battalion returned to France and Belgium to visit the sites of their exploits. Although all the 'Stockbrokers' have now died their memories, thoughts and words are being preserved by family members who have contributed material for this book.

Wilkinson's list of equipment taken to France 31 July 1915

In addition to the clothes I stand up in:

  1 rifle with oiler & pull through
  1 bayonet and scabbard
  1 entrenching tool
  1 entrenching tool handlebar
  1 waterbottle (quart)
  1 mess tin (containing ration bags*)

1 haversack containing:
  1 gas helmet
  1 knife, fork and spoon
  Towel and soap (aluminium box)
  Ration bag (with food)
  1 First Aid Manual *
  1 box chocolates*
  1 pair bootlaces*

Sewn in tunic:
  2 First Aid Field Dressings
  Iodine in metal case**

1 jack knife on lanyard containing
  Tin opener
  Spike
  Blades

1 pair field glasses and case*

In pockets:
  Field Service Pay Book
  Kitchener's Message
  1 Ingersoll Watch*

1 Compass*
1 Diary*
1 New Testament*
1 small antiseptic soap*
1 penknife*
1 leather purse and money*
1 pair nail clippers*
Photo of scouts*

1 pack containing
    1 Greatcoat
    1 rubber groundsheet
    1 cardigan jacket
    1 sleeping cap
    1 shirt
    1 pair pants
    1 pair socks
    1 pair plimsoll shoes**
    1 housewife
1 holdall containing:
    Razor and soap
    Mirror*
    Shaving brush
    Comb

1 can rifle oil
Supply of rifle rags

1 pair of aertex pants*
1 writing pad complete*
4 handkerchiefs*
1 piece of soap (washing clothes)

Set of leather straps etc
Pouches filled with large amount of ammunition (120 rounds)

2 Brass RFs on shoulder
2 Brass grenades on shoulder
1 Brass 10 on collar

* Personal not issued
** Presented to us

Appendix 2

Movement and Actions of the Battalion

1914   Colchester:

1915   Andover: Ludgershall: Boulogne: Armentières: Foncquevillers

1916   Bailleulval: Mezerolles: Berles-au-Bois:
        Somme Fighting: La Boiselles: on Pozières: Bazentin, Mametz Wood, High
        Wood, Loos, Ham.

1917:   Hulloch: Buneville:
        Arras Push **Attacks** on Monchy-le-Preux and Gavrelle:

        Messines Operations **Attack** North of Wytschaete, **Attack** in Tower Hamlets
            sector of Ypres Salient: Menin Road

1918   Wardreques: Dickebusch: Polderhoek:

Counter-attack on Joppa, Foncquevillers: Rossignol Wood: Hébuterne: Ablainzevelle:
Bucquoy: Foncquevillers (Gas Bombardment): Villers Bretonneux:

German Retreat: **Attack and capture** of Ablainzevelle: Bihucourt: Logeast Wood and
Havrincourt Wood: **Counter-attack** on Favreuil: Canal de Lescaut: **Attack** on Belaise
and Hindenburg Line: Ligny **Attack** on Beaurain and Louvignies:

Armistice: Caudry

Appendix 3

Awards and Casualties

Decorations:

Victoria Cross	1	L/Cpl Charles Robertson
Distinguished Service Order and Bar	1	
DSO	5	
Military Cross and Bar	5	
MC	35	
Distinguished Conduct Medal and Bar	2	
DCM	18	
Military Medal and Bar	13	
MM	149	
Meritorious Service Medal	3	
Foreign Decorations	2	
Commander of the Bath	1	
Commander of St Michael and St George	1	

Casualties:

	Killed in Action	Died of Wounds	Wounded	Missing
Officers	32	17	92	5
Other Ranks	408	232	1866	48

Bibliography

Maxwell, William B. *Time Gathered* Hutchinson 1937
O'Neill, H.C. *The Royal Fusiliers in the Great War* Heinemann 1922
Holland, C. & Phillips, R. *The Great War Letters of Roland Mountford* Matador 2009
Messenger, C. *Call to Arms, The British Army 1914-1918* Cassell 2006
Messenger, C. *The Day we won the War* Weidenfeld and Nicholson 2008
Cornish, P. *Machine Guns in the Great War* Pen & Sword 2009
Chapman, G. *A Passionate Prodigality* Buchan & Enright 1983
Reed, P. *Great War Lives* Pen & Sword 2010
Reed, P. *Walking the Somme* Pen & Sword 1997
Fox, C. *Monchy le Preux* Leo Cooper 2010 (Pen & Sword)
Cornish, P. *Machine Guns and The Great War* Pen & Sword 2009
McCarthy C. *The Somme The day-by-day Account* Brockhampton Press (1998)
Gliddon, G. *Somme 1916 Battlefield Companion* Sutton 2006
Germains, V.W. *The Kitchener Armies* Naval & Military reprint
Hay, I. *The First Hundred Thousand* Forgotten Books Reprint
Barker, S. & Boardman, C. *Lancashire's Forgotten Heroes* History Press 2008
Murray, N. *The Red Sweet Wine of Youth* Little, Brown. London 2010
Stand To Journal of Western Front Association May 2012

Papers and Documents
From the Collection of Documents and Sound Section, Imperial War Museum, London. Reproduced with permission of the Trustees of the Museum. Every effort has been made to contact individual copyright holders.
>   Papers of G.A. Wilkinson
>   Papers of R.D. Mountfort
>   Papers of Percival Maurice Sharp, with permission of Mr Robin Sharp
>   Extracts from the Diary of Brigadier General The Hon R. White CB, CMG, DSO edited by F.W Dimbleby
>   Life and letters of George Knight Young, edited by Florence E. Cole
>   R.S. Whiteman - Memoir of the attack on Monchy le Preux
>   P.R. Zealley - 10th Fusiliers, Somme 1916

Crown Copyright
10th Battalion Royal Fusiliers War Diary TNA WO95/2532

Websites
Stephen Booth's Trench Art www.trenchartofww1.co.uk
Diary of Alfred Mills with permission of Graham Morley owner of www.tome.at
Pictures and records of individuals, courtesy of Jane Jones, www.ww1photos.com
Reproduction Trench Maps available from G.H. Smith & Son www.ghsmithbookshop.com
Great War Forum http://www.1914-1918.invisionzone.com/forums/index.php?
Long Long Trail http://www.1914-1918.net
Information about the men in the battalion and contact the author http://www.10throyalfusiliers.co.uk

Notes

1 The Royal Fusiliers used abbreviations for numbering members of specific New Army battalions. The 10th was named Stockbrokers with the abbreviation Stk, the Public Schools prefix, abbreviated to PS, covered four battalions. This practice continued until 1916 when all new recruits were viewed as joining the regiment and were numbered sequentially to be sent as drafts to individual battalions as they were needed.

2 Pencilled notes while writing *Memoirs of an Infantry Officer* (1930) quoted in Murray, N. *The Red Sweet Wine of Youth (The Brave and Brief Lives of the War Poets)* page 122. Published by Little, Brown. London 2010

3 Diary of Alfred Mills at www.tome.at

4 Son of the Earl of Albemarle. His wife, Alice, had been a mistress of Edward VII.

5 Later 4th Baronet Boileau, of Tacolneston Hall, Norfolk.

6 If payment is not made for the gift of a knife the recipient will cut themselves.

7 Shown in census of 1881, 1891, 1901 as coming from Herefordshire.

8 Private George Rothschild Stk218 later Major, Royal Sussex Regiment DSO, MC.

9 A tonic wine to build up the system.

10 Possibly Francis A. Dudley see Chapter 4.

11 Lady Augusta Fane, wife of Cecil Fane, Member of the Stock Exchange, mother of Lt Charles Fane, 10RF.

12 Charles Shurey, Maxwell describes him as a 'rich young man'. His father in 1901 was a newspaper proprietor who lived in Brighton, with wife and two of his sons. Charles, the oldest son, then aged 9 was a boarder in a lodging house in the same road, Kings Road, Brighton. His mother and brothers were living in Eastbourne in 1911; she was then a widow.

13 Manager at Million Guiet, the car maker George had worked for.

14 White mentions this in his diary 'Very good march through thick wood by compass'.

15 Worth about £1500 in 2013 based on average salaries

16 The Defence of the Realm Act included provisions to reduce the amount of alcohol consumed in the country, partly by introducing licensing hours. There was particular concern over the effect of drinking in munitions factories and near army barracks. In March 1915 Lloyd George, then Minister of Munitions, began a campaign to strengthen the effect of the Act. He gained the support of the King who announced that no alcohol would be drunk by the Royal Household for the duration of the war.

17 'Young officers' newly appointed subalterns who need to practise drilling squads and platoons as part of their training and induction to the battalion.

18 Francis M. Taylor, age 18 was 781, private, in Inns of Court. Gazetted second lieutenant 12 September 1914.

19 A game of chance. Players pitch (throw) coins towards a post or wall. The winner is the one landing nearest the target. He can then toss all the coins, winning those which land head side up.

20 Actress and singer in musicals. Became engaged to Paul Rubens but he died of TB in 1917 before they could be married.

21 Appendix 1

22 This was the route used for horses and freight using the commercial docks in Southampton and Le Havre, leaving Folkestone and Dover for troops.

23 The combined power of up to 64 Vickers machine guns of a division firing over the advancing troops. In one barrage in 1916, to support an advance, ten guns fired just under one million bullets, which rained down on the defenders, who afterwards described the fire as 'devastating'. Barrage fire was equally effective in breaking up concentrations of troops assembling for a counter-attack.

24 Possibly Sergeant Frederick Clapp formerly East Surrey Regiment.

25 Dormor, Mountfort's brother serving with the Surrey Yeomanry.

26 The mail was dealt with by the Royal Engineers (Postal Section) which took on Royal Mail employees who had the necessary experience. It was not so much the increasing volume that led to the rationing to two letters but the pressure on the censors at Base who had to check outgoing letters. Both Wilkinson and Young complain at the restriction. It was possible to send unlimited open field postcards.

27 See Chapter 7

28 Mother's name = SARAH: Reverse without first letter = ARAS becomes ARRAS: 5 letters times 3 = 15 miles S of Arras.

29 Presumably Second Lieutenant Philip Knox, age 40, an actor with family ties to Trinidad in the incident described in Chapter 6.

30 About 1 litre

31 Waterproofed cotton, light but capable of keeping the water off the legs when marching with a greatcoat.

32 Metal barriers with stakes placed in front of the trenches.

33 Major Ralph Cobbold, see Ch 1: 10th Loyal N. Lancs Regt was in 112 Brigade 37th Division, 10RF was in 111th Brigade of the same Division: later career Lieutenant Colonel; Air Force Munitions Unit Lt Col; 112 Brigade Brigadier General.

34 Popham became Lieutenant. Colonel of a battalion of the Kings Own Royal Lancaster Regiment.

35 The City of Coventry collected to send parcels to the men from the city who were in the army. It appears from his letters that Mountfort never got his.

36 De Ruvigny, The Roll of Honour, Volume 4 (no date, no publisher), p 126. Quoted in Reed, P, *Great War Lives.*

37 Stk731 John Kortright, aged 22, a bank clerk living in East Ham with his family in 1911. He had married Margaret Rosenberg in Romford in the autumn of 1915.

38 Insurance Clerk, age 23, lived in Camberwell with his family, his father a corn dealer and baker.

39 English potter and designer, friend of William Morris.

40 Stk475 Albert Montague, aged 22, an Old Boy of Christ's Hospital School. In 1911 census a Stockbroker's clerk living with is mother and four brothers in West Ham.

41 Stk518 Henry G.G. Rutherford, son of Reverend H. & Mrs Rutherford, 10 Portland Road, Remuera, Auckland, New Zealand.

42 Stk431 Robert Hember, aged 21. In 1911 census a schoolboy living with his family in Greenwich, his father a company secretary.

43 Stk554 George Tutt, later Lieutenant MGC .

44 A reference to Kitchener's career as an officer in the Royal Engineers.

45 Now a CWGC Cemetery.

46 Captain Hall lost an eye in this attack.

47 Royal Mail Steam Packet Company ship, launched 1908, converted to a hospital ship. Saw service between France and England and in the Eastern Mediterranean. At 12000 tons taking over 800 casualties. She was one of the largest ships to be torpedoed when hit off Start Point 20th March 1917. She was salvaged and repaired.

48 Probably 29-year-old Stk835 James Sowerby, a solicitor born in Beverley, Yorkshire.

49 Quotation from 'Dray Wara Yow Dee' a short story by Rudyard Kipling with the theme of friendship.

50 Reginald C. Penfold, formerly of the London Regiment, later awarded MC, he survived the war.

51 Robert Geoffrey St John commissioned 20 November 1914, a stockbroker, born 1879 living with wife and daughter in Bishops Stortford, Hertfordshire (1911).

52 See Messenger: *Call to Arms* pp489-495

Index

DROITWICH

POINTON. M.R.   ~~759.29/AYC~~

759/DYC

1 5 MAR 2003

2 0 MAY 2005

- 7 JUN 2005

27 JUN 2005

- 2 AUG 2005

2 4 NOV 2005

1 4 DEC 2005

- 4 JAN 2006

1 9 APR 2006

2 0 NOV 2007

1 5 DEC 2007

10/12

2 2 AUG 2005

- 8 SEP 2005